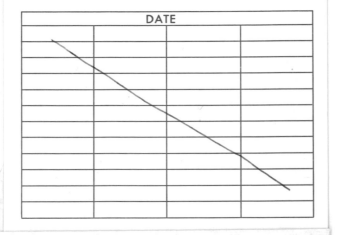

DATE			

THE ETHICAL FOUNDATIONS
OF MARXISM

THE ETHICAL
FOUNDATIONS
OF MARXISM

by

EUGENE KAMENKA

Routledge & Kegan Paul
LONDON AND BOSTON

First published 1962
Second edition 1972
by Routledge & Kegan Paul Ltd
Broadway House, 68–74 Carter Lane,
London EC4V 5EL and
9 Park Street,
Boston, Mass, 02108, U.S.A.

Printed in Great Britain by
Redwood Press Limited
Trowbridge, Wiltshire

ISBN 0 7100 7360 7

Contents

CONTENTS

Part IV: Ethics and the Mature Marx

Part V: Communism and Ethics

Conclusions

Preface to the Second English Edition

IT is now almost ten years since this book was first published. I still hold, without significant reservations, what I take to be the book's main theses in the area of Marx scholarship. These are:

(1) The underlying ethical and logical assumptions of Marx's work are to be understood in terms of a technical metaphysical concept of freedom, involving the associated philosophical notions of 'universality', 'rationality' and 'self-determination'.

(2) The internal logic of Marx's intellectual development is to be understood as the attempt to realise his concept of freedom by 'overcoming' the dualisms of universal and particular, society and individual, civil society and state, autonomy and heteronomy.

(3) Marx's work thus reveals no radical break between his early philosophical concern with freedom and alienation and his subsequent exposition of an allegedly scientific theory of social change and social development. After his 'discovery' of the materialist interpretation of history in the spring of 1845 we find a certain change in style and a growing socio-historical concreteness. Marx's concern shifts from proclaiming the philosophical nature of freedom to ever-deepening studies of the social and historical conditions that produce alienation, but we do not find a change of theoretical structure or a major revision of his philosophical premises.

These three theses, which go to make up and explain the assertion that alienation is a central concept in Marx's work, are now very much more familiar to an educated English-speaking public than they were ten years ago. As set out in this book, they may not command universal assent; nevertheless it seems to me that they have survived unscathed the widespread scholarly discussion of these issues, a discussion that takes up material in this book and in other books. Certainly, these theses have gained much wider acceptance than they had ten or fifteen years ago and among the scholarly the place of ethics in Marx's intellectual development and in his mature 'scientific' system is now very much better understood. For a period, under the influence of such men as Robert Tucker, Fromm and Marcuse, this led, *intra et extra muros*, to an excessive moralisation of Marx, to a tendency to 'expose' him as a moralistic religious ideologist or to deify him as a philosopher of the human condition whose relevance is eternal and largely independent of the concrete social and historical details of his work. In my more recent writings on Marx and Marxism, no doubt in reaction against this tendency and the growing misuse of Marx's name by peasant anarchists, romantic nihilists and revolutionary Jacobins, I have put greater stress on the nineteenth-century European context and on the specific socio-historical content of Marx's work, on his numerous social insights, on his concern with modernisation, with revolutionary realism, with the educative role of the industrial process, and with the social *base* of a revolution. Nevertheless, the eliciting of Marx's philosophical and ethical assumptions does remain of central importance to an understanding of the total thrust and direction of his work, to a grasp of the interrelation of its parts, to a deeper appreciation of the force and point of his key categories, from 'exploitation' and 'dehumanisation' to 'free labour' and the proletariat as a 'universal class'.

With all this in mind, I have thought it best to allow this book to go into a second edition unchanged, except for the correction of misprints and some minor improvements in the Index. To write in the historical dimension of Marx's work at this stage would be to open up new concerns more appropriate to another book and to destroy the unity and coherence that I have striven to give this one. Similar considerations have made me resist the temptation provided by a new edition to expound in somewhat greater detail my views on the extent of Marx's debt to Kant, to Fichte, to Hegel, to Feuerbach, to Moses Hess, to French Socialism and French historiography, to Ferguson and to classical English economics. The determination of Marx's precise position in the movement of ideas is both exciting and difficult; Marx's work is part of many intellectual histories. The careful reader of this book will note a certain emphasis on the Young Hegelian character of Marx's interpretation of Hegel and on his consequent debt to Kant and Fichte and to the aesthetics of German Romanticism. This is part of what is now often discussed under the heading 'Marx's Prometheanism' and Marx's handling of alienation in many respects owes more to Fichte than it does to Hegel. I have said and am saying something more on these matters in other works. Here, I was concerned to refer to Marx's intellectual antecedents and to his cultural debts only in so far as such reference was necessary to an understanding of Marx's work; it seems best to leave it thus.

EUGENE KAMENKA

Canberra,
1971

Preface to the Japanese Edition (1965)

MARXISM, as a theoretical system, is a product of nineteenth-century north-western Europe, which nevertheless looks beyond Europe and its nineteenth century. In the name of science and of man it seeks to transcend the specific divisions of climate, race and creed, of nation-state and language-group, in order to chart a common future for mankind.

The bases for this transcendence, as Marx himself emphasised, were being laid by the industrial developments and the economic expansion that were primarily associated with Europe and the United States. Marx, no doubt, grossly overestimated the rate at which Africa and the Orient would be socially and economically 'Europeanised': the creation of a world in the image of the bourgeoisie is not yet complete, and in many areas of the world it has followed, instead of preceding, the spread of Marxism. Marxist ideology, in these circumstances, has lost most of its connection with the existing industrial proletariat: Marxism, once to be the heir of industrial civilisation, has become, in such countries as Russia and China, its pre-condition.

Marx, in seeking to transcend national ideologies and national concerns, was somewhat too cavalier in gauging the influence of national, social and geographical distinctions on the long-term trend of historical development. The age of the nation-state was not over when he died, even in Europe, let alone in the non-European world. The rise of sociology as an academic subject at the turn of the nineteenth and twentieth centuries, though given a decided impetus by Marx and Marxist thinking, owed equally much to the concern of German and French intellectuals with the conditions of nationhood. Max Weber and Emile Durkheim were consciously looking for the factors that weld a society and a nation together: the factors that make men a *community*. Marxism, as a theoretical system and as a practical movement, thus now finds itself in an age of nationalism and of internationalism, of One World and of many. The technological progress that has brought men all over the face of the globe into ever closer contact with each other has also made men more aware of the differences in social and economic circumstance, and of the resultant differences of temperament and attitude, that distinguish one society from another. Much as mankind has suffered from the recognition (and especially from the over-emphasis) of human differences, the study of society has benefited enormously from our new-found acquaintance with an even wider range of social settings. To have a theory of society forged in London or in Paris tested in the circumstances of China and Japan is a scientific experiment beyond the wildest hopes of a Vico or a Hobbes.

For me as author, then, the translation of my *Ethical Foundations of Marxism* into Japanese is at once an exciting and a humbling experience. We are all, as Marx said, an ensemble of social relations: apart from the individual blindnesses my book may display, the reader reared in somewhat different circumstances may find in it further examples of social and cultural blindness. To have this book translated into Japanese and presented to the Japanese reader is thus to put it to an important double test. It is to extend, in the first place, the company of men who will read and judge the book as men. It is to subject the book in the second place to the extra dimension of criticism that can be provided by readers who, at least in some respects, will have been raised in traditions and circumstances very different from my own. It is not in the common content of what we know, but in the common standards of discussion and the common aim of truth, that the international character of the community of scholars is to be found.

EUGENE KAMENKA

Canberra,
November 1964

Preface to the First Edition (1962)

KARL MARX, I shall argue in this book, came to Communism in the interests of freedom, not of security. In his early years he sought to free himself from the pressure exercised by the mediocre German police state of Frederick William IV. He rejected its censorship, its elevation of authority and of religion, its cultural Philistinism and its empty talk of national interest and moral duty. Later he came to believe that such pressures and such human dependence could not be destroyed without destroying capitalism and the whole system of private property from which capitalism had developed.

At the end of his *Economico-Philosophical Manuscripts* of 1844, Marx paints a picture of the society of Communism, of the society of true and ultimate human freedom. Sympathetic critics have called it the picture of a society of artists, creating freely and consciously, working together in perfect harmony. In such a society, Marx believed, there would be no State, no criminals, no conflicts. Each man would be 'caught up' in productive labour with other men. The struggle would be a common struggle; in his work, and in other men, man would find not dependence and unpleasantness, but freedom and happiness, just as artists find inspiration in their own work and in the work of other artists. Truly free men will thus need no rules imposed from above, no moral exhortations to do their duty, no 'authorities' laying down what is to be done. Art cannot be created by plans imposed from outside; it knows no authorities and no discipline except the authority and the discipline of art itself. This discipline and authority every artist accepts freely and consciously; it is this and this alone that makes him an artist. No government authority, no patron or overseer, can make him one. What is true of art, Marx believed, is true of all free, productive labour.

This vision of Communism remained with Marx all his life. It

xii

comes out clearly in the *German Ideology* of 1846, in the notes and drafts he made between 1850–9, in his *Critique of the Gotha Programme* of 1875. It runs through all three volumes of *Das Kapital*. It is a vision of freedom, of spontaneous co-operation, of men's conscious self-determination. It is not a vision of economic plenty or social security. Engels may have seen Communism that way; Marx did not. Freedom, for Marx, lay in struggle, but in conscious, co-operative struggle. The desire for security under the protection of authority would have seemed to him a base desire, born of 'inhuman' conditions.

Marx's vision, I shall argue, rests on a sound if unworked-out perception of positive ethical distinctions, of the difference between the spontaneous co-operation of goods and the forced and extrinsic temporary alliances possible to evils, of the tension between the producer's morality of freedom and enterprise and the consumer's concern with ends, with securities, profits and returns. The fundamental weakness of Marx's thought lies in his failure to work out the distinction between freedom and servility in positive terms, in terms of the *character* of the processes and movements involved. It is only because Marx glosses over the positive character of social movements and ways of living that he is able to believe in a classless society, in a society in which the *conflict* of movements and ways of living has disappeared. The *transition* to socialism thus becomes something he simply cannot afford to examine seriously: the precise character of the 'dictatorship of the proletariat', the 'values' and ways of living represented by the people in whose hands it would lie, have to be left out of account. Here he is driven back on a crude economic reductionism: the abolition of private property destroys the foundation on which competing interests rest.

Socialism, on Marx's view, would be born out of capitalism. But socialist or Communist society would be the society of true freedom and enterprise, in which capitalist morality had been entirely destroyed. Marx was right in the first proposition and wrong in the second. Socialism was born of capitalism. But it was not the result of the catastrophic collapse of capitalism. On the contrary, it sprang from the very ideology fostered by capitalism: from the concern with economic ends over ways of living, from the belief in the universal exchange-ability and rational control of all things as mere means to a common commercial end. The socialist's vision of society, as Rosa Luxemburg once said of Lenin, is the capitalist's vision of a factory, 'efficiently' run by an overseer. The conception of economic planning is a capitalist conception: the capitalist manager is the prototype of the socialist administrator. Both depend in their ideology on the commercial morality of utilitarianism: on the conception that all things can be treated and assessed as means to ends and that ends can be reduced to a common measure.

Marx had a strong desire to believe that the proletariat, in its misery yearned for initiative, enterprise and freedom, that it rejected servility, careerism and the concern with security as Marx himself had rejected them. It would not be bought off with ameliorated conditions, with prospects of higher rewards or of 'opportunities' for the individual to 'better' himself. But Marx was not prepared to make such a claim part of his theory, to see socialism as the extension and culmination of the freedom and enterprise already displayed by the worker. Essentially, he stuck to his negative view of the proletariat as the *most suffering class*;[1] a class whose future was determined not by its character, but by its deprivation. This prevented him from paying serious attention to freedom and enterprise as historic traditions operating in any society, strengthened and not necessarily weakened in the struggle against adversity. It prevented him from seeing the importance of other forms of production and of other manifestations of the productive spirit in social life: of artistic and scientific production, for instance, as continuing traditions capable of supporting and strengthening the productive spirit in industry. Instead, Marx chose to rely on 'history', to hold out to the proletariat the vision of a classless society *made safe* for goods, where enterprise and freedom would be *guaranteed* by the economic foundations of society itself, where freedom would not lie in struggle, but follow from mere existence. It is a servile conception, appealing, however unwittingly on Marx's part, to the demands for security and sufficiency, to the longing for certain returns. Its servile character was strengthened even further by the fact that it was Engels, with his blindness for alienation, with his crude evolutionism and his utilitarian concern with economic satisfaction, who became the 'ideologue'—the propagandist and populariser—of Marxism.

It is obvious that the labour movement, and even the socialist movement, were at no stage wholly given over to enterprise. The search for security, for welfare and economic sufficiency, was always a powerful motive within them. But it is also obvious that propaganda

[1] This was the accusation which Marx and Engels, in the *Communist Manifesto*, flung at the Utopian socialists; yet they themselves remained open to the same accusation.

of a Marxist colour, with its insistence on ends and aims, its elevation of economic rewards, did much to destroy what enterprise there was. In their controversies with anarchists and syndicalists, Marxists may have been able to expose much that was utopian in both movements. But against the anarcho-syndicalist elevation of the free and enterprising character of the existing working class, Marxists were upholding a servile and unfree morality.

Partly as a result of Marx's failure to deal positively with ethical questions, as a result of his failure to highlight ways of life and organisation over 'ends' and policies, ethical distinctions did not play a central part in the splits and controversies that racked Marxism. The revisionists in the 1890's, it is true, made much ado about their Kantian ethics. Bernstein proclaimed his seemingly sound slogan: 'The movement is everything, the goal is nothing.' But Bernstein, for all this, preached security and sufficiency all his life. The real issue confronting Marxists was not ethics, but the consequences of their neglect of ethics. Marx had been wrong in forecasting the imminent collapse of capitalism and the growing pauperisation of the worker; no longer driven by needs, Western workers were displaying their preference for rewards and security over freedom and struggle. If one wanted to follow the worker, the Marxist vision of a radically new society born of struggle had to be abandoned. Socialism became a matter of negotiation and of demand for improved conditions and greater security within the existing society. This was the path of reformism. Notably, the Marxist neglect of ethics prevented Marxists from attacking reformism for its elevation of rewards and security: the orthodox Marxists had to argue instead, quite implausibly, that the reformists were bound to fail, that increased rewards and greater security could not last under capitalism.

Orthodox Marxists, clinging to the vision, had to find a substitute for the proletariat. Lenin, drawing on Russian populism, found it in the revolutionary intelligentsia and the centralised, hierarchical party of professional revolutionaries acting as the 'vanguard' of the working class, driving it beyond the bread-and-butter politics at which the working class by itself would always remain. Enterprise was not to be won by the worker, but for him.

The bringing of freedom and enterprise *to* somebody is not a free but a despotic conception. Yet Marx, too, had seen freedom as something that would be brought *to* the worker by 'history'. Marx's work laid no foundations for thoroughly exposing the course the Communist Party under Lenin was soon to follow. Indeed, his failure to see freedom as a force within history, his treatment of it as merely a final end, made it possible to erect despotism in his name. The erection of this despotism points not to the worthlessness of Marx's vision, but rather to its half-heartedness. A radical of genius, Marx was, in the end, not radical enough.

Karl Marx is still best known for the political and economic writings of his maturity that were published in his own lifetime. These, and these alone, form the popular corpus of Marx's work; they have been widely disseminated in English translations. For any thorough understanding of Marx and his thought they are not enough. The ethical enquirer, especially, must take into account Marx's earlier, more philosophical, writings and the notes and drafts not meant for publication as they stood which Marx habitually made throughout his life. Marx's mature writings notoriously eschew any direct consideration of ethical or philosophical questions; it is in the earlier writings and private drafts that we shall find the key to his ethical views and their puzzling place in his mature beliefs. The study that follows therefore draws heavily on those of Marx's writings that preceded the publication of the *Communist Manifesto* in 1848 and on the notes and drafts that Marx compiled between 1850 and 1859. The former have been published in the language of composition (usually German) in the *Marx-Engels Gesamtausgabe*, brought out by the Marx-Engels Verlag, Frankfurt–Berlin, between 1927 and 1932. The latter, first published in Moscow in 1939 and 1941, have been republished in the original German by the Dietz Verlag, Berlin, under the title *Grundrisse der Kritik der politischen Oekonomie* (1953). The major portion of these writings has not been translated into English; the rendering of those writings that have been translated is not always satisfactory. Greater space than would otherwise be necessary has therefore been devoted to the translation and presentation of relevant passages from these works. Where the source reference is a foreign-language text, the translation is my own unless otherwise indicated.

The *Marx-Engels Gesamtausgabe* was not completed, though it contains all of Marx and Engels' extant writings down to 1848 and the entire Marx-Engels correspondence. Its original editor, the Communist D. Riazanov, was removed; he died in a Stalinist prison. Some of Marx's writings had been tampered with in earlier editions and were to be tampered with again in later Soviet editions; the *Marx-Engels Gesamtausgabe*, most scholars agree, shows no signs of any conscious unfaithfulness to the originals.[1] Despite its incompleteness, it is still indispensable. From Marx's mature political writings I cite verbatim less frequently; here I have found the current English translations quite adequate. I have preferred, however, to use the German text in citing from *Capital* since I was largely looking for philosophical terms and overtones that might unwittingly be lost in any translation. In making these citations, I append references to the (Kerr) English edition for comparison.

Accuracy in translating Marx's more philosophic writings is extremely important to a sound understanding of his views. His constructions are involved; his language is studded with philosophical terms; his sentences are often ungrammatical. He plays with words and makes deliberate use of their overtones or their ambiguity. He sets out a sequence and then fails to follow it; he poses questions and leaves them unanswered. I have thought it neither illuminating nor proper to 'tidy up' the young Marx's writing, to turn a clumsy, Hegelian German into elegant empirical English that eschews vagueness, metaphysics or ambiguity. To do that would be to present as Marx a man who is not Marx.

Presenting the metaphysical side of Marx faithfully and yet convincingly in English is not easy. Words like 'essence', 'true reality', 'actuality' and 'objectification' do not sit readily on an English tongue. Those raised in traditional German culture will read their German counterparts without the least unease, often even without stopping to ask what they mean. Most Englishmen, faced with these words in English, will not. To translate Hegel into English, it has been said, is to rob him of much of his plausibility. The same is often true of the early Marx. But to shear Marx of his metaphysics, or to translate his earlier Hegelian conceptions as though they were his later Communist ones, as many translators have done, is to misunderstand and to misrepresent Marx's thought. At the risk of leaving a Hegelian clumsiness where many previous translators have felt justified in substituting a pamphleteering simplicity, I have striven not to do so.

The genius displayed in Marx's writings—the suggestive power of his leading ideas, the illumination afforded by his subsidiary insights,

[1] Professor Lieber, of the Free University, Berlin, has very recently drawn attention to a number of errors in the *Gesamtausgabe* version caused, he claims, by the fact that Riazanov was working from photostat copies. None of the suggested errors affects the citations or conclusions given below.

xvii

the interest of his very inconsistencies—has made writing this book as exciting and stimulating as it has often been difficult. No author could wish for a more interesting body of work, or for a more impressive man, as his subject.

Work and thought requires time. The main work on this book was done—under the supervision of Professor P. H. Partridge—in the two-and-a-half years that I held one of the generous research scholarships awarded by the Australian National University in Canberra; the manuscript of this book has been accepted as a thesis for the degree of Doctor of Philosophy in that University. Without the opportunities for untroubled research offered by what is now the A.N.U.'s Institute of Advanced Studies, the writing of this book would have taken many more years.

Intellectually, I owe my greatest debt to John Anderson, Emeritus Professor of Philosophy in the University of Sydney, under whom I read as an undergraduate and for whom I retain the highest admiration, friendship and respect. Many younger men who have worked on Marx—Georg Lukács and Sidney Hook, for instance—have tended to see in Marx the doctrines of their first teachers. No doubt I have done the same. But Anderson's social theory and ethical position, on which I have drawn heavily, still seem to me to illuminate both Marx and the subjects with which Marx is dealing. Specific debts to Anderson are acknowledged in the text; though his influence on my thought has been wider than these acknowledgments indicate, this should not be taken to imply that he necessarily agrees with my interpretation of Marx or with the formulation and applications his own doctrines are given here. Those interested in Anderson's position should consult Anderson's work.

Alice Erh-Soon Tay has shared in all the trials that accompanied the writing of this book. Chapter 3 on 'The Natural Law of Freedom' and Chapter 16 on 'Law and Morality in Soviet Society' are based on articles dealing with Marxism and law which we published jointly; she has read and re-read the drafts that became the rest of this book with untiring patience. Without her steadfastness and encouragement during the difficult period when I lectured in the University of Malaya in Singapore and amid the uncertainties of a far more stimulating year in London, this book would hardly have been completed.

In London, too, I gained much encouragement from new but warm friendships with men working in or around my field—notably with Dr. George L. Kline of Bryn Mawr, Mr. Leo Labedz, Mr. Walter Z.

Laqueur, Mr. George Lichtheim, and M. Maximilien Rubel of Paris.

Preliminary drafts and studies for this book have been published in the *Australasian Journal of Philosophy*, the *Hibbert Journal*, the *Indian Journal of Philosophy* and *Soviet Survey*. I am grateful to the editors of these journals for permitting me to draw freely on the material published by them, and to Professor John Anderson and Professor A. K. Stout, editor of the *Australasian Journal of Philosophy*, for allowing me to cite from Anderson's contributions to that journal.

EUGENE KAMENKA

Canberra,
March 1962

Citations and Abbreviations

THE bibliography of works cited at the conclusion of the text indicates the editions used; page references are to these editions. Where two sources are given together, the citation is from the first and the second is given for comparative purposes only.

I have used the following abbreviations for works frequently cited in the text (see bibliography for details of editions):

AD—Engels: *Herr Eugen Dühring's Revolution in Science (Anti-Dühring)*, trans. E. Burns.

A.J.P.P.; A.J.P.—Australasian Journal of [Psychology and] Philosophy.

C—Marx: *Capital*, Aveling-Moore trans., vols. I–III, Kerr edition.

CPE—Marx: *A Contribution to the Critique of Political Economy*, trans. I. N. Stone.

CWF—Marx: *The Civil War in France*, trans. for Marxist-Leninist Library.

EPM—Marx: *Economic and Philosophic Manuscripts of* 1844, trans. Martin Milligan.

GI—Marx and Engels: *The German Ideology*, Parts I and III, ed. R. Pascal.

HF—Marx and Engels: *The Holy Family or Critique of Critical Critique*, trans. R. Dixon.

HM—Emile Burns (ed.): *The Handbook of Marxism*.

K—Marx: *Das Kapital*, vols. I–III, German text.

M—*Marx-Engels Gesamtausgabe*, Section I, vols 1–7, Section III, vols. 1–4.

M-E Soch.—Marx-Engels: *Sochineniia* (The collected works in Russian, publ. 1939 f.).

PP—Marx: *The Poverty of Philosophy*, English trans. by Foreign Languages Publishing House, Moscow.

SC—Marx-Engels: *Correspondence 1843–1895*, ed. Dona Torr.
SW—Marx-Engels: *Selected Works*, vols. I and II, Foreign Languages
   Publishing House, Moscow.

Arabic numerals directly after the abbreviation indicate page
numbers; if a Roman numeral precedes them it normally refers to the
volume. The *Marx-Engels Gesamtausgabe*, however, is divided into
sections as well as volumes, and volume I of Section I appeared in two
sub-volumes (*Halbbänder*). In citations from this edition, therefore,
the large Roman numeral refers to the Section, the Arabic numeral
that follows to the volume within that section, a small Roman numeral
to the sub-volume (if any) and the final Arabic numeral to the page.
Thus M I, 1–ii, 435 refers to page 435 of Section I, volume I, sub-
volume ii of the *Gesamtausgabe*.

Where other English translations of material here translated from
the *Gesamtausgabe* are available, I have generally cited them after the
M reference for purposes of facilitating comparison.

References to other parts of the present work are to the Part
(Roman numeral) and chapter (Arabic numerals). The chapters cited
are generally brief and I therefore hope that the omission of page
numbers—for technical reasons—will not prove too burdensome.

Preliminaries: Marx, Marxism and Ethics

THE relationship between Marxism and ethics is often alluded to and rarely explored. The disputes that surround it have produced little precision or clarity concerning the issues involved; so far they have generally illuminated neither Marxism nor ethics. Marx himself wrote nothing devoted directly to the problems of moral philosophy. Nowhere did he analyse critically the meaning of moral terms or the basis of ethical distinctions; nowhere did he consider carefully the concept of moral obligation or the criteria for distinguishing moral demands from other demands. He did, it is true, emphatically reject the conception of ethics as a normative science; he denied completely the existence of 'values', 'norms' and 'ideals' above or outside the empirical realm of facts. He prided himself that he had not asked what *ought* to be, but only what *is*. Yet the answers he gave to his question have seemed to many of his disciples and critics implicitly ethical and/or advocative. He called feudalism a state of bondage; he described the dehumanisation of the worker under capitalism in terms highly reminiscent of ethical writing; he identified the empirical culmination of history with the emergence of 'rational' and 'truly intelligible' human relations. Many of the 'contradictions' that play so large a part in his exposure of capitalism smack of moral as well as logical 'contradictions'. His life and work seem to proclaim a unity of theory and practice, of science and advocacy, that characterises the ethical *Weltanschauung* rather than the positive 'value-free' science. Even his own disciples seem uncertain whether Marx revolutionised the foundations of ethics or showed that it could have no foundation.

The tensions that appear to lie beneath the surface of Marx's work, and to which he may have had a coherent solution, break out as crass inconsistencies in the 'philosophical' works of his leading collaborator and disciple, Friedrich Engels. The 'co-founder' of Marxism asserts in one ill-considered breath that all moral judgments are relative and that moralities have in fact progressed: he rejects all absolute moral values and yet foretells the rise of 'a truly human morality' (AD 104–109). Under his influence, dogmatic Marxists have vacillated helplessly between the belief that Marxism is a 'value-free' science which destroys the very basis of moralism and exposes moral demands as no more than economic interests in disguise and the belief that Marxism is the most progressive, the most humane ar.1 the most ethical of all world-views. Hilferding, it is true, sought to resolve the contradiction ruthlessly. 'The theory of Marxism, as well as its practice,' he wrote in 1910,[1] 'is free from judgments of value. It is therefore false to conceive, as is widely done, *intra et extra muros,* that Marxism and socialism are as such identical. For logically, regarded as a scientific system and apart from its historical effect, Marxism is only a theory of the laws of movement of society formulated in general terms by the Marxian conception of history; the Marxian economics applying in particular to the period of commodity-producing society. But insight into the validity of Marxism, which includes insight into the necessity of socialism, is by no means a matter of value judgments and just as little an indication to practical procedure. For it is one thing to recognise a necessity, and another thing to work for this necessity. It is quite possible for someone convinced of the final victory of socialism to fight against it.' Whatever the logical position may be, Hilferding's analysis has not commended itself to Marxist writers and does not fit readily into a Marxist system. Marx himself would not have conceded the distinction between 'facts' and 'values', 'science' and 'attitude', in the crude terms suggested by Hilferding. Thus the doyen of contemporary Soviet moral philosophers, A. F. Shishkin, writes: 'Marxist ethics does not "prescribe" norms, it deduces them from the social being of men; it does not divorce "values" from facts, the "ought" from the "is".'[2]

---

[1] In the preface to his *Finanzkapital,* p. 10. I cite the translation by Sidney Hook in his *Towards the Understanding of Karl Marx,* pp. 33–4.

[2] *Osnovy kommunisticheskoi morali (The Foundations of Communist Morality),* p. 103. In an earlier article in *Voprosy Filosofii* on 'The Decay of Anglo-American Ethics', Shishkin wrote: 'The chief struggle [in Anglo-American ethics] is against Marxist ethics and its objective and rigorous norms and principles derived from a scientific understanding of society; ethical relativism was implicit in the thought of Rosenberg and Goebbels.' (Cited by H. B. Acton, *The Illusion of the Epoch,* p. 195, from *Soviet Studies,* vol. I, no. 3, January 1950.)

The attempt to combine description and advocacy, to claim scientific objectivity and yet 'deduce' moral 'norms' and social 'principles', appeared cautiously in the work of Marx and crassly in the work of Engels; it has remained, despite Hilferding, the most obvious feature of subsequent Marxist writing on ethics. Kautsky, for instance, proclaimed[1] that 'it was the materialist interpretation of history which first completely deposed the moral ideal as the directing factor of social revolution', and added, in the same sentence, that this theory has 'taught us to deduce our social aims solely from the knowledge of the material foundations', i.e., it has shown us what we ought to do. Lenin insisted that Marxism 'contains no shred of ethics from beginning to end'—and then went on to speak of 'the simple and fundamental rules of every-day social life'[2] and of 'the revolutionary consciousness of Justice'[3] to be established by Communism. More recently, the Soviet philosopher P. A. Sharia wrote:[4] 'The founders of Marxism had no need to separate out a special science of ethics, since the scientific theory of social development created by them already provided a scientific foundation for morality as one of the forms of social consciousness as well . . . One must not confuse two things: the basing of socialism on ethics, which the classics of Marxism-Leninism attacked bitterly, and the ethical nature of Marxism itself, as the most progressive, scientific world-view, striving toward incessant progress, toward the liberation of exploited and suffering humanity.' Consciously or unconsciously, virtually every Marxist has sought to have it both ways.

Marxism has become a dogma. Like Christianity, it speaks in the name of its founder more frequently than it speaks with his voice. Its sacred texts–'the great classics of Marxism-Leninism'—are not confined to the writings of Marx; its most general conclusions and simplified catechisms were not formulated by him. Marx's life-long friend and collaborator, Friedrich Engels, was elevated (partly by himself) to the status of co-founder of Marxism and intellectual *alter ego* of Marx. Lenin and then Stalin were proclaimed 'disciples of genius',

---

[1] *Ethics and the Materialist Interpretation of History*, p. 201.
[2] *State and Revolution.*
[3] Letter to Kursky preceding the enactment of the 1922 Civil Code, quoted by R. Schlesinger: *Soviet Legal Theory*, p. 140.
[4] P. A. Sharia: *O nekotorykh voprosakh kommunisticheskoi morali (Concerning Some Questions of Communist Morality)*, pp. 30 and 31–2.

clarifying the thought of the Master and building on its foundations. A world-wide political party, fighting or governing in his name, has claimed to be the sole repository of orthodox Marxism and the final arbiter of 'what Marx really meant'. 'Since the publication of Comrade Stalin's new works on linguistics, intended to provide the basis for all scientific knowledge and not only for Soviet-Marxist linguistics, many debatable questions of logic have been automatically settled.' Thus wrote one of the ablest and *most independent* of Soviet philosophers, the Georgian S. K. Bakradze, in *Voprosy Filosofii* for 1950–1. Was Stalin speaking in his own name or Marx's? It was not a question a Soviet Marxist could ask. As the number of 'Marxist' pronouncements and 'classics' increased, Marx steadily slipped from one's grasp. The abundance of followers and interpreters obscured rather than illuminated his thought. 'Joint founders', 'inspired disciples' may carry the prestige of numbers; they do not make for a single view.

Marx has been widely read as the great founder of 'scientific socialism' for at least seventy years—he has been dead for seventy-eight. Yet there is still no complete, scholarly edition of his work; there is no definitive biography, no monumental study of his thought. His early, more philosophical writings had been printed in the minor journals and newspapers for which they were written or left in manuscript to 'the gnawing criticism of the mice'; their systematic publication did not commence until 1927. The tireless notes, comments and drafts that formed a considerable part of Marx's mature output and that throw important light on the basis and development of his thought have attracted increasing attention in the recent revival of Marxian scholarship; most of them were unavailable and almost unknown before 1939; some, at least, are still unpublished. In the decisive years that saw the building of Communist ideology, Marx's unalloyed influence rested on his political pamphlets dealing with concrete contemporary affairs and on the detailed economic and economico-historical studies culminating in *Das Kapital*. Marx, in his serious work, propounded no general principles as a substitute for detailed knowledge. It was Engels who became at once the populariser, the systematiser and the 'philosopher' of Marxism. It was he, and not Marx, who compressed Marx's thought into a few simple principles. To Marx, few things were simple. For those who wanted to master his thought, he provided no short course, no quintessence of Marxism. To do this was the work of other, less able, minds.

All this is not to say that there is no connexion between the works of Marx and the corpus of Marxism. It is rather to warn that the connexion must be examined carefully and never taken on trust. 'The ideology of Marxism-Leninism-Stalinism' is a legitimate field of enquiry. It is neither synonymous with the study of Marx nor of the same intrinsic intellectual interest. The subtle ambiguities and suppressed conflicts in Marx's position are often made evident by the clumsy restatements of his disciples; none of these disciples can be regarded as an equal partner of Marx's in the building of a Marxian system and a Marxist philosophy. Where these disciples claim, like Engels, to speak on Marx's behalf, or to expound a view shared by him, they must be treated with the suspicion appropriate to dealing with any disciple 'expounding' a master. For the first and most profound distinction between Marx and his disciples is a distinction in intellectual capacity.

Marxism, Georges Sorel argues in his *La Décomposition du Marxisme*, is not the simple, coherent and purely empirical science it sometimes pretends to be. For Sorel it is in fact three things: a set of *dogmas*, a *canon* of historical interpretation and a heroic social *myth* meant to promote working-class education and strength. The dogmas, Sorel thought, were absurd; the canon could be very useful; the myth was to be judged in terms of its effectiveness, not of its truth. The word 'dogmas', of course, is pejorative: Marx was aggressive, self-confident and much given to regarding his opponents as fools; he was neither a believer in dogmas nor an expounder of them. (Herein lies a second distinction between him and his followers.) But for all his intellectual caution, for all his dislike of generalities 'abstracted' from concrete facts, his leading works between 1845 and 1875 unmistakably—if not unambiguously—embody the set of general propositions and conclusions which Marxists have summarised as the fundamental principles of Marxism and treated as political dogmas. There is the 'materialist interpretation of history'—the proposition that 'the mode of production in material life determines the general character of the social, political and intellectual processes of life'.[1] There is his distinction between the forces of production and the relations of production and his belief that social change takes place—violently—when the relations

[1] This is Marx's formulation in the Preface to his *Contribution to the Critique of Political Economy*, CPE, 11. Both the phrase 'mode of production' and the vague 'general character' suggest immediate difficulties, but at least Marx's formulation is significantly different from Engels' inept reduction of this statement to the individualistic claim that man's desire to eat controls his other desires.

of production cease to correspond with the forces of production and become fetters upon them. There is his allied doctrine that society is divided into competing classes, whose struggle for mastery is reflected in the political institutions and theoretical life of any given period. There is his suggestion that the capitalist state is merely the executive committee of the bourgeoisie. Finally, there is his detailed analysis of the economic processes of capitalism—his belief that the capitalist system must inevitably collapse through the very logic of its own development and give way to a dictatorship of the proletariat to be followed by the unflowering of the rational society of Communism. These are the doctrines most commonly associated with Marx's name and the chief link between him and his 'orthodox' disciples. They formed the basis of the Communist *Weltanschauung*; they were for many years, and officially are even now, *the* test of Marxist orthodoxy.

Apart from the detailed analysis of the economic processes of capitalism, all the propositions outlined above suggest a general philosophy of history and the basis of a universal view. Marxists, indeed, have treated them as such. But virtually every one of the propositions is surrounded by ambiguity and qualified or contradicted by some of the most brilliant of Marx's specific insights in specific fields. Time and time again, critics who assume quite fairly from these general propositions that Marx could not have foreseen or accounted for the emergence of fascism, the rise of capitalist managers, the existence of a state bureaucracy or the economic effects of law find that Marx did foresee them or mention them, at whatever cost to his general theory. The 'materialist interpretation of history' and the materialist reduction of ideologies have become Marxist dogmas, but their precise content has always been, and remains, far from clear. To Marx himself, they were not even dogmas to be followed at all costs.

Marx's conclusions concerning the fate of capitalism are unquestionably at first sight the most specific of his doctrines; they also seemed to his immediate followers the doctrines most pregnant with contemporary significance and the most conclusive in establishing that Marxism is the most 'advanced' of all sciences.[1] Beginning with the Ricardian theory that the value of a commodity is the amount of labour 'embodied' within it, Marx sought to show that the capitalist's profit

---

[1] 'If the theory correctly estimates the course of development and foresees the future better than other theories, it remains the most advanced theory of our time, be it even scores of years old,' wrote Leon Trotsky in *The Living Thoughts of Karl Marx*, p. 14.

depended upon the extraction of 'surplus value' from hired labour by paying the labourer less than the values the labourer produced. The well-being of the bourgeois thus necessarily implied the misery of the proletarian. The very nature of capitalist competition, Marx was understood to be saying, would lead and was leading to recurrent crises, to the concentration of wealth in fewer and fewer hands, to the proletarianisation of unsuccessful capitalists, petty bourgeoisie and other intermediate classes and to ever-increasing misery for the proletariat. Goaded by its destitution, the proletariat would rebel against a bourgeoisie no longer capable of supporting society or itself. It would establish a dictatorship of the proletariat, abolish private property, socialise the means of production, distribution and exchange and usher in the ultimate truly human society of rational economic planning and free associative production.

For a period, such doctrines seemed more than an intellectual *tour de force*; they carried conviction and appeal. Capitalist crises, unemployment and the miseries attendant upon rapid industrialisation were real and disturbing phenomena, belying the moralistic optimism of classical economists and the pious hypocrisy of Protestant industrialists. There seemed no reason why uncontrolled competition should not lead precisely where Marx said it would lead; the human debasement and destitution it had brought in its wake were all too evident.

As the basis for an ideology and a social myth, Marx's doctrines skilfully if unconsciously combined the messianic faith of a future state of bliss with the growing prestige of objective empirical science, the wistful longing for the community and fellowship of the feudal-agrarian past with the realistic acceptance of the inescapable process of ever-increasing industrialisation. What anarchists and utopians strove to make possible, Marx seemed to prove inevitable. Where they posited a conflict between the proletarian's work and his hopes, Marx showed the proletarian's work leading inevitably to the fulfilment of his hopes. History only seemed to crucify man; in fact, it was working toward his restoration.

The effectiveness of the myth even was weakened—though not completely destroyed—as the doctrines on which it rested became less convincing. Precisely that dynamic quality of capitalism which Marx had been the first to appreciate thoroughly, its continual transformation of the social background in which it operated, quickly made his analysis too simple, too primitive, too crude. The catastrophes he predicted did not occur; there are some indications that in the last years of his life

Marx may no longer have expected them to occur. Kautsky, it is true, in drawing up the *Erfurter Programm* of 1891, still envisaged a bleak future of mounting class tensions, increasing centralisation of wealth and the certainty of 'growing insecurity, misery, oppression, enslavement, debasement, exploitation' for the proletariat and the sinking middle class. Eduard Bernstein only eight years later saw evidence of increasing order, security, tranquillity, prosperity and a more equitable distribution of wealth. Statistics, he argued in his *Voraussetzungen des Sozialismus und die Aufgaben der Sozialdemokratie* (*The Presuppositions of Socialism and the Tasks Facing Social Democracy*), proved that the middle classes were holding their own and that the incomes of wage-earners were actually rising, small-scale enterprise were still flourishing alongside the industrial giants, business cycles were continuing to flatten out, social tensions were lessening, ownership of property was becoming more widespread.[1] Bernstein's statistics were hotly contested; nevertheless, Marxist attention shifted from the unprofitable expectation of internal economic collapse to the national economic rivalries between competing capitalist countries, thus implicitly confirming Bernstein's analysis of the situation. The Austrian Marxists discovered that capitalism was moving into a new state of 'finance-capitalism' in which the banks were assuming the power previously held by the great industrialists; Lenin, basing himself on the work of J. A. Hobson, proclaimed in 1916 that this period of 'finance-capitalism' or imperialism was the final stage preceding the collapse of the entire capitalist system. The more developed countries, he argued in his pamphlet *Imperialism: The Highest Stage of Capitalism*, had already reached the point where they were producing more goods than their home markets could absorb; they were therefore driven to find markets in backward countries where they could get raw materials in exchange. These countries were then annexed, while the 'super-profits' derived from the exploitation of their peoples were used to bribe the proletariat in metropolitan countries with better wages and conditions that seemed to belie the Marxist prognosis. But the struggle for markets in a world where there were no new territories to be discovered implied an inescapable series of imperialist wars, while the creation and exploitation of a proletariat in the backward countries only added a further nail to the coffin of capitalism.

Lenin's thesis became and remained of vital importance to the

[1] See George Lichtheim: *Marxism: An Historical and Critical Study*, pp. 278–300, where these and other examples are cited.

Communist movement—not because it successfully explained the failure of Marxist expectations of a world-wide capitalist collapse, but because it provided a theoretical justification for Communist revolution in such industrially backward countries as Russia and because it enabled Communists to mobilise totally new forces and different resentments into the 'national-liberation' Communism preached in Asian countries. But as proof that the inevitable, catastrophic collapse of capitalism through its own 'contradictions' has merely been delayed, the Austro-Marxist and Leninist thesis has also ceased to convince. However great the underlying tensions in a system resting largely on private capitalism, the Marxian picture of an uncontrolled competitive capitalism propelling itself inexorably towards catastrophic collapse has proved quite false. Even conceding that Marx had been somewhat more cautious about the pauperisation of the proletariat than many of his disciples, and had recognised various countervailing tendencies, Marx had erred basically and most seriously in neglecting the rise in the real value of wages that could and did occur under capitalism as a result of technological advance. At the same time, legislative interference with working conditions gathered pace within a few years of the publication of the first volume of *Capital* in 1867; the trade union movement overcame its legal disabilities and grew in strength and bargaining power. The skilled worker has thus moved slowly but steadily toward a middle-class standard of living and a middle-class ideology; even the living conditions and purchasing power of the shrinking class of unskilled labourers have patently risen and continue to rise.

Arguments can still be adduced in favour of the validity of some of Marx's long-range predictions. The movement toward more and more social control, not only through Communist expansion but also within the Western 'capitalist' world, is an obvious feature of our time; Marx's suggestion in the third volume of *Capital* that the nature of the capitalist process of production and the emergence of a class of capitalist managers would produce a certain 'socialisation from within' under capitalism seems today peculiarly striking and relevant. The tremendous strides made by Soviet technology are seen by some, at least, as vivid proof of the fact that socialist production is more 'rational' and therefore bound to triumph in economic competition. But by and large, despite the prevision and suggestiveness of many of his insights, the leading themes in Marx's analysis of capitalism have become irrelevant to the economic problems and economic conflicts of our time. Even thirty years ago, a serious book on Marx would have largely consisted of a detailed examination and criticism of the central Marxist dogmas outlined above. To the mature Marx, unquestionably, these were the central and most important aspects of his work; to us their interest has already become largely historical.

Truly great men and truly great works have something to say to each generation. They do not come back as unrecognised elements of a cultural inheritance; they come back, as Schumpeter put it, 'in their individual garb with their personal scars which people may see and touch.'[1] Each generation finds in them new features, new sources of illumination. The specific predictions Marx made, which seemed so important and challenging to earlier generations, now seem to us false. The general canons that permeate Marx's work—his recognition of the relatedness of all social phenomena, his emphasis on the existence of social conflict, on the impossibility of standing outside or of manipulating society and on the importance of production in social life—still need to be hammered home against voluntarists, individualists and social engineers; but poorly learnt as they may have been, they bring us today no new, unsuspected insights. Yet Marx still has much to say to us.

While the Marxist picture of capitalism still appeared to the less able or more fanatical to be truthful and relevant, West European Marxists were largely immersed in the task of 'exposing' the contradictions of capitalism. The relation of Marxism to ethics and the foundations of a positive morality of Communism did not seem burning practical issues. When Marxists in the advanced industrial countries did deal with ethics, they tended to concentrate on the Marxist *critique* of morality, using it to distinguish their 'scientific socialism' from the woolly, unscientific humanitarianism of liberals, social democrats and revisionists. Even the serious critics of Marxism in this period, unless themselves moralisers, mostly thought the Marxist relation to ethics a side issue. On the whole, the attitude taken by Marxists accorded well with the intellectual climate in capitalist countries. It could draw on the science-worship of the late nineteenth century[2] and the scientific

[1] *Capitalism, Socialism and Democracy*, p. 3.

[2] Sorel is certainly right in suggesting that much of the appeal of Marxism from the 1880's and 1890's onward is connected with this growing prestige of science, whether or not we accept Sorel's belief that the prestige resulted from public recognition of the role played by German technological superiority in the Franco-Prussian War.

positivism of the earlier part of the twentieth century; it could mobilise, quite effectively, the young intellectual's contempt for moralism, cant and hypocrisy. At the same time, it was useful to a party leadership which, from the time of Lenin, began increasingly to pursue a course of unprincipled, opportunistic tactics and consistently refused to consider the *character*, rather than the *aim*, of the proletarian movement.[1]

The anti-moralistic strain in West European Marxism did not lead, as we have seen, to a thorough-going rejection of norms, duties and principles, or to a shedding of all ethical assumptions. Marxists continued to speak of society evolving towards something 'higher', 'more magnificent'; they were neither willing nor able to discard the Messianism, the mingling of logic and ethics into an optimistic *metaphysic* of history, which had given Marxism so much of its popular and intellectual appeal. They wanted to have it both ways. But when speaking directly of ethics, they tended to protest their amoralism.

The development of the Soviet Union, as we shall see in Chapter 16, created new problems and with them new attitudes and new interpretations of Marx. The Soviet radicalism of the early twenties was soon abandoned; dangerous tensions were discovered between moral scepticism and party and national discipline. A period of the glorification of economic planning (and of stringent secret police controls) was followed by a frank insistence from the late thirties onward on traditional means of ensuring social stability. Soviet propaganda increasingly emphasised the importance of patriotism, obedience to the 'will of the community', respect for Soviet law and for the norms of Soviet morality. As conventional moral slogans became more and more part of the Soviet machinery of government, even the materialist interpretation of history was steadily reinterpreted to give greater prestige and independence to 'ideological' factors.[2]

---

[1] The opponents of such a course, e.g. Rosa Luxemburg, were inevitably drawn into having to counterposit an *ethic* and thus helped to keep alive some interest in the question of Marxist morality. But their influence on those who remained 'orthodox' was not great.

[2] Although some recent Chinese Communist pronouncements suggest that the Chinese wish to be regarded as 'purer' and more radical Marxists than the Russians under Khrushchev, Chinese Communism is even more moralistic than Soviet Communism. I would feel quite strongly, however, that Chinese Communists have made no significant contribution to Marxism as an intellectual system and that any consideration of the morality preached in China today would

Soviet party leaders and theoreticians have begun to emphasise the importance of ethics in Marxism for patently political reasons and because the radical Marxism of the twenties has become increasingly irrelevant to their problems and purposes. From a different angle, Marx critics in Western Europe and Communist revisionists in Eastern Europe have displayed growing interest in the philosophico-ethical conceptions that underlie the work of the younger Marx. Chief among these conceptions is that of 'alienation': the notion that in modern capitalist society man is estranged or alienated from what are properly his functions and creations and that instead of controlling them he is controlled by them. This concept is never mentioned in the well-known mature works of Marx; but the Hungarian Marxist Georg Lukács suggested with impressive insight in his *Geschichte und Klassenbewusstsein* (1923) that the Hegelian concept of alienation was nevertheless an underlying theme of Marx's mature work. A few years later, the publication of Marx's early manuscripts was to document fully the development Lukács had postulated. The publication of these works no doubt gave a new fillip to philosophical examinations of Marx; but the main cause is again political and ideological. Precisely because Marx's leading economic and social doctrines no longer make the impact they did, radical critics seek comfort or enlightenment in his metaphysics. To left-wing radicals in the West, the concept of alienation suggests a subtler and more plausible critique of contemporary society than the Marxist slogans of the past; to the revisionist philosophers in Eastern Europe Marx's philosophical concepts offer support in the struggle for freedom against the Party machine and the doctrinaire Marxism of the Party theologues.

Two recent trends thus again highlight the problem of the relation between Marx, the Marxism preached in his name and ethics. Neither trend, I should argue, has led to its solution. From the Soviet side there has been a refusal to face up to the distinctions between Marx and his disciples, including Engels, as well as a refusal or inability to grasp the fundamental difficulties that have to be solved by a moral philosophy or science of ethics. The work of the non-Soviet radicals and recent philosophical Marx critics deserves far greater respect; but the willingness it displays to examine Marx freshly and critically

---

have to be almost entirely in terms of its relation to Confucian tradition and Chinese social structure. I have therefore left Chinese Communism entirely out of account in the pages that follow as throwing no light upon Marx and the intellectual problems of Western Marxism.

is not generally matched by a similar willingness to deal with the nature of ethics freshly and critically. To throw truly penetrating light on the relation between Marx, Marxism and ethics we must be willing to do both.

PART ONE

The Primitive Ethic of Karl Marx

1. The Philosophy of the Concept

IN autumn, 1835, the 17-year-old Karl Marx, recently matriculated from the Trier *Gymnasium,* entered the University at Bonn as a student of jurisprudence. The family intention was that he should become a lawyer like his father. His conduct at Bonn was not exemplary; he was arrested by the police and punished by the University authorities for 'nocturnal noisiness and drunkenness', involved in a duel in Cologne and investigated for possessing 'forbidden weapons' (i.e., duelling pistols instead of the permissible swords). By October, 1836, he had persuaded his father to allow him to transfer to the great centre of critical thought, the University of Berlin. Here he quickly became a Left or Young Hegelian, infected with the philosophy of radicalism. Beside his courses in law, he attended lectures in philosophy, history and the history of art; when his father died in May, 1838, he openly proclaimed his intention of abandoning his training for a legal career and of concentrating on philosophy. For the next three years he worked on his doctoral dissertation, *The Differences Between the Democritan and the Epicurean Philosophies of Nature.* It was finished in 1841 and accepted for the degree by the University of Jena, where Marx had sent it to avoid the new anti-Hegelianism in Berlin and, possibly, to secure an easier degree. His confident hopes of a lectureship in philosophy at Bonn, promised him by his friend and fellow-Left-Hegelian Bruno Bauer, were dashed when Bauer himself was dismissed from the theological faculty in consequence of his radicalism. Meanwhile, Marx made his public political debut in 1842 with two contributions to Arnold Ruge's radical journal, *Anekdota*: a lengthy criticism of the Prussian King's new instruction to censors and a brief theological note in support of Feuerbach's exposure of miracles. There followed a spate of political articles for the radical newspaper newly formed in Cologne, the *Rheinische Zeitung,* which had been permitted by the Prussian authorities in the belief that it would uphold Prussian culture against Rhenish Roman Catholic separatism. On November 14, 1842, Marx was appointed editor—his first paid employment. On March 17, 1843, he resigned in a vain attempt to help the shareholders stave off the newspaper's threatened suppression. He occupied himself with a detailed criticism, paragraph by paragraph, of those sections of Hegel's *Philosophy of Right* which deal with the constitutional law of the State, the princely power, the executive power and the legislative power. (This incomplete manuscript, first published in 1927, I call his first Hegel critique.) In the later half of 1843, immediately after his marriage to Jenny von Westphalen and just before their emigration to Paris, Marx was working on his contributions to the *Deutsch-französische Jahrbücher,* published in Paris by Marx and Ruge in February, 1844. In these contributions Marx proclaims for the first time his espousal of the socialist cause and his discovery of the proletariat as the class which will provide the 'material force' of revolution and usher in the rational society and State. By then, as I shall seek to show, Marx had formed certain philosophical theories and ethical attitudes which continued to mould and direct his hopes and beliefs.

Throughout the period that ends with the completion of his first Hegel critique, Marx seems not to have been, in any useful sense of the word, a socialist. He certainly was a radical critic of the authoritarian Prussian State, of its censorship, its privileges, its revival of the system of estates. He believed firmly in the existence of common human interests and of rational law, and in their supremacy over class and individual privileges. He spoke occasionally of a popular will and warned that the exercise of authority from above might produce revolution from below. He was not unaware of poverty, as his articles on the wood theft law debates show,[1] and interested in socialism as an opposition movement proclaiming his own ideals of freedom and rationality. But Marx's fundamental ideals at this stage were intellectual and theoretical rather than social or practical. 'His path,' as Rosenberg writes,[2] 'had its beginning in his own intellectual and spiritual qualities, and his choice was influenced by the ideas that Hölderlin had implanted

---

[1] M I, 1–i, 266–304. See also his emphasis on the material hardships of the Mosel District in his *Vindication of the Correspondent from the Mosel* (M I, 1–i, 355–83).

[2] Arthur Rosenberg, *History of Bolshevism,* p. 3.

in the young German intellectuals of the *Vormärz*. He sought to free himself from the pressure exercised upon him and his intellectual equals by the mediocre German police state.' Marx's concern was with freedom and rationality, not with poor relief or factory legislation. He judged socialism—of which he confessed he knew little—harshly for its theoretical woolliness, and he judged it decidedly from outside. Until the end of 1843, he saw the poor as living examples of the irrationality of the existing State, not as a special moral indictment of that State or as vehicles for its overthrow. The separate class or estate was to him an anomaly to be abolished in the name of the truly popular sovereignty required by the rational State; he did not yet see it as the ground of a conflict to be developed until it found its dialectical conclusion. It was rather the movement of intellectual liberalism—the party of the concept, as Marx called it in his dissertation—that would usher in the rational State. That State would come, Marx believed, as the result of the blossoming forth of the rational and universal human spirit in history—working through *philosophy*, i.e., theoretical criticism. Philosophy was for Marx, even then, practical, in the sense that it criticised actual states of social affairs, but its function was to expose their theoretical presuppositions, to lay bare their inner contradictions. It was by exposing the discrepancy between the 'truly real' (i.e., the rational) and the existing state of affairs that philosophy would transform society.[1] The implication is clearly that the philosophically educated middle classes, and not the theoretically ignorant poor, will be the vehicles for such a transformation. This, at any rate, was Marx's position in his doctoral dissertation and at the beginning of his activity on the *Rheinische Zeitung*. His experience on that newspaper, as we shall see, no doubt helped to open his eyes to other possible allies in the fight against the Prussian State, but only after the wave of newspaper suppressions ousted Marx from his post and demonstrated the practical impossibility of further effective criticism of the Government did Marx turn to the proletariat.

[1] Thus he writes in his dissertation: 'It is a psychological law, that the theoretical spirit which has become internally free is turned into practical energy, and coming forth as will from the shadow kingdom of Amenthes, turns against the mundane reality that exists without it . . . But the *practice* of philosophy is itself *theoretical*. It is criticism.' (M I, 1–i, 64.) Cf. Hegel in his letter to Niethammer of October 28, 1808: 'I am daily growing more convinced that theoretical work brings more about in the world than practical work; once we have revolutionised the kingdom of ideas, actuality can no longer resist.' (Quoted by Hans Barth, *Wahrheit und Ideologie*, p. 83.)

If Marx was not a socialist at this stage, he was even more emphatically not a 'scientist', concerned with 'brute facts' rather than logical or ethical 'principles'. He did like to think of himself, from the beginning of his intellectual quest, as an opponent of logical *a priorism* and empty speculation. He saw himself as a man who derives logical principles from reality and not reality from logical principles. As early as 1837, he wrote in one of his verse epigrams:

> Kant und Fichte gern zum Aether schweifen,
>   Suchten dort ein fernes Land,
> Doch ich such' nur tüchtig zu begreifen,
>   Was ich—auf der Strasse fand!
>
> (M I, 1–ii, 42.)

But what Marx finds in the street is a logical 'principle', and generally one of the most abstract and metaphysical kind. He does, of course, criticise Hegel for *a priorism*; at least he does so in the first Hegel critique if not yet in the dissertation. In the critique he attacks Hegel vigorously for performing his deduction in the logical mind instead of the actual mind and for treating world history as a mere illustration of the mysterious life history of the Idea. He complains tellingly that Hegel develops the world out of the logical concept, instead of developing the logical concept out of the world. Of Hegel's discussion of the constitution, Marx exclaims: 'Hegel gives us the constitution of the concept instead of the concept of the constitution' (M I, 1-i, 420). But it is with the *concept* of the constitution, or with the 'concept' of any other thing, that Marx himself is concerned at this stage—not with the actual existing thing itself. Nor is the 'concept' for Marx a 'mere' recognition of the common features of certain existing things. For him, as for Hegel, it is their inner principle, the logical essence that determines their development, but which in fact may not yet have broken through into 'empirical' existence.

Marx, in fact, has as much contempt as Hegel for the 'merely empirical', for treating things just as they are or 'appear'. To do so, Marx believed with Hegel, would be to see only the outer appearance, and to see this one-sidedly, with the inevitable result of being caught in seemingly irresolvable contradictions. True understanding can only be gained by looking at the concept, the motive power which is in things and yet outside them as their aim, the 'energising principle' which determines their character and development, not by external compulsion, but as an inner self-realisation.

The alleged inadequacy of the 'mere empirical generalisation' as opposed to the speculative grasp and development of the 'concept' seen as energising principle is the fundamental theme of Marx's doctoral work. He contrasts Democritus, who saw the atom simply as existent, with all its contradications, and Epicurus, who allegedly saw it as absolute concept, grasping its apparent contradictions and giving them their full speculative development and ultimate reconciliation. For Democritus, says Marx in his final summing up, 'the atom remains pure and abstract[1] category, a hypothesis which is the result of experience and not its energising principle and which therefore remains unrealised just as it fails to determine subsequent actual science' (M I, 1-i, 52). It is because of this, Marx took his dissertation to show, that Democritus' philosophy of nature is inadequate.

The unresolved contradictions in Democritus' account of the atom are epitomised in the two contradictory accounts of truth with which he is credited. On the one hand, he proclaimed that truth is hidden— 'it lies at the bottom of a well'. On the other hand, as he says elsewhere, truth is all that appears. In pursuit of truth in this sense Democritus travelled throughout the ancient world collecting and ordering facts. Yet he was never able to resolve the contradiction between the atom as inaccessible to perception and as yet logically presupposed by the existence of reality. Epicurus is able to resolve this and other contradictions in the concept of the atom because he develops it speculatively, finds the necessary logical synthesis, instead of wandering off blindly on the paths of science. He does this in precisely that part of his theory —the seemingly illogical doctrine that atoms swerve capriciously— for which he has been most criticised. In the doctrine of the swerve, according to Marx, Epicurus resolves the contradiction between the atom as a free point and as a determined line; for the atom moving mechanically, as in Democritus, is the atom determined from without, that is, the atom not itself. Epicurus' doctrine of the swerve thus makes the atom free and self-determined. His theory of knowledge and of time, by placing the atom under the form of the inner sense, makes the atom conscious. Individual self-consciousness thus 'steps from her concealment and confronts Nature in the independence she has just attained'.[2] The free spirit's final obstacle is the heavenly bodies, seen by thinkers before Epicurus as eternal and unchangeable. These bodies

---

[1] *Abstract* throughout Marx's early work has the Hegelian sense of one-sided, something seen from a specific but inadequate point of view that fails to reveal the logically relevant whole.   [2] M I, 1–i, 41–44.

represent abstractly individual matter confronting a self-consciousness still conceived as abstractly individual. They are the symbols of the free spirit's greatest foe, physical necessity. Thus its final step on the march to freedom is to throw off the yoke of these heavenly bodies seen[1] as independent, as foes of the *ataraxia* of the human spirit. The human mind, armed with its own self-consciousness in which the independence of Nature is reflected and overcome, can now assert its own freedom and throw off the mechanistic determination imposed by external physical laws just as it threw off the Gods and divine heavenly bodies that symbolised man's subjugation. In their place, it erects its own 'natural science of self-consciousness', whose subject matter is the march of human self-consciousness toward the rational whole, independent, free and self-determined.

On this ground, and this ground alone, Marx argues, can the necessary contradictions of the Democritan atomic theory be resolved. Marx proceeds to resolve them with a Hegelian sophistry almost breath-taking in its substitution of verbal analogies for real connexions. At least as sophistical as his identification of the atom with self-consciousness (through its 'placing under the form of the inner sense') is his resolution of the contradictions threatened in Epicurus' theory by the problems of the atom's weight, shape and size. The question whether the attraction and repulsion between atoms does not destroy their 'freedom' receives similar short shrift. In being repelled or attracted by another *atom,* the atom is simply repelled or attracted by *itself,* since one atom is indistinguishable from another. It thus remains self-determined and therefore free.[2]

The critical position with which Marx is working here, and throughout his earliest writings, is frankly, even aggressively, Hegelian. To understand the world is to see its energising principle, to grasp the concept working dialectically through things toward an ultimate

---

[1] Marx, like Hegel, insists throughout his dissertation on equating *what* is seen or conceived with our seeing or conceiving it. We are thus left with the impression that when the Greeks changed their theory of the heavenly bodies the heavenly bodies themselves changed. But this, of course, outrageous as it may seem, is precisely what the Idealist denial of independence tends to suggest.

[2] The above, necessarily brief, outline of Marx's dissertation emphasises his philosophical position rather than the mere anti-religious sentiment which it helped to support and which was strongly expressed in Marx's 'Promethean' preface, where those who rebel against the Gods were treated as the true heroes of philosophy. For a fuller English summary of the dissertation see H. P. Adams, *Karl Marx in His Earlier Writings,* pp. 27–41.

harmony that represents the truly real come to empirical existence. To see this, for Marx as for Hegel, is to overcome the apparent conflict between what is and what ought to be, to see them reconciled in the rational that is coming to be, the rational which will establish both true freedom and lasting harmony.

It is clear then, that for the young Marx as for Hegel, philosophy is a normative study, and that the notion of the 'rational' provides them with a moral as well as an historical end. It is thus that for both of them the criteria of rationality become at the same time the criteria of what is ultimately moral or good. These criteria, as we saw, are freedom and harmony. For Marx, as for Hegel, freedom meant self-determination in accordance with one's inner constitution; it meant not being determined from without, by one's relations to other things, but by the logical principle of one's own development. Harmony meant above all the lack of inner contradiction, in that curious Hegelian sense of contradiction that confuses it with exclusion and treats it as a character of—imperfect—existing things, thus holding that two contradictories may both be 'partially' true and both exist. Since contradiction is held to be the necessary basis of historical change, the truly harmonious is also the stable, the ultimately durable. It represents the truly real as against the 'mere' dependently existing thing which, by its dependence, is not itself. To be truly self-determined and free from contradiction is to be truly real and truly good.[1] To exhibit dependence (determination from without), division, instability, and 'self-contradiction' is to fall short, to be evil in a sense that sees evil merely as a negative appearance, a one-sidedness, rather than as a positive quality. The conflict between good and evil, for both Marx and Hegel, is not irreconcilable or eternal—the evil is simply the partial, a one-sidedness that will be taken up and dissolved in the inevitable progress toward the rational.

There are certain important differences between Marx and Hegel even at the time of Marx's completion of his dissertation. Hegel and Marx both saw thought as an essence, and not as a relation, but in Hegel's doctrine of the thought in things, and in his treatment of the Absolute Idea as that which ultimately contains all its manifestations, both social and 'natural', thought loses its specifically human character and the Absolute Idea becomes an impersonal, non-human force, at

---

[1] 'That which is the Best,' Marx quotes approvingly from Aristotle in his dissertation, 'has no need of action but is itself the end.' Like the gods of Epicurus and of Greek plastic art, it expresses the unlimited freedom of the subject in dealing and grappling with objects.

once the dynamic form of all reality and its ultimate totality. Marx, on the other hand, followed the Left Hegelians in identifying thought with *human* self-consciousness, and the motive power of history with a specifically *human* spirit or essence. We shall see later how Marx, in consequence, rejects the non-human Absolute Idea as something alien to humanity and to man, and regards its alleged social manifestations (e.g., Hegel's rational State and its organs) as attempts to erect authoritarian social institutions 'dominated by a spirit not their own'. This, too, is why Marx can take the Hegelian criteria of rationality at face value, and actually use them against Hegel's complicated structure of rights and duties. Similarly, Marx rejects Hegel's notion of philosophy as *Nachdenken*, as the passive analysis of the progress of the Idea after the event. 'The owl of Minerva', Hegel had written in a famous passage in his preface to the *Philosophy of Right*, 'spreads its wings only with the falling of dusk.' Marx, on the other hand, by identifying the motive power of history with *human* self-consciousness, could see philosophy as the critical activity of that consciousness, and hence as itself part of the motive power. For Marx, at any rate when he wrote his dissertation, philosophy was thus the force which would change the world, and not merely register its changes.

Marx's rejection of Hegel's attempt to straddle the issue between immanent self-realisation and external necessity has one fundamentally important result: it brings out even more clearly the Rousseau-Kantian strain in Hegel, the emphasis on freedom as self-determination and on the free will as the universal and universalisable will. To the youthful Marx, the goal of human history is the free society—the universal kingdom of ends—and men and institutions are judged by the Kantian criterion of universalisability, with self-determination strongly emphasised and the concept of duty entirely omitted. Marx believed, of course, that, as Hegel had shown, the Kantian dualism must be overcome: the dichotomies of noumenal and phenomenal, of speculative and practical reason, of duty and inclination, would disappear in the 'truly human' man and 'truly human' society. But the dualism, Marx believed, was about to be overcome—the rational society was hovering in the wings of the theatre of history. Not until the end of 1843, when his confidence in the immediate, almost unaided, coming of the rational society had waned, did Marx pay any serious attention to the dialectic process that would bring it about. Before that, he was not interested in tracing historical progress through its succession of partial forms. The rational society was at hand—it was no longer necessary to study the contradictions of empirical existence. All that needed to be done—and all that Marx did in his first year of political writing—was to hold up the truly rational before the empirical, and watch the latter disintegrate. This is why, in his earliest work, Marx could confidently hold up, against the perfidy and privilege of the Prussian State, the positive morality and the natural law of the free man and the free society.

2. The Free Individual

THAT the young Marx took his criteria of freedom and harmony to establish positive moral and ethical 'principles', eternally and immutably true, his earliest work leaves no doubt. Thus, in his *Remarks on the Most Recent Prussian Instruction to Censors* (one of the *Anekdota* contributions, written in January–February, 1842), Marx notes that the instruction has substituted the words 'decency, propriety and external decorum' for the words 'morality and the decent proprieties' in the original law. 'We see', writes Marx, 'how morality as morality, as the principle of the world, which obeys its own laws, disappears, and in place of the essential character we have external appearance, a decorousness imposed by the police, a conventional propriety' (M I, 1–i, 161). But for Marx, positive morality does not disappear, nor can it be explained away. After arguing that censorship is evil in all its aspects, he concludes: 'That which is in general bad, remains bad, no matter which individual is the carrier of badness, whether a private critic or an employee of the Government. Only in the latter case, the badness is authorised and regarded from above as necessary in order to bring to realisation the good from below.' (M I, 1–i, 165.) This, for Marx, is no excuse. 'We have shown', he writes in his *Rheinische Zeitung* articles on the debates on freedom of the press in the sixth Rhenish Diet, 'that the press law is a right and the censorship law a wrong. The censorship, however, itself admits that it is not an end in itself, that it is not in itself good, that it therefore rests on the principle: "the end makes holy the means." But an end which necessitates unholy means is not a holy end.' (M I, 1–i, 211.) Again, when the representative of the knights in the Diet argues that all men are imperfect and need guidance and education, Marx insists that we cannot abandon objective standards merely because all things are allegedly imperfect:

26

'If then all things human are imperfect by their very existence, shall we therefore jumble up everything together, respect everything equally the good and the bad, the truth and the lie?' (M I, 1–i, 201).

The positive distinction between the good and the bad stems for Marx from the positive distinction between self-determination and dependence. In his comment on the Prussian censorship instruction, Marx emphatically distinguishes true morality from the spurious, evil morality of religion: 'Morality rests on the autonomy, religion on the heteronomy of the human spirit' (M I, 1–i, 161). Again, in the *Rheinische Zeitung* discussion of press freedom and censorship, he writes:

From the standpoint of the Idea, it is self-evident that freedom of the press has a justification quite different from that of censorship, in so far as it is itself a form of the Idea, of freedom, a positive good, whereas censorship is a form of bondage, the polemic of a *Weltanschauung* of appearance against the *Weltanschauung* of the essence. It is something merely negative in character.

(M I, 1–i, 201.)

The identification of self-determination and good comes out still more strongly a little later in the same article:

The censored press remains bad, even if it brings forth good products, for these products are good only in so far as they represent the free press within the censored press, and in so far as it is not part of their character to be products of the censored press. The free press remains good, even if it brings forth bad products, for these products are apostates from the character of the free press. A eunuch remains a bad man, even if he has a good voice. Nature remains good even if it brings forth abortions.

(M I, 1–i, 205.)

and again when Marx rejects the view that freedom of the press can be defended as a case of freedom to exercise a craft:

The freedom to exercise a craft is just the freedom to exercise a craft and no other freedom, because within it the nature of the craft takes form undisturbed according to its inner rules of life; freedom of the courts is freedom of the courts, if the courts follow their own rules of law and not those of some other sphere, e.g., of religion. Every specific sphere of freedom is the freedom of a specific sphere, just as every specific way of life is a specific nature's way of living.

(M I, 1–i, 221.)

For Marx, as for Spinoza, then, 'to act absolutely in obedience to virtue is nothing else but to act according to the laws of one's own nature.'[1] As much a determinist as Spinoza, Marx sees quite rightly that a theory of freedom could not be erected coherently on the basis of indeterminacy, and no conception is further from his mind when he is writing about morality than that of absolute, or unlimited, 'freedom of the will'. What is for Marx the closest empirical approach to such a conception, the *capricious* action not in harmony with man's essential being, is as destructive of freedom on his view as 'passions' were on Spinoza's. But freedom, on rather traditional grounds which Marx never examines thoroughly, is taken by him as necessarily and exclusively of the essence of man. Freedom distinguishes man—the potential master of his environment—from the animal—necessarily the slave of its environment. Thus Marx contemptuously rejects, in the preliminary notes to his dissertation, Plutarch's treatment of fear of the divine as a means of bettering the unjust: 'In so far as in fear, and namely in an inner, unextinguishable fear, man is treated as an animal, then in an animal it is a matter of complete indifference how it is kept in restraint. If a philosopher does not consider it the height of infamy to regard man as an animal, then he cannot be made to understand anything at all.' (M I, 1–i, 114.) For Marx, 'freedom is so thoroughly the essence of man, that its very opponents bring it into actuality even while they struggle against its reality . . . No man fights freedom, at most he fights against the freedom of others' (Discussion of press debates, M I, 1–i, 202).

If Marx's belief in freedom was largely moulded by Hegelian philosophy and the intellectual climate of the *Vormärz*, it received powerful reinforcement from his outstanding character trait—his almost Nietzschean concern with dignity, seen as independence and mastery over things.[2] The strain breaks out already amid the high-flown idealism of his school examination essay, *Reflections of a Youth in Choosing a Career*:

Dignity is that which raises man the most, which lends to his actions, to all his strivings, a higher nobility, which leaves him unimpaired, admired by

[1] Spinoza, *The Ethics*, Part IV, Proof of Prop. XXIV (p. 207). Marx's preliminary notes for his dissertation, where he calls Aristotle, Spinoza and Hegel the more intensive philosophers, make clear the extent to which he is attracted by Spinoza's ethical views.

[2] This trait, I have argued elsewhere, like Marx's irascibility and contempt for Judaism and Jews, is connected with the insecurity imposed upon him by his Jewish origins and the equivocal nature of his status until his baptism at the age of six. See Eugene Kamenka, 'The Baptism of Karl Marx', in the *Hibbert Journal*, vol. LVI (1958), pp. 340–51, esp. pp. 344–5.

the multitude and elevated above it. Dignity, however, can be afforded only by that position in which we do not appear as servile instruments, but where we create independently within our circle.

(M I, 1–ii, 166.)

It is this psychological trait, too, which accounts for the fire in passages like the following from his discussion of the debates on press freedom:

A country which, like the old Athens, treats boot-lickers, parasites, toadies as exceptions from the general standard of reason, as public fools, is the country of independence and self-government. A people which, like all people of the best of times, claims the right to think and utter the truth only for the court fool, can only be a people that is dependent and without identity.

(M I, 1–i, 184.)

Time and time again his aggressive independence and his moral commitment to freedom burst out, in passages that punctuated his work long after he had ceased to be a Young Hegelian, long after he had stopped proclaiming a rational morality and had turned from philosophy to his 'scientific work'. 'The social principles of Christianity', he wrote angrily in the *Deutsche-Brüsseler Zeitung* in 1847,[1] 'preach cowardice, self-contempt, debasement, subjugation, humility, in short, all the properties of the *canaille*, and the proletariat, which does not want to be treated as *canaille*, needs its courage, its consciousness of self, its pride and its independence, far more than its bread.' Six years later Marx was writing in the *New York Daily Tribune*[2] on the village communities of India:

We must not forget that these little communities were contaminated by distinctions of caste and by slavery, that they subjugated man to external circumstances instead of elevating man to be the sovereign of circumstances, that they transformed a self-developing social state into never-changing natural destiny, and thus brought about a brutalising worship of nature exhibiting its degradation in the fact that man, the sovereign of nature, fell down on his knees in adoration of *Kanuman*, the monkey, and *Sabbala*, the cow.

Twenty years after that, when one of his daughters handed him a

---

[1] 'The Communism of the Rheinischer Beobachter' (September 12, 1847) M I, 6, 278.

[2] 'The British Rule in India', published on June 25, 1853, reprinted in *Marx and Engels on Britain*, pp. 383–4.

Victorian questionnaire asking him, *inter alia,* to state the vice he detested most, he wrote: 'Servility.'[1]

It was on behalf of the free, self-determined man, then that Marx rejected the repressive Prussian police State. It was on behalf of the free man that late in 1843 he became a socialist and joined Ruge and Bakunin in issuing the *Deutsch-französische Jahrbücher* of 1844. Ruge speaks for them all when he writes to Marx in the 'Correspondence of 1843', published in the *Jahrbücher* as a prefatory statement of the journal's *raison d'etre*: 'I call revolution the conversion of all hearts and the raising of all hands on behalf of the honour of the free man, the free State which belongs to no master, but which is itself public being, which belongs only to itself' (M I, 1–i, 558). Bakunin, too, speaks of 'the State, whose principle now finally is really man' (loc. cit., p. 566), while Marx proclaims precisely those principles which we have seen in his earliest work:

> The criticism of religion ends in the teaching that *man is the highest being for man,* it ends, i.e., with the categorical imperative to overthrow all conditions in which man is a debased, forsaken, contemptible being forced into servitude, conditions which cannot be better portrayed than in the exclamation of a Frenchman at hearing of a projected tax on dogs: Poor dogs! They want to treat you like men!
>
> ('Towards the Critique of Hegel's *Philosophy of Right:* Introduction',[2]
> M I, 1–i, 614–15.)

> Man's self-esteem, freedom, must be awakened once more in the heart of these men. Only this feeling, which disappeared from the world with the Greeks and from the blue mists of heaven with Christianity, can once more make from a society a fellowship of men working for their highest purposes, a democratic State.
>
> ('Corr. of 1843', M I, 1–i, 561.)

For the social conditions that would produce the free man Marx was to struggle for the next forty years. In the intensity of the struggle he never again turned to ask what the 'realm of freedom' might mean. That problem, he thought, he had solved before the struggle began.

---

[1] The incident is related by E. H. Carr, *Karl Marx—A Study in Fanaticism,* p. 7.

[2] This article, published in the *D.-f.J.*, though written shortly after the manuscript criticism of Hegel's *Philosophy of Right* which I have called Marx's first Hegel critique, is quite distinct from it. I shall refer to it in future as his second Hegel critique.

From 1844 onward Marx's primary interest was not in the nature of freedom, but in the developments by which it would come about.

In his earliest work, this problem does not yet occupy his mind at all. (The conditions of censorship under which he worked no doubt helped to keep him away from it.) Against what he believed to be the disintegrating conditions of servitude around him, he is concerned to hold up the truly human morality, law and society. His conception of the latter two we shall now examine.

3. The Natural Law of Freedom

THAT Marx should have begun his political activity by upholding natural law is hardly surprising. We have already seen the strength of Marx's rationalism. At Berlin, Marx had attended lectures on jurisprudence by Gans, the Hegelian opponent of Savigny, and as an undergraduate Marx had planned a major work demonstrating the rational foundations of jurisprudence—a work which he abandoned as soon as he had realised that his plan depended upon the separation of what ought to be from what is.[2] Soon after graduation, Marx wrote for the *Rheinische Zeitung* a vicious attack on the historical school of jurisprudence and on the morals[3] of Hugo, whom Marx regarded as its real founder. To treat law as an expression of the historical power of the 'irrational', as the tradition of a people or as an organic growth always true for its society, Marx insists, is to abandon all legal standards, to treat whatever occurs as legally and morally right. For Marx, law is Reason—seen not as an abstract faculty, torn out of history, but as the rational exposition of the necessary rules involved in the very nature of the activities with which law is concerned. In his discussion of a new Prussian divorce bill,[4] Marx writes confidently:

---

[1] Portions of this chapter are drawn directly from 'Karl Marx's Analysis of Law', by Alice Erh-Soon Tay and Eugene Kamenka, with the co-author's permission. Cf. *The Indian Journal of Philosophy*, vol. I (1959), pp. 17–38, esp. pp. 23–30.

[2] Marx, then nineteen, describes the ill-fated project and his reasons for abandoning it in a letter written to his father on November 10, 1837 (M I, 1–ii, 213–21).

[3] With special reference to polygamy. See M I, 1–i, 251–9.

[4] Published in the *Rheinische Zeitung* in December 1842. For a complete English translation of this article and some comment see Alice Erh-Soon Tay and Eugene Kamenka, 'Karl Marx on the Law of Marriage and Divorce—A Text and a Commentary', *Quadrant*, no. 15 (Winter, 1960), pp. 17–29.

The legislator must regard himself as a scientist. He does not *make* laws, he does not invent them, he only formulates them, he enunciates the inner laws of spiritual relationships as conscious positive laws.

(M I, 1–i, 318.)

It is this view which a little later—in the first Hegel critique—enables Marx to give a short answer to the antinomy that worried Hegel: the fact that the legislator derives his authority from a constitution itself created by legislators. 'The legislative power,' Marx retorts, 'does not make the law; it only discovers and formulates it' (M I, 1–i, 468).

The process of 'discovering' the rational natural law is not one that Marx is able to describe clearly. As in morality, so in law his position makes it easier to state what is not moral or truly legal, than what is. There is much vague talk of 'concepts'—the 'concept' of the press (which is taken logically to exclude censorship), the 'concept' of the public service, the 'concept' of marriage—from which positive rules of law are supposed to flow with logical necessity. Marx's most serious attempt at a concrete treatment is in the article on divorce. Marriage, he argues, is 'according to its concept' indissoluble—but some human relationships no longer correspond to their 'concept', i.e., are no longer marriages. The State may therefore dissolve them in law, but only because they are already dissolved in fact.

The dissolution of a marriage is nothing but the declaration: this marriage is a *dead* marriage, whose existence is a snare and a delusion. It is self-evident of course, that neither the capricious will of the legislator nor the capricious will of a private person, but only the *essence of the matter*, can decide whether a marriage is dead or not, for it is well-known that a declaration of death depends on the facts of the case and not on the *wishes* of the parties concerned. But if in the case of *physical* death you demand precise and unmistakeable proofs, must not a legislator lay down a *moral death* only after the most incontestable symptoms?

(M I, 1–i, 319.)

What these 'incontestable symptoms' are, how we derive them logically from the 'concept' of marriage, or how we would defend any particular criterion against those who reject it, Marx is unable to indicate. Conscious of the deficiency, he falls back on a vague popularism:

The *guarantee* that the *conditions* under which the *existence* of a moral relationship no longer corresponds with its *essence* will be laid down truly, in accordance with the state of knowledge and of universal opinion, without preconceptions, can be found only when law is the conscious expression of the will of the people, created with the people and through it.

(M I, 1–i, 319.)

Fundamentally, Marx is working with the general—truly universal and truly universalisable—will of Rousseau and Kant. For all the talk about concepts and specific spheres, both law and marriage become mere expressions of the human essence and its allegedly universal will. This indeed is Marx's basic position:

Where the law is true law, that is, where it is the existence of freedom, it is the true existence of the freedom of man. The laws, therefore, cannot fore-stall man's actions, for they are the inner rules of life of his activity itself, the conscious mirror images of his life. Law hence retreats before man's life as a life of freedom, and only when his actual actions have shown that he has ceased to obey the natural law of freedom, does the State force him to be free.

(Debates on press freedom, M I, 1–i, 210.)

The apparent assertion of positive codes of natural law is confined to Marx's earliest work. We do not meet it again. But his main view that 'true law' is freedom, the inner moral consciousness of the truly human and truly self-determined man, remains at the core of his mature belief in the withering away of the State and of the official Communist doctrine that under Communism law will wither away to be replaced by the inner moral consciousness of the Communist citizen.[1] So does his insistence that man must throw off anything that determines him from outside. This is why Marx utterly rejects the intrusion of religious conceptions into law, why he rejects the lawgiver who 'does not regard human morality but spiritual holiness as the essence of marriage, and thus puts in place of self-determination determination from above, in place of the inner natural inspiration a supernatural sanction, in place of the loyal submission to the nature of the relationship a passive obedience to decree.'[2] As we have seen, throughout his life Marx insisted that religion, by seeking to make man submit to illusions which man himself created, turns the free and self-determined man into a debased animal, determined from without. Two years later, in *The Holy Family*, Marx discusses the penal theory of moral regeneration which Eugene Sue seeks to exemplify in his

[1] Cf., for recent reaffirmations of this view, A. Y. Vyshinsky, *The Law of the Soviet State*, p. 52; P. A. Sharia, *O Nekotorykh voprosakh kommunisticheskoi morali*, p. 88; A. Shishkin, *Osnovy kommunisticheskoi morali*, p. 38.

[2] Marx's editorial note (1842) to another contributor's article on divorce, M I, 1–i, 315.

novel *The Mysteries of Paris* and makes this point time and time again. Each one of Sue's characters who goes through 'moral regeneration', according to Marx, comes out the less a *man* (or woman) in a moral sense. Each 'criminal', originally full of vitality, is made dependent or cringing, robbed of his or her talents, brought to anguish and submission:

As Rudolph [the moral regenerator] kills *Fleur de Marie* by handing her over to a priest and to consciousness of sin, as he kills *Chourineur* by robbing him of his human independence and debasing him to a bulldog, so he kills the gangleader by having his eyes gouged out so that he can learn to '*pray*'.[1]

Marx's own theory of punishment and regeneration rests squarely on his belief in the truly human society of the truly self-determined man. Marx contrasts what he considers to be Hegel's merely apparent demand that the criminal become the judge of his own crime with the genuine fulfilment of this demand under 'human' conditions:

Hegel holds that the criminal must as a punishment pass sentence on himself. *Gans* developed this theory at greater length. In Hegel this is the *speculative disguise* of the old *ius talionis* that Kant developed as the *only legal theory of punishment*. Hegel makes self-judgment of the criminal no more than an '*Idea*', a mere speculative interpretation of the *current empirical penal code*. He thus leaves the mode of application to the respective stages of development of the State, i.e., he leaves punishment as it is. Precisely in that he shows himself more critical than his Critical echo. A *penal* theory which at the same time sees in the criminal the *man* can do so only in *abstraction,* in imagination, precisely because *punishment, coercion,* is contrary to *human* conduct. Besides, this would be impossible to carry out. Pure subjective arbitrariness would take the place of the abstract law because it would always depend on official 'honest and decent' men to adapt the penalty to the individuality of the criminal. Plato admitted that the *law* must be one-sided and must *make abstraction* of the individual. On the other hand, under *human* conditions punishment would *really* be nothing but the sentence passed by the culprit on himself. There will be no attempt to persuade him that *violence* from *without,* exerted on him by others is violence exerted on himself by himself. On the contrary, he will see in *other* men his natural saviours from the sentence which he has pronounced on himself; in other words the relation will be reversed.

(M I, 3, 356; cf. HF 238–9.)

Marx began, as we have seen, with a positive conception of rational law and rational legal rules, which courts could and should apply.

---

[1] All the passages quoted here were written by Marx.

Yet, almost in the act of stating this conception, he finds it disintegrating in his hands. For if law is the expression of freedom, if the criminal must suffer no violence from *without,* then, under truly human conditions, law must simply disappear. This, indeed, is what the mature Marx believed would happen. He was able to do so because he saw true freedom as necessarily requiring the truly co-operative, truly human, society.[1]

[1] Marx reverts to the problem of law and punishment on two subsequent occasions: in his review of Peuchet's book on suicide, which he wrote for Moses Hess' *Gesellschaftsspiegel* in the latter half of 1845 (M I, 3, 391–407), and in an article published in the *New York Tribune* in 1853 (cited in French by Maximilien Rubel in his translation and selection of *Karl Marx: Pages Choisies pour une Ethique Socialiste,* pp. 117–18, from *Gesammelte Schriften von Marx und Engels,* edited by Riazanov, pp. 80 et seq.). In the former he is concerned to show the pointlessness of discussions whether suicide is the product of bravery or cowardice and of a moralism which constantly speaks of man's social *duties* without ever mentioning his social *rights.* The true lesson we can learn from the prevalence of suicide is quite clear to Marx: 'What sort of a society is it, in truth, where one finds several millions in deepest loneliness, where one can be overcome by an irresistible longing to kill oneself without anyone discovering it. This society is not a society; it is, as Rousseau says, a desert populated by wild animals.' (M I, 3, 394.) In the *New York Tribune* article Marx again rejects Kant and Hegel's theory of punishment as the *lex talionis* in philosophical guise. Their argument that the criminal, in denying other people's rights, calls down on himself the denial of his own, has the merit of treating him as a being worthy of respect. But it treats the whole question *abstractly;* it considers only the 'free-will' of the criminal and the violation of rights in general; it does not consider the motives and temptations of the criminal as a specific human being in a concrete social situation. The conclusion is thus the same as he reached in his review of Peuchet: 'Punishment, at bottom, is nothing but society's defence of itself against all violations of its conditions of existence. How unhappy is a society that has no other means of defending itself than the executioner.' (Cf. Acton, *The Illusion of the Epoch,* pp. 210–11.) Marx, as many critics have noted, seems to hold that every criminal is driven to crime either by economic necessity or by a 'truly human' feeling of protest against the pressures of the class society. Hence, on this basis he could again believe that law and crime would wither away once economic necessity and class pressures had disappeared.

4. The 'Truly Human' Society

NOWHERE in Marx's early discussion of rational morality and rational law do we find Marx treating these as *means*, as principles of conduct meant to ensure the production of the maximum 'good' possible in any given situation. He was not interested in the 'moral' problems of the individual faced with inherently 'evil' situations, conditions in which someone must suffer, have his desires thwarted, be dominated or constrained. The fear of a Burke that sound moral intentions, in political life, could produce evil results, the problem of a Godwin forced to choose between saving Archbishop Fénelon or his mother, would have seemed to Marx nothing but an attempted piece-meal accommodation with evil. As long as such 'contradictions' were possible, Marx would have retorted, society is not yet rational, man is not yet free, true morality is still impossible. There can be no rational principles for dealing with 'contradictions' except by resolving these contradictions. 'Rights and duties', Marx writes in the *German Ideology* (M I, 5, 192), 'are the two complementary sides of a contradiction which belongs only to civil society.'

For Marx, morality and law represented the unflowering of man's essential being (*Wesen*) and an essence, according to Marx, is always truly universal. The human essence or spirit is what is common to all men: their eternal nature. It must therefore express itself above all in the unity of men, in overcoming the divisions created by their empirical particularity. Conflict for Marx stems from the empirical particularities and distinctions among men; but these distinctions for Marx are secondary, destined to be overcome by the unflowering of the human essence. 'What is the kernel of empirical evil?' asked Marx in the preliminary notes for his dissertation. 'That the individual locks himself into his empirical nature against his eternal nature.' (M I, 1–i,

111.) No doubt, traditional moralists and legal theorists, with their dualism of facts and standards, had sought to erect moral and legal norms based on an attempted accommodation between man's empirical divisiveness and rational unity. But such an accommodation, Marx firmly believed, was pointless, necessarily incoherent and unstable, doomed to be swept away in the historical progress toward rational freedom. Only with the full fruition of the human spirit or essence could morality arise. Since the essence is universal, its first and primary condition is the rational society, in which the traditional problems of morality and law are entirely resolved. The true basis of morality is not individual conduct, but social organisation. On this ground Marx proclaimed the rational society, 'the concretisation of human freedom' (M I, 1–i, 248). 'Philosophy,' he said in the same article—an attack, written in July, 1842, on the editorial opinions of the rival *Kölnische Zeitung*—'interprets the rights of man, it demands that the State shall be the State of human nature' (M I, 1–i, 247).

In such a rational State, a universal 'political intelligence' rules:

The question is whether special interest shall represent political intelligence or whether political intelligence shall represent special interest. Political intelligence will regulate the ownership of land according to the maxims of the State,[1] it will not regulate the maxims of the State according to the ownership of land; it will enforce the ownership of land not according to its private egoism, but according to its civic nature; it will not determine the universal being according to this or that particular being, but it will determine this or that particular being according to the universal being.

(Article on 'The Committee of Estates in Prussia',
M I, 1–i, 333.)

The divided State, the unfree State, stands to the rational State just as the unfree animal stands to the rational man:

The unfree condition of the world demands rights of bondage, for while human right is the existence of freedom, animal right is the existence of bondage. Feudalism in the broadest sense is the spiritual kingdom of animals, the world of divided humanity in contrast with the world of self-distinguishing humanity, whose inequality is nothing but the spectrum of equality.

(Discussion on wood theft laws, M I, 1–i, 272.)

[1] Just what these maxims are, or what precisely the 'civic nature' of the State is, never appears. At best, one might treat the passage above, like Kant's universalisability principle or Mill's statement of liberty, as creating a presumption against certain actions.

In the first Hegel critique Marx takes up the same point. The Middle Ages, which represented the form of bondage, which divided man from his universal being, he says, 'are the animal history of humanity, its zoology' (M I, 1–i, 499).

Civic morality and the criticism of the State, then, reveal the same ethical categories as Marx's examination of the individual, whom Marx indeed sees as above all a universal, social being. In the rational State, man, as individual and as universal essence of the State, is self-determined—the State is harmonious, stable and free from self-contradiction. 'A State, which is not the concretisation (*Verwirklichung*) of rational freedom, is a bad State' (M I, 1–i, 248). The imperfect or bad State is characterised by incomplete self-determination, division, instability and self-contradiction.[1]

Above all, the rational State is the State of a truly unified humanity. Its chief enemies, for the young Marx, are special interests, privileges and the estate or class, all of which elevate social divisions into a principle of social organisation:

> In general, the significance of the *estate* is that it treats *difference, separation*, as the existential content of the individual. Instead of making him a member, a function, of society, his manner of life, activity, etc., make him an *exception* from society; they constitute his privilege. The fact that this *difference* is not merely an *individual* one, but entrenches itself as a *common way of being* (*Gemeinwesen*), as estate or corporation, not only fails to dissolve the exclusive nature of the difference, but is actually its expression. Instead of each individual function being a function of society, this makes the individual function a society in itself.
>
> Not only is the *estate* based on the *separation* of society taken as a governing principle, but the estate separates man from his universal being, it makes him an animal . . .
>
> (M I, 1–i, 499.)

Similarly, Hegel's rational monarchy is for Marx the very reverse of rational or truly free, for 'in monarchy, a part determines the character of the whole' (M I, 1–i, 434). Monarchy represents a State divided against itself, just as the class represents man divided against himself.

Privilege is for Marx the most obvious expression of such division.

---

[1] One must not forget that within the imperfect State, however, division is also the condition of progress to the higher form. Thus Marx writes at the end of his polemic with the *Kölnische Zeitung*: 'Without parties, no development, without division, no progress' (M I, 1–i, 250). To the actual mechanism of the social dialectic Marx had at this stage devoted no serious attention.

In his contributions to the *Rheinische Zeitung*, especially in his discussions of the debates on press freedom and the wood theft laws, it becomes a synonym for lawlessness, for apparent freedom as opposed to true freedom, for man divided against himself (i.e., against another man, which for Marx is the same thing). 'The customary rights of the privileged in their content rebel against the form of the universal law. They cannot be formed into laws, because they are formations of lawlessness.' (M I, 1–i, 273.) Even in a small footnote to a contributed article advocating protective tariffs because of their success in England, Marx finds the philosophical criterion applicable:

The example of England refutes itself, because it is precisely in England that we see the appearance of the pernicious results of a system which is not the system of our times, but which corresponds rather to the conditions of the Middle Ages, conditions which were based on separation and not unity, which had to give special protection to every special sphere because they did not have the universal protection of a rational State and a rational system of individual States.

(M I, 1–i, 308–9.)

Now in this concept of the rational State as the State of the human essence, of truly unified humanity, there are obvious difficulties. Basically, they resolve themselves into the general difficulty of determining and describing the relationship between men as individuals, as particular, empirical beings, and the State that is supposed to be a form of their essence, the concretisation of their freedom. Marx himself draws attention to the way this difficulty arises in paragraph 261 of Hegel's *Philosophy of Right*, the paragraph with which Marx begins the extant portions of his first Hegel critique. In that paragraph Hegel says:

In contrast with the spheres of private rights and private welfare (the family and civil society), the State is from one point of view an external necessity and their higher authority; its nature is such that their laws and interests are subordinate to it and dependent on it. On the other hand, however, it is the end immanent within them, and its strength lies in the unity of its own universal end and aim with the particular interests of individuals, in the fact that individuals have duties to the State in proportion as they have rights against it.

Here, according to Marx, we already have a crucial antinomy, the conflict between the State as external necessity acting on men and as immanent principle within man. To speak of the State as external necessity is to imply that in a conflict between public and private interest, private interest must give way. Admittedly, Hegel does not speak of such a conflict, he portrays the situation rather as a relationship of spheres. But even so, Marx insists, Hegel's use of words like 'subordinate' and 'dependent' implies clearly that the character of the lower sphere is constrained from outside—we are still left with the unresolved antinomy between external necessity (for Marx, though not so simply for Hegel, normally a sign of evil) and immanent purpose.

In the rest of the critique, Marx does not go on to tackle the antinomy directly, but gets drawn into a more detailed criticism of Hegel's 'systematic' exposition of politics, in which he is able to show well enough how Hegel's careful logical deductions are consistently empty, the formal premises providing no real ground for the empirical content of the institutions he pretends to deduce from them. Soon, however, we begin to see that this antinomy forms the crux of the political issue between Marx and Hegel, and that the whole of the first Hegel critique is in fact an attempt to resolve that antinomy. Already Marx has rejected the Absolute Idea, because, like God and the external physical laws of a mechanical science, it marked the subjugation of man to an external determination, to something that was not a form of his essence. Now, for that same reason, he wants to reject a State that is not entirely *human*, not solely a form of man's essence, but also a form of the non-human Absolute Idea, an external necessity acting on man from outside.

Marx obviously feels that there are no major difficulties in the way of resolving that antinomy once we reject the Absolute Idea as a metaphysical form logically outside man and the world, and accept instead, as the motive power of history and the logical concept that manifests itself in the rational State, the universal spirit or essential being of man. Thus for Marx the State is not the concretisation of an empty, non-human, metaphysical, rational will, but the concretisation of essential human nature. It *is* immanent principle, and it is not *external* necessity at all.

Marx still has to give an account of that obvious basis of social conflict which makes Hegel treat the State as also representing external necessity: the conflict between private interests, divisive groups, all that which Hegel calls civil society, and the unified system which Marx and Hegel call the rational State. Hegel, despite the not unjustified sneer by Marx and Feuerbach that he makes the State the subject and society the predicate, does begin with the divisiveness of particular interests, with the assumption that civil society by itself never rises above particularity, dependence and necessary contradiction, and deduces from this its necessary logical completion by the State, which brings order, universality and freedom where there was instability, particularity, dependence and increasing misery. Admittedly, Hegel wants to say that civil society is 'taken up' into the rational State, and that the resultant order is in some sense *its own* order. But the very emphasis on external necessity, dependence and subordination which Marx criticises, the concern with the individual's 'rights' and 'duties', make it clear that Hegel does not simply dissolve the particularity of interests, but tries to mould them into a rational system. The whole *Philosophy of Right* becomes a study of the methods and institutions by which the State can keep civil society *in check*.[1] Marx, on the other hand, in making the rational State the State of the human essence, and thus ultimately completely identifying it with civil society in a way that the later Hegel did not, does not even try to grapple with man's 'particularity', with the relationship of specific activities, interests and strivings to man's 'human essence'. For Marx, once the essence has come to its full self-determination, the conflicting, divisive, features of human activities simply disappear—in place of division comes the distinction that is 'the spectrum of equality'.[2] We have seen how Marx had solved in his doctoral dissertation the apparent antinomy of the free Epicurean atom which is nevertheless determined from the outside because it is repelled by other atoms. In being repelled by another atom, said Marx, it is simply related to another *atom*, that is, to itself; hence it is not unfree at all. Similarly, Marx obviously feels, in the rational State, man, in being related either to other men or to the State, is simply related to the human essence, that is, to himself.

[1] Marx is quite right, however, in insisting that 'the only "final consequence" of Hegel's assertion of the ultimate unity of individual and universal being, of citizen and State, 'is the harmony of discord with harmony' (*The German Ideology*, M I, 5, 465).

[2] Here, as in many other places, Marx is unconsciously supporting a view held by the younger Hegel against the view held by the older Hegel. Marx's position against the *Philosophy of Right* was put admirably by the twenty-six-year-old Hegel himself in his *Erstes Systemprogramm des deutschen Idealismus* (1796), where he wrote: 'I shall demonstrate that, just as there is no idea of a machine, there is no idea of the State, for the State is something mechanical. Only that which is an object of freedom may be called an idea. We must, therefore, transcend the State. For every State is bound to treat free men as cogs in a machine. And this is precisely what it should not do; hence the State must perish.' (Quoted by Herbert Marcuse in *Reason and Revolution*, p. 12 from *Dokumente zu Hegels Entwicklung*, ed. J. Hoffmeister, Stuttgart, 1936, pp. 219f.)

Neither in the first Hegel critique nor anywhere else in his work does Marx make any real attempt to get to grips with the problem of relating and distinguishing man's universal essence, his *Wesen,* and his existence as a particular, empirical, being. He does take up in the critique, however, a political question connected with this problem: the question of the relationship between the State as a concrete manifestation of human freedom and the individual person within the State. Marx rejects sharply Hegel's view that the 'rational will' can be embodied in a single individual (the Monarch) and argues instead that the rational State, to be free, must be democratic. What Marx means by democracy, however, must be examined carefully.

In his relatively popular polemical work for the *Rheinische Zeitung* Marx was constantly fighting against the conception that civic affairs could be the prerogative of a certain class or group. Often he sounded as though he were demanding democratic control as something requiring merely representative control. This was emphatically not his conception. Like Rousseau, he would have conceded that the will of the majority and the rational will are not necessarily identical, though, again like Rousseau, he was not always anxious to stress the differences. But the notion of representation Marx rejects emphatically, both on the grounds that to be free is to be active, self-determining, and on the grounds that representation undermines the truly universal character of the State.

To be represented is in general something miserable; only the material, spiritless, dependent, insecure need representation; but no element of the State can be permitted to be material, spiritless, dependent, insecure.

('On the Committees of Estates in Prussia', M I, 1–i, 334.)

In the first Hegel critique Marx reinforces this with a more general point—representation converts civic affairs into sectional affairs, into special interests, and thus destroys the very basis of the rational State. It is the product of the divorce between political or civic affairs and human affairs in general, of the gulf between the State and civil society. This divorce, this 'abstraction' (in the Hegelian sense) of the political State, Marx sees as a modern phenomenon. The medieval State, even though the State of human nature in bondage, was nevertheless a State of human nature, though not in its rational form. 'Folk life and civic life were identical' (M I, 1–i, 437.)[1]

---

[1] Marx's development of this point and his general conception of the relationship between civil society and political State will emerge more clearly in the following Part. In the material dealt with here, his views are still sketchy.

Hegel, however, had posed the problem in the form of an antinomy: If citizens are not to participate in the State through representatives then each citizen must take part as an individual. This would be impossible:

To hold that all persons should share, as individuals in deliberating and deciding on political matters of general concern on the ground that all individuals are members of the State, that its concerns are their concerns and that it is their right that what is done should be done with their knowledge and volition, is tantamount to a proposal to put the democratic element without any rational form into the organism of the State, although it is only in virtue of the possession of such a form that the State is an organism at all.
(*Philosophy of Right*, para. 308).

Marx seeks to solve the problem by cutting through and rejecting both alternatives:

The antinomy in its essential form is: all the individuals do it, or the individuals do it as *some*, as *not-all*. In both cases allness remains only *external* multiplicity or totality of individuals. Allness is not an essential, vital, actual quality of the individual. Allness is not something through which he loses the character of abstract individuality; allness is only the full *number* of *individuality*. *One* individual, *many* individuals, *all* individuals. The one, many, all—none of these descriptions changes the *essential being* of the subject, of individuality.

(M I, 1–i, 539–40.)

The contrast here is between universality as a mere collection, universality treated extensionally, and universality as an intrinsic character, universality treated intensionally. It is the same distinction as the distinction between Rousseau's 'truly general' will and what is merely the common will of a majority, or even of an entire totality. The rational State is the State of this intensional universality. Its universality rests on the fact that it is a form of the human essence, of man's essential being, which is, in virtue of its character as an essence, common to the entire species. Its universality does not rest on any voting by its members, on any counting of supporters and opponents.

What then *is* the relationship of particular, empirical men to their universal essence and to the rational State? The essence and State, according to Marx, ultimately permeate their entire being: social life and citizenship, civil society and State, become one; man's every action is an expression of the universal essence, and a part of his civic being. Thus, immediately after rejecting representation, in his article on the Prussian Committees of Estates, as something required by the spiritless and insecure, Marx writes:

Representation must not be understood as the representation of some stuff, which is not the people itself, but only as the self-representation of the people. It must be understood as a civic act which differs from the other expressions of the people's civic life only by the generality of its content; it must not be understood as the people's only, exceptional civic act. Representation must not be regarded as a concession to defenceless weakness, to impotence, but rather as the self-confident vitality of the highest power. In a true State there is no landed property, no industry, no gross stuff, which, as such raw elements, could make a bargain with the State; there are only spiritual [*geistige*] powers, and only in their resurrection in that State, in their political re-birth, do the natural powers qualify for a voice in the State. The State pervades all of nature with spiritual nerves, and at every point it must become apparent that what dominates is not matter but form, not nature without the State but the nature of the State, not the unfree thing, but the free man.

(M I, 1–i, 335.)

According to Marx, when

civil society is the true political society, it is nonsense to make a demand which arose only from the conception of the political State as having an existence divorced from that of civil society . . . In these circumstances the significance of the *legislative* power as a *representative* power disappears wholly. The legislative power is representative here in the same sense as *every* function is representative, in the sense, for instance, that the cobbler, in so far as he fulfils a social need, is my representative, in the sense that every specific social activity, as a species of activity, represents only the species, i.e., a character of my own being, in the sense that every man represents the other. He is a representative in this case not through something else, which he symbolises, but through that which he *is* and *does*.

(M I, 1–i, 542.)

This, then, is Marx's vision of the moral and historical end of man: the rational State which is the State of a human essence that is qualitatively and essentially universal. As such, it is self-distinguishing, but absolutely precludes separation or conflict. We do find in it a division of functions, but one that arises 'naturally' and spontaneously. Since each function is a manifestation or activity of the human essence, since each truly represents man's universal being, all functions are naturally harmonious components of a united social life. There is no call for an external power to apportion or to harmonise their various roles; there is no need for a coercive political State outside or above the society that rationally arranges itself. The conflict of rights and duties, of 'private' and 'public' wills, of individual and society, disappears from the arena of history.

The first Hegel critique, written soon after Marx's resignation from the *Rheinische Zeitung* and just before his emigration to Paris and Brussels, marks the end of one brief period of relatively popular writing by a very young man and forms the beginning of the new stage of intensive work and thought which was to make Marx a Communist. In the critique, Marx had to make clear to himself why he rejected the coercive State envisaged by Hegel and on what grounds one could proclaim the free society of the truly human man. Marx believed that he had done so. From then on, the problem that occupied him was how that society would necessarily come about. Its final nature occupied him less and less. In the *Paris Manuscripts* of 1844 and in the *German Ideology* two years later he presents a detailed view of the rational society of Communism for the last time. His language is already increasing economic, but his metaphysical assumptions remain: 'The fully realised society produces man in the full richness of his being, it produces the *rich* man, genuinely equipped with all his senses [*der tief allsinnige Mensch*].'[1] Wants and enjoyments lose their egoistic nature and utility becomes human, universal, social utility. Man is united not only with himself but even with Nature, which he makes part of his being and function.

The radicalism of Marx's position, as well as its concrete merits, which are discussed in Part III below, is somewhat obscured by the fact that Marx so far still speaks of rational law and a rational State—i.e., of freedom as a system of rules. Certainly, he cannot give such a position any concrete content. He cannot show on what 'rational' basis a court would decide precisely the point where a marriage ceases to be one; he cannot show what are the rules of 'political intelligence' by which a truly rational society would be dominated. It seems to me that there is little point in driving these arguments home against Marx at length. The conceptions of rational law and of a rational State which he proclaims at this period are confused versions of his position—residues of a moralism he is soon to abandon entirely. The view he is working toward is a far subtler and sounder view. A true 'marriage'—i.e., a genuine love between two persons—unifies the persons involved, brings them together in a co-operative relationship that transcends

[1] *Paris Manuscripts*, M I, 3, 121; cf. *German Ideology*, M I, 5, 185–217.

concern with purely individual ends. Such a relationship is not created by laws or rules and cannot be maintained by them when it has ceased to exist. (Marx's talk of 'caprice' only confuses this issue and reduces his position to the vulgar moralism he decries in theology.) Again, a truly free and co-operative society is one in which people *participate* in free and co-operative activities: a system in which people 'participate' only through *representatives* is not a free and co-operative society, but one in which people are in dependence, in which they lack the enterprise characteristic of freedom. What Marx means by the 'rational' State, then, is no State at all; what is implied by his conception of 'rational' law is no law at all. As long as either law or the State remain 'necessary' society is neither truly co-operative nor truly free. This is the view at which Marx was soon consciously to arrive.

PART TWO

Karl Marx's Road to Communism

5. The New Social Dialectic

IN the first Hegel critique Marx, following Hegel and an eighteenth-century tradition, had decomposed social life into civil society—the material and economic life of man, the divided and conflicting world of his private desires and activities—and the political State, which represents man's recognition of social interdependence and his striving for unity. Hegel, according to Marx, had sought to impose the latter on the former. Marx, on the other hand, insisted that the entire dualism would have to disappear in the rational society which would be at once spontaneously co-operative and materially all-embracing. Precisely how such a rational society would come about, Marx, as we have seen, had not yet asked. Between his resignation from the *Rheinische Zeitung* in March, 1843 and the publication of the *Deutsch-französische Jahrbücher* in February, 1844, he was both to ask the question and to emerge with an answer that was to direct and canalise the whole of his subsequent thought. The rational society would come about through the dialectical conflict, ultimate dissolution and 'taking up' of civil society and the political State. The bearers of the transformation, its 'material base', would be the proletariat: the class which is within civil society and yet outside it.

For Marx in his earliest writings, philosophy was the activity that finally overcomes man's empirical nature and the divisive, incoherent institutions based on this nature. It brings about the rational State. In the final stage, Marx had argued in his dissertation, philosophy is 'fired with the drive to make itself concrete'; it turns, in the form of will, against the empirical world. The resultant conflict ends, and can only end, in that final rational reconciliation in which the world becomes philosophical and philosophy worldly.

At the opening of his career, philosophy becoming worldly meant

51

two things to Marx. Firstly, it meant that philosophical concepts would ultimately become concrete existences. The rational reality which philosophy discovers as the necessity behind the one-sidedness of current empirical reality would itself burst into empirical being. The actual would become also the rational or truly real. Secondly, philosophy becoming worldly meant that even before this rational reconciliation philosophy enters the fray against the one-sided empirical reality. It turns on 'the world itself' and struggles to change it. 'But the practice of philosophy', Marx had insisted, 'is itself theoretical. It is criticism.' (M I, 1–i, 64.)[1] Philosophy becoming worldly thus did not mean for Marx, at this stage, that philosophy abandoned the philosophic method of criticism for some other form of struggle. It meant simply that philosophy turned from the discussion of abstract, metaphysical issues and took actual worldly institutions for the objects of its criticism. In the first two years of his critical writing, as we saw, Marx appeared to believe that it was sufficient to expose the 'contradictions' of empirical reality and to hold up against them the truly rational. The growing reaction in Prussia, culminating in the wave of newspaper suppressions that lost Marx his job in March, 1843, was to show Marx that it was not enough. The 'party of the concept' had been proved utterly powerless when faced by the material forces of the State.[2] On most of the 'philosophical radicals' the situation had a politically shattering effect. It drove them back into the examination of individual consciousness, of religion and theories of culture, and away from a practice of politics that showed all the signs of leading to nothing but despair. Only Marx, Ruge and Hess threw themselves with new energy into political effort. Marx, above all, with his pugnacious belief in freedom and dignity, was not the man to shrink from the struggle. On January 25, 1843, immediately on hearing that the *Rheinische Zeitung* is to be suppressed, he writes to Ruge:

I see in the suppression of the *Rh. Z.* a step forward for political consciousness and am therefore resigning. Apart from that, the atmosphere had become too oppressive for me. It is bad to perform servile tasks, even for freedom, and to fight with pins instead of clubs. I am tired of the hypocrisy, stupidity and bullying authority, and of our capping and cringing, our evasion and

---

[1] See also Marx's preliminary notes for his dissertation at M I, 1–i, 131–2. For a similar interpretation of Marx's position at this stage see H. Barth, *Wahrheit und Ideologie*, pp. 81–6 and H. Popitz, *Der entfremdete Mensch*, pp. 5–7.

[2] For a brief account of the relevant events, see Nicolaievsky and Mänchen-Helfen, *Karl Marx, Man and Fighter*, esp. pp. 61–2.

hair-splitting with words. In other words, the Government has set me free again.

(M I, 1–ii, 294.)

Typically enough, Marx was already on the look-out for possible allies. Thus on March 13, 1843, the eve of his retirement from the paper, he writes again to Ruge:

The head of the local Israelites has just come to me seeking my signature for a petition to the *Landtag* on behalf of the Jews, and I shall give it. Repellant as I find the Israelite belief, Bauer's notions[1] seen too abstract to me. We must riddle the Christian State with as many holes as possible and smuggle in the rational . . . We must at least try this—and *bitterness* grows with every petition rejected amid protests.

(M I, 1–ii, 308.)

By the end of that year Marx had proclaimed an ally more powerful than these poor Rhenish Jews—the proletariat.

'The weapon of criticism', Marx had discovered, 'can certainly not supplant the criticism of weapons: material force must be overthrown by material force.'[2] Thus, in the *Deutsch-französische Jahrbücher,* Marx proclaims his new political programme, the necessary union of philosophic criticism and class agitation, the alliance of thinking humanity which suffers and suffering humanity which thinks.[3]

Revolutions need a *passive* element, a material basis . . . It is not enough that the thought strives to be made real, reality itself must strive toward the thought.

(Second·Hegel critique, M I, 1–i, 615–16.)

Where, then, lies the *positive* possibility of German emancipation? Answer: In the formation of a class with *radical chains* . . . the proletariat . . . Philosophy finds in the proletariat its material weapons.

(Ibid., pp. 619–20.)

[1] That disfranchisement of the Jews is perfectly logical in a Christian State, and that the emancipation of Jews can therefore only *follow* the emancipation of the State from Christianity.

[2] *Toward the Critique of Hegel's philosophy of Right: Introduction* (the second Hegel critique, published in the *D.-f. J.*), M I, 1–i, 614.

[3] Compare his second letter to Ruge, dated May 1843 and published in the 'Correspondence of 1843': 'The existence of a suffering humanity which thinks and of a thinking humanity which is oppressed will necessarily be unpalatable for the passive animal world of the Philistines . . . The longer circumstances give thinking humanity time to reflect and suffering humanity time to rally, the more finished when born will be the product that the world carries in its womb' (M I, 1–i, 565–6).

Marx had discovered that he needs the proletariat, but he has not abandoned philosophy:

> Just as philosophy finds in the proletariat its material weapons, so the proletariat finds in philosophy its intellectual weapons, and as soon as the lightning of thought has penetrated thoroughly into this naive popular ground the emancipation of the German into a man will be complete . . . The head of this emancipation is philosophy, its heart is the proletariat. Philosophy cannot translate itself into reality without taking up and dissolving the proletariat, the proletariat cannot rise and dissolve itself without making philosophy real.
>
> (Ibid., pp. 620-1.)

Unquestionably, Marx was pushed toward the proletariat and toward the study of the concrete conditions of social development by his realisation of the impotence of a struggle that used ideas alone. But if the search for 'material' allies and foundations arose out of the practical climate in which Marx worked and out of his own aggressive temperament, it was equally necessary to him as part of a more detailed working out of the views he had sketched in his dissertation, his contributions to the *Rheinische Zeitung* and his first Hegel critique. He did there, and still does to some extent in the passages quoted immediately above, portray the climax of history as the confrontation of, and ultimate reconciliation of the 'contradiction' between, an unphilosophical world and an unworldly philosophy. He had begun by emphasising that philosophy, in the final stage, sheds its unworldliness and enters the dialectical struggle by seeking to make itself concrete. Now, political events had made Marx realise that the thought striving toward reality was not enough. Reality would also have to strive toward the thought. Marx's strong realisation of this at this particular stage may have stemmed mainly from the practical situation, but it enabled him to come to grips with what had been in any case a major weakness in his earlier position. For the dichotomy of thought and reality which runs through Marx's earliest views is a weak expression of what he himself believed. Philosophical criticism was for him the manifestation of man's universal, generic being in conflict with the one-sidedness and egoism of man's particular, empirical being. Such a conflict is not merely a conflict between 'thought' and 'reality'. It is a conflict within (social) reality between public and private being. To that conflict Marx now devotes his attention.

In his first Hegel critique Marx, following Feuerbach, had insisted that all thought is social or 'natural' in content, that that which is allegedly above 'the world' can always be reduced to a reflection of something within 'the world'. In the *Deutsch-französische Jahrbücher* he is able to develop this view. 'Material' life is something which he still sees as distinct and separate from the 'theoretical' life of men;[1] but he insists—quite rightly—that the supraterrestrial is always reducible to the terrestrial.[2] Thus he treats religion as expressing on the one hand real misery and on the other the protest against real misery (second Hegel critique, M I, 1–i, 607), and insists that in dealing with philosophy we are dealing with 'a copy, not an original' (ibid., p. 608).[3] Marx, who had constantly seen philosophy as an expression of man's real essence, now plants it firmly in its social context and ceases to treat it loosely as conquering reality from outside. From now on he treats the fundamental conflict and movement toward rationality as taking place *within* society, as a necessary consequence of social features and forms of development.

Although Marx has turned to the proletariat for succour, he does not yet see the dialectical conflict in society primarily as a conflict between economic classes. The central feature of modern society for him, at this stage, is not the separation between various economic groups in society. It is the separation, within each man himself, between his empirical being and his generic, social being, between his civil,

[1] Thus, in the 'Correspondence of 1843', Marx writes: The whole socialist principle is . . . only one side that affects the true human existence. We must concern ourselves just as much with the theoretical existence of man, i.e., make religion, science, etc., the object of our criticism.' (M I, 1–i, 573–4.)

[2] 'We do not convert questions about the world into theological questions. We convert theological questions into questions about the world.' ('On the Jewish Question', M I, 1–i, 581.)

[3] Here we already find that unfortunate metaphor of reflection which has raised the well-known difficulties in interpreting Marx's mature views on the character of ideologies and the social 'superstructure'. The insistence that the supraterrestrial (i.e., that which claims to be non-empirical) can only be made sense of in terms of the 'terrestrial' (i.e., the empirical) implies neither an untenable economic reductionism nor a doctrine that ideologies are purely passive; the word 'copy' tends to suggest the latter here and both in Marx's later work. Yet if Marx were really upholding the view that ideologies are purely passive, it would be difficult to see why he should think it important not to neglect criticism of the 'theoretical existence of man'. Much of the difficulty here, I think, is caused by the fact that Marx had not entirely emancipated himself from a Lockean representationalism; he had certainly not considered carefully either the nature of belief or the social role of beliefs. In spite of the generality of his later doctrines on this subject (considered in Part IV, Chapters 12 and 13) he was never to do so.

material life and his political life. It is the separation between civil society and the political State, between private, egoistic interest and common interest:

The consummate political State is in its essence the generic life of man in contrast with his material life. All the presuppositions of this egoistic life remain in civil society, as properties of civil society outside the sphere of the State. Where the political State has reached its true form, man leads a double life, a heavenly one and an earthly one, not only in thought, in consciousness, but in reality, in life itself. He leads a life within the common unity [*Gemeinwesen*], in which he is himself a common or generic being, and he leads a life in civil society, in which he acts as a private person, regarding other people as means and demeaning himself into a means, so that he becomes the football of alien powers.

(On the Jewish Question', M I, 1–i, 584.)

Here, then, is Marx's new social dialectic—the hostile confrontation of civil society and political State, each of them abstracted, one-sided, unstable and logically incomplete, powerless, within its present form, to express its 'true nature' or to achieve logical completion. In the Hegelian destruction of these forms, and in the raising of their respective contents into a new form where both are harmoniously reconciled, the rational society will be born:

Every emancipation consists of leading the human world and human relationship back to man himself . . . Human emancipation will be complete only when the actual existing individual man takes back into himself the abstract citizen, when, as individual man, he has become a generic social being [*Gattungswesen*] in his everyday life, in his individual work and in his individual relations, when man has recognised and organised his own forces [*forces propres*] as social powers, and thus no longer severs this social power from himself in the shape of political power.

('On the Jewish Question, M I, 1–i, 599.)

The conflict between civil society and political State, then, is seen primarily as the expression of a conflict within man himself, as an example of that *alienation* which Hegel sees as an essential step in the development of mind, and which Feuerbach strikingly developed in the field of religion. Just as Hegel had argued in the *Phenomenology of Mind* that the feeling of estrangement between man and certain of his own externalised powers becomes particularly acute at certain periods of history, so Marx argued that the hostile confrontation of civil society and political State is a modern phenomenon, the necessary precondition of the final rational society and the product of political emancipation from feudalism. In his first Hegel critique he had already argued that in medieval times the strict division between civil society and political state did not exist. The whole of man's material life was pervaded by religious and political forms. Men carried on their 'private' pursuits in guilds, estates, corporations. 'The material content of the State was determined by its form, every private sphere had a political character, or was a political sphere' (M I, 1–i, 437).

Now, in his essay on the Jewish question, Marx proceeds to develop the point and to show how history has set the stage for the final dialectical conflict:

Political emancipation is the *dissolution* of the old society on which the sovereign power, the alienated political life of the people, rests. The political revolution is the revolution of civil society. What was the character of the old society? One word describes it. *Feudalism*. The old civil society had a *directly political* character, i.e., the elements of civil life, such as property, the family and ways of earning a living, were raised to the level of being elements of civic life in the form of seignorial rights, estates and guilds. In this form they determined the relationship of the single individual to *the State as a whole*, i.e., they determine his *political* situation, i.e., his separation or exclusion from the other constituent parts of society. For this organisation of the life of the people did not raise property or labour to the level of social elements. It rather consummated their *separation* from the civic whole and formed them into *particular* societies within society. Nevertheless, the functions and conditions of life in civil society remain political, even if political in the feudal sense, i.e., excluding the individual from the civic whole, transforming the *particular* relationship between his guild or corporation and the civic whole into a general relationship between the individual and social life, just as they transformed his private, particular activity and situation into a general activity and situation. In consequence, the State as a unity, and the consciousness, will and activity of the State—the general political power—appear as the particular concern of a ruler separated from the people and of his servants.

The political revolution which overthrew the power of these rulers and made affairs of state affairs of the people, which made the political State a matter of *universal* concern, i.e., which made it a true State, necessarily smashed all estates, corporations, guilds and privileges as just so many expressions of the separation of the people from its communal life. The political revolution thus *destroyed* the *political character of civil society*. It smashed civil society into its simple constituents: on the one hand, *individuals*, on the other, the *material* and *spiritual or cultural elements* which form the life-content, the social situation, of these individuals. It liberated the political spirit, which, distributed in the various blind alleys of feudal society, had been worn down and decomposed; it gathered together the scattered fragments, liberated the political spirit from its amalgamation with civil life and constituted it into the sphere of common social being [*Gemeinwesen*], of *universal* public affairs, theoretically divorced from the *particular* elements of civil life. *Specific* activities and specific social situations sank to merely individual significance. They no longer constituted the universal relationship between the individual and the State totality. Public affairs as such became the universal affair of every individual; the political function became his universal function.

This perfection of the idealism of the State was at the same time the consummation of the materialism of civil society. Shaking off the political yoke meant at the same time shaking off those bonds which held fast the egoistic spirit of civil society. Political emancipation was at the same time the emancipation of civil society from politics, from even the *appearance* of a universal content.

Feudal society was broken up into its basic element, into *man*. But [it was broken up] into man in the shape in which he really was its basic element, into the *egoistic* man.

(M I, 1–i, 597–8.)

Here, then, is the basic structure of Marx's new social dialectic. The struggle between the particular, empirical nature of man and his rational, universal essence is the struggle between his private, material pursuits in civil society and the unity and universality expressed in the political State. In feudal society the struggle was still unclear. Man's material life and his political life were welded together, everything he did was treated as legitimately coming within the sphere of religious and political life. As a result, the feudal structure did to some extent inhibit and suppress the naked divisiveness and individual conflict of civil society, of man's economic and material life. It tolerated no economic 'freedom' to indulge openly in the *bellum omnium contra omnes;* it bound serfs to the land, fettered the 'free' land-holder in the political chains of homage and fealty, controlled retail prices and standards of workmanship through the guilds, forbade usury as an offence against the Christian faith. But the unity and universality proclaimed by feudalism were not the unity and universality of free men, co-operating spontaneously. Feudal unity was an artificial, illusory unity: a unity in bondage. Instead of overcoming division, feudalism elevated it into a political principle and temporarily stabilised it by force. Precisely because feudal society had not yet split human nature into two, because the rational universal being of man had not yet liberated itself from man's particularity and division, man under feudalism could not yet recognise his potentialities. The struggle was not yet clear. Then came the political revolution against feudal tyranny which ushered in modern society. It overthrew the political bondage of feudalism; but at the same time it also overthrew feudalism's political and religious control of economic life. It liberated man as a political citizen; it also liberated man as a self-seeking economic unit. The contradiction in social life thus emerged openly for all to see: on the one hand, the unified, universal political state, the fellowship of man as a citizen: on the other, the divisive, conflicting civil society, the material world of greed and competition, the *bellum omnium contra omnes*. 'The word "civil society" ', Marx writes in the *German Ideology* (M I, 5, 26), 'emerged in the eighteenth century, when property relationships had already extricated themselves from the ancient and medieval communal society [*Gemeinwesen*]. Civil society as such develops only with the bourgeoisie.'

6. The Critique of Politics

IN the *Deutsch-französische Jahrbücher*, as we have seen, Marx does not yet treat his social dialectic as consisting simply of the struggle of economic classes or as arising from economic 'contradictions'. His detailed investigation of civil society, of the world trade and industry, is only about to begin. For the moment, his analysis of civil society is still fairly perfunctory, particularly in relation to his far more detailed critique of the political State. But he does, in his article on the Jewish question, take the all-important step of connecting the evils of modern civil society specifically with the power of money, thus both laying the foundation for his coming critique of economics and bringing out clearly once more the ethical categories with which he works. Civil society, he insists, is 'the world of riches', and money is that power which turns man into a servile, dependent being, determined from without. It makes man into a *commodity*. Precisely in that, for Marx, lies its absolute moral evil.

> Money lowers all the gods of mankind and transforms them into a commodity. Money is the universal, self-constituting value of all things. It has therefore robbed the whole world, both the human world and Nature, of its own peculiar value. Money is the essence of man's work and existence, alienated from man, and this alien essence dominates him, and he prays to it.[1]
>
> ('On the Jewish Question', M I, 1–i, 603.)

Marx is able to bring these points into a review of Bruno Bauer's pamphlets on Jewish emancipation because he treats Judaism as the

---

[1] Here we have Marx's first economic application of Hegel and Feuerbach's doctrine of alienation. For Marx it simply means that man takes one of his own powers or functions, objectifies or reifies it by infusing it into an object or treating it as though it has separate existence from himself and then, instead of dominating it, allows it to dominate him.

religion of money,[1] as the practical expression of the egoism of the world of riches. Christianity he regards as the witting or unwitting partner of Judaism, as the religion which puts all of man's moral and social relationships into heaven, makes them external to his social being, and thus enables civil society to achieve its current arrogant independence:

Judaism reaches its highest point with the perfection of civil society; but civil society consummates itself only in the *Christian* world. Only under the sway of Christianity, which makes *all* national, natural, moral and intellectual relationships *external* to man, could civil society separate itself entirely from the life of the State, rend all social bonds [*Gattungsbande*] of men, put egoism, self-interested wants, in place of social bonds and break up the human world into a world of atomistic mutually hostile individuals.

Christianity arose out of Judaism. Once again it has flown back into Judaism.

Christ was patently the theorising Jew; the Jew therefore is the practical Christian and the practical Christian is become Jew again.

Christianity overcame actual living Judaism only in appearance. It was too *respectable,* too spiritualistic, to overcome the brutality of practical needs except by raising itself into the sky.

Christianity is the sublime thought of Judaism and Judaism is the mean practical application of Christianity, but this practical application can become universal only after Christianity as the consummated religion has completed *in theory* man's self-alienation from himself and from Nature.

Only then could Judaism gain universal dominion and turn externalised and estranged [*entäussert*] man and externalised and estranged Nature into objects fallen into servitude to egoistic needs, into objects of barter.

Making things saleable is the practical side of alienation. Just as man, so long as he is still caught within the limitations of religion, can only objectify his essential being by making it into an *alien,* phantastic being, so under the domination of egoistic wants he can only act practically, he can only create objects in practice, by putting his products as well as his activity under the domination of an alien being and giving them the significance of an alien being—the significance of money. . .

As soon as society succeeds in destroying the *empirical* essence of Judaism, buying and selling and its presuppositions, the Jew will become *impossible,* because his consciousness will no longer have an object, because the subjective basis of Judaism, practical wants personified, and the conflict of the individual–sensual existence with the existence of man as a member of the species will have disappeared.

[1] He was not the first Jew to display *jüdischen Selbsthass*—Jewish self-hate.

The *social* emancipation of the Jew is the *emancipation of society from Judaism.*

('On the Jewish Question', M I, 1–i, 604–6.)

Such, then, for Marx is modern civil society—egoistic, atomic, particular, logically precluded by its form from true universality and leading inevitably to servility, self-alienation, dependence and increasing internal tensions and misery. It is the animal world from which there can be no further development but to negate its basis and pass over to the 'human world of democracy' ('Corr. of 1843', M I, 1–i, 564).

The modern political State—Marx means by this the constitutional democracies established by the French and North American revolutions—suffers from a similar incoherence. According to Marx, it does embody the demands of reason, it points to the future, but only with the inevitable limitations imposed by its form and by its separation from civil society.

Reason has always existed, but not always in a rational form. The critic can therefore seize upon any form of the theoretical and practical consciousness and develop out of the special forms of existing reality the true reality of that which ought to be, of that which is reality's final aim. So far as actual life is concerned, it is just the *political State,* even where it is not consciously permeated by socialist demands, that contains in all its *modern* forms the demands of reason. And it does not rest there. Everywhere it supports reason coming to be reality. Equally, however, it falls everywhere into the contradiction of its ideal characters with its presuppositions.

('Corr. of 1843', M I, 1–i, 574.)

For Marx at this stage the political State is not yet merely an instrument of class control, nor is it a mere reflection of the state of civil society. On the contrary, like religion, it is not a reflection of civil society but a compensation for it, an ideal completion of it. Just as Marx regards Christianity as expressing not only real misery, but also the protest against real misery, a ghostly rationality in another world (second Hegel critique, M I, 1–i, 607), so he treats the political State as an ideal assertion of the universal human essence, of that striving toward universality, self-determination and natural co-operation which has been entirely banished from modern civil society.

Just as *religion* is the table of contents of the theoretical struggles of man, so the *political State* is that of his practical struggles. The political State within its form therefore expresses *sub specie rei publicae* all social struggles, needs, truths.

('Corr. of 1843', M I, 1–i, 574.)

The political State, however, is fatally limited by its form, by its separation from civil society and from the actual, empirical being of man with that society. It remains an *ideal* expression of his universal being, powerless to conquer the actualities of man's existence. It is hence one-sided, logically incomplete and incoherent in precisely those principles which it professes to apply to human society. The proof of this, says Marx, can be seen in the French and American revolutions. Professedly, they achieved the *political* emancipation of mankind. They proclaimed man's freedom, independence from religion and his rationality—*as a political citizen*. But as a *man*, they left him in bondage, thus contradicting their own basis, bringing out their one-sidedness and incoherence:

The boundary of political emancipation reveals itself immediately in the fact that the State can free itself of a certain limitation[1] without men becoming truly free of this limitation, in the fact that the State can be a free State without man being a free man.

('On the Jewish Question', M I, 1–i, 582.)

Thus, Marx argues, men proclaim themselves atheists politically by declaring the State to be secular yet guarantee themselves the 'right' of worship and so remain in religious bondage. Man decomposes himself into the *man*, follower of a specific religion, and the *citizen*, member of the atheistic State. The resultant tension expresses the real, this-worldly tension between civil society and the political State, between the *bourgeois* and the *citoyen*, between the private interest and the common interest (M I, 1–i, 583–91). Nor is this product accidental. It arises from the very character of political emancipation, which robs religion of even that limited connexion with man's universal being which it had in the feudal State and transforms it into an expression of the very spirit of civil society. The same considerations apply to private property:

The political annulment of private property [through the removal of property qualifications for voters and candidates] does not destroy private property

1 Marx uses the word 'limitation' [*Schranke, Beschränktheit*] here and elsewhere in the *D.-f.J.* to mean both the limitation or narrowness that prevents a subject from being truly 'universal' and the limitation that sets limits to the subject from without and thus makes it determined and not truly free. Both meanings are essential to his argument.

63

but presupposes it. The State destroys distinctions of *birth, estate, education* and *occupation* in its own way, when it takes distinctions of birth, estate, education and occupation to be *unpolitical* distinctions, when it makes every member of the people an *equal* participant in the sovereignty of the people without reference to these distinctions, when it treats all elements of actual civil life from the point of view of the State. For all that, the State nowise prevents private property, education and occupation from *acting* and making their *specific* being felt in *their* own way, i.e., as private property, as education, as occupation. Far from resolving these distinctions *of fact*, the political State exists only by presupposing them, it sees itself as a *political State* and imposes its *universality* only in opposition to these, its elements.

(Op. cit., M I, 1–i, 583–4.)

This contradiction, says Marx, runs through the whole doctrine of human rights, fundamental to the political State in its modern form. It breaks out clearly in the distinction made between political rights, the *droits du citoyen,* and the rights of man or natural rights, the *droits de l'homme*:

Who is the *homme,* as distinguished from the *citoyen?* No one but the member of civil society. Why is this member called 'man', simply man; why are his rights called the rights of man? How shall we explain this fact? By the relationship of the political State to civil society, by the essential character of political emancipation.

Above all, we assert the fact that the so-called rights of man, the *droits de l'homme,* as opposed to the *droits du citoyen,* are nothing but rights of the member of civil society, i.e., of egoistic man, of man separated from man and from the common life and being.

(Op. cit., M I, 1–i, 593.)

We can see this clearly, says Marx, if we examine the rights of man and of the citizen as laid down in the most radical constitution, the French Constitution of 1793, which names the rights of freedom, property, equality and security.

Freedom [if we examine the definition given in the Constitution] is therefore the right to do everything which harms no one else. The borders within which every man can move harmlessly are determined by the law, just as the border between two fields is determined by a fence. The concern is with the freedom of man as an isolated monad withdrawing into itself . . . The human right of freedom is not based on the connexion of man with man but rather on the separation of man from man. It is this right of separation, the right of the *limited* individual, limited unto himself. . .

Man's right of private property is the right to enjoy one's property and to dispose over it arbitrarily [*à son gré*], without considering other men, independently of society. It is the right of self-interest. Such individual freedom, like this application of it, forms the basis of civil society. It allows every man to find in other men not the realisation, but the limitation, of his freedom . . .

Egalité, in its non-political sense, is nothing but the equality of the liberty described above i.e., that each man is regarded equally as such a monad, based on itself . . .

Security is the highest social conception of civil society, the conception held by the police force that all of society exists only in order to guarantee to each of its members the preservation of his person, his rights and his property . . .

Civil society does not through the concept of security raise itself above its egoism. Security is rather the guarantee of egoism.

None of these so-called rights of man goes beyond the egoistic man, beyond man as a member of civil society, as a man severed from the common social life and withdrawn into his private interests and private caprice. Far from man being conceived in these rights as a generic being [*Gattungswesen*], the life of the genus itself [*Gattungsleben*], society, appears in them as a frame external to individuals, as a limitation of their original independence. The sole thread that keeps them together is natural necessity, needs and private interest, the preservation of their property and of their egoistic person.

(Op. cit., M I, 1–i, 593–5. I have omitted in this and in many subsequent quotations those of Marx's over-frequent italicisations which seem to me merely pointless.)

This, then, is the result of a political emancipation confined to the realm of politics, an emancipation based on the separation of political State and civil society:

A people which is just beginning to free itself, to tear down all the barriers between various members of the people and to found a common political fellowship [*politisches Gemeinwesen*] . . . solemnly proclaims the vindication of the egoistic man, severed from his fellow-man and from the common fellowship . . .

The political emancipators lower the citizen and the common political fellowship to the level of a mere means for preserving these so-called human rights, so that the *citoyen* is made the servant of the egoistic *homme*. The sphere in which man conducts himself as a universal, social being is degraded, put below the sphere in which he conducts himself as a sectional being and, finally, man as a bourgeois and not man as a *citoyen*, is taken for the essential and true man.

(Op. cit., M I, 1–i, 595.)

Thus egoistic man, the member of civil society, now stands revealed as 'the basis, the pre-supposition of the political State, which recognises him as such in the rights of man' (op. cit., p. 598). The political man, on the other hand, remains only 'the abstracted, artificial man, man as an allegorical person' (ibid.). Because the political State is such an allegory, such an ideal construct, based on the factual presupposition of egoistic man in civil society, it is in fact powerless before civil society. This is why, according to Marx, the Jews who are denied the right to vote in the smallest European hamlet control the bourses of the great European capitals.

The contradiction between the practical political power of the Jew and his political rights is the general contradiction between politics and the power of money. In thought, the former stands above the latter, in fact it has become the latter's slave.

(Op. cit., M I, 1–i, 602.)

We have seen, then, the formal, logical, necessary limitations of political emancipation and the political State. Both deny civil society, yet rest upon it. The historical reason for this 'contradiction' Marx suggests in his second Hegel critique, where he approaches his later class doctrine most closely:

Upon what does a partial, merely political revolution rest? Upon this, that a part of civil society emancipates itself and attains universal dominion, upon the fact that a particular class, working from a situation particular to itself, undertakes the universal emancipation of society. This class does free the whole society, but only under the proviso that the whole society find itself in the situation of this class, i.e., for instance, that it possess money and education or that it can at least attain these.

(M I, 1–i, 617.)

There are, indeed, moments of political enthusiasm when the demands of reason, embodied in limited form within the political State, seek to fulfil themselves. They press, within the form of the political State for the dissolution and supercession of such cardinal symptoms of man's bondage as religion and private property. But within the form of the political State this proves impossible:

In the moments of its specific feeling for itself, political life seeks to suppress its presuppositions—civil society and its elements—and to constitute itself as the true, contradictionless generic or social life of man. It can do this only through the forcible negation of its own conditions of existence, through declaring the revolution to be permanent; the political drama therefore necessarily ends with the re-establishment of religion, of private property and of all the elements of civil society, just as war ends with peace.

('On the Jewish Question', M I, 1–i, 586–7.)

A few months later, in his article 'Critical Glosses on the Article: "The King of Prussia and Social Reform. By a Prussian" ',[1] Marx again insists on the *necessary* impotence of the political State:

The State cannot overcome the contradiction between the good intentions of the administration on the one hand and its means and possibility of action on the other without overcoming and destroying itself, for the State rests on the contradiction. It rests on the contradiction between public and private life, between universal interests and special interests. The administration therefore has to confine itself to formal and negative action, for where civil life and its work begin there the power of the administration ends. Impotence *vis-a-vis* the consequences which spring from the unsocial nature of civil life, from private ownership, trade, industry and the mutual plundering engaged in by the various bourgeois circles is the natural law governing the administration. This fragmentation, this oppression, this slavery to civil society, is the natural foundation on which the modern State rests, just as the civil society of slavery was the natural foundation on which the ancient State rested . . . If the State wanted to overcome and destroy the impotence of its administration, it would have to overcome and destroy the private life of to-day.

(M I, 3, 14–5.)

Thus, according to Marx, we can see the necessary incompleteness, the merely illusory character, of political emancipation. But he still believes with that Young Hegelian optimism that sees the rational society about to burst upon the world that the chain of events begun by political emancipation cannot be halted. Its own logic drives it relentlessly forward at tremendous pace. Because each class that presses for political emancipation liberates society only from its own point of view, the rôle of emancipator in spirited countries like France, if not in Germany, passes in dramatic sequence from one class to another.

Finally it reaches the class which no longer realises social freedom under the presupposition of particular conditions that lie outside man but were

---

[1] The original article by 'a Prussian' was written by Arnold Ruge and published in *Vorwärts* (Paris) on July 27, 1844. Marx's reply appeared in the same paper on August 7, 1844. Ruge's text is reprinted in MI, 3, 587–9 and Marx's article in M I, 3, 5–23.

yet created by human society. This class on the contrary organises all the conditions of human life under the presupposition of social freedom.
(Second Hegel critique, M I, 1–i, 619.)

In France, Marx believes, such a class might be activated by enthusiasm. In Germany the French revolution took place only in ideas, in the philosophy of Kant, and not in reality; the middle classes remained powerless; here such a revolutionary class will be activated only by needs. But there is such a class—

a class in civil society which is not a class of civil society, an estate which represents the dissolution of all estates, a sphere endowed with universal character because of its universal suffering and claiming no particular rights because the wrong it is made to suffer is not a particular wrong but simply wrong as such . . . a class which represents the utter loss of humanity and which can therefore regain itself only by fully regaining the human. This dissolution of society as a particular estate is the proletariat . . . When the proletariat announces the dissolution of the social order that has existed hitherto, it thereby only expresses the secret of its own existence, for it is the effective dissolution of this order. If the proletariat demands the negation of private property, it is only making into a principle of society that which society has made into a principle of the proletariat.
(Op. cit., 619–20.)

If Marx turned to the proletariat from practical considerations, through realising the impotence of the German middle classes, he has here given it the 'speculative development' which he claims Epicurus gave to the atom. He sees in it not just the empirical existence, but the logical category. The proletariat occupies a necessary place in the dialectical schema; it is driven by 'the secret of its own existence' to accomplish the dissolution and raising up into a new form of the old order. And just as contradictions in the atom could not be resolved without treating it as *free*, so the contradictions of the proletarian's position cannot be resolved without restoring to mankind its freedom, its 'universal soul'.

The fellowship [*Gemeinwesen*] from which the worker is isolated is a fellowship of a scope and order of reality quite different from that of the political fellowship. The fellowship from which his own labour separates the worker is *life* itself, physical and intellectual life, morality and customs, human activity, human satisfaction, being human. Being human [*Das menschliche Wesen*] is the true fellowship of men. Just as irremediable isolation from this fellowship is incomparably more pervasive, unbearable, horrible and full of contradiction than isolation from the political fellowship, so the dissolution of this isolation from being human, or even a partial reaction or uprising against it, is as much wider in scope as man is wider in scope than the political citizen, as human life is wider in scope than political life. Thus, no matter how sectional an industrial uprising, it carries within it a universal soul; a political uprising, no matter how universal, hides in the hugest form a narrow soul . . .

A social revolution therefore takes place from the standpoint of the whole, even if it takes place only in one factory district, because it is the protest of man against the dehumanised life, because it starts off from the standpoint of the single, real individual, because the fellowship against whose separation from himself the individual is reacting is the true fellowship of man, the fellowship of being human. The political soul of a revolution, on the other hand, consists in the tendency of a politically uninfluential class to break asunder its isolation from the State and the ruling power. Its standpoint is that of the State, an abstracted whole which arises only through separation from empirical life, which is unthinkable without the organised contradiction between the universal idea and the individual existence of man. A revolution permeated with the political soul therefore organises, in accordance with its limited and dualistic nature, a ruling circle in society at the cost of society . . .

Revolution in general—the overthrowing of the existing power and the destruction of old relationships—is a political act. But without revolution socialism cannot be carried out. Socialism needs this political act in so far as it needs destruction and dissolution. But as soon as its organising activity begins, as soon as its essential purpose, its soul, steps forward, socialism tosses away the political shell.

('Critical Glosses', M I, 3, 21–3.)

7. The Critique of Economics

HIS critique of politics, as we have seen, led Marx to the conclusion that the universality of the political State was contradicted by the egoism of economic life. He is not content, however, to develop the inevitability of the rational society out of the 'dialectical' conflict between the political State and economic life alone. For though he does not yet treat politics as a mere reflection of productive relations, he does already ascribe to it a certain impotence. He sees the political State as dominated by civil society, by the naked, atomic economic man. It is for this reason, no doubt, that Marx now turns to an examination of civil society itself and seeks to find within economic life the dialectical motive force toward change which political life alone is too weak to provide. For the first time, Marx plunges into detailed economic studies. He makes copious excerpts from de Boisguillebert, Eugene Buret, Lord Lauderdale, John Law, Friedrich List, MacCulloch, James Mill, Osiander, Ricardo, Say, Schüz, Skarbek and Adam Smith. The *Economico-Philosophical (Paris) Manuscripts* of 1844 were the first results of this work. In them, Marx sought to show the dialectical break within economic life itself, the inescapable contradictions which made its continuance or free development within the same 'form' impossible. He sought to do so by submitting the entire structure of contemporary political economy, its categories and its fundamental laws, to the most searching philosophical criticism.

Philosophical criticism, for Marx, still meant logico-ethical criticism. It did not mean patently normative criticism. Marx expounds no moral 'principles' or standards according to which political economy is tried and found wanting. But logical 'contradictions', to Marx, are the inevitable result of evil; they are part of the very nature and way of working of the egoistic, the alienated, the unfree. Engels, who had

70

acquired from the Young Hegelians roughly the same views, had already preceded Marx in the task of subjecting political economy to such criticism by publishing in the single issue of the *Deutsch-französische Jahrbücher* of February, 1844 his 'Outlines of a Critique of Political Economy'. Marx thought highly of the article and became interested in Engels, whom he knew only slightly, as a result. Yet a comparison of Engels' article with Marx's manuscripts brings out how much more thorough-going is Marx's conception of the relation between logical and ethical criticism. For Engels, political economy is something he attacks both morally *and* logically; for Marx, these attacks are not complete until they have been brought back to a single base. Thus Engels begins with a moral-advocative onslaught: 'Political economy, or the science of becoming rich, arisen out of the mutual envy and greed of merchants, carries on its brow the marks of the most revolting self-seeking' (M I, 2, 379); he ends (M I, 2, 400) by seeing in man's dependence on private property, competition and conflicting interests his most complete degradation. His logical indictment is complementary but distinct, mostly untinged by moral or ethical overtones. It rests on the necessary vacillation in economic theories of value, the 'contradiction' between a high 'national income' and the overwhelming poverty of the nation as a set of individuals, as well as on the contradiction between the allegedly harmonious operation of the laws of supply and demand and the increasing number of trade crises. Marx, on the other hand, insists that ethical deficiency and logical contradiction are necessarily connected. The criticism is not complete until they have been shown to arise from a single cause, from a 'one-sided' treatment of man or from a failure to see the human content of social institutions which have been illegitimately ripped out of their human context and treated as dead things. His whole *tour de force* in the *Paris Manuscripts* is to proclaim that political economy cannot be an ethically neutral study of so-called 'objective' relations between non-human things or laws and to bring it back into the ethical sphere by reducing it once more to its human content. The fundamental categories of political economy, Marx insists, are not labour, capital, profits, rents, land. The fundamental category is man, man and his human activities. These activities cannot be abstracted from man; they must be seen as integral expressions of his humanity. The categories of which traditional political economists speak are nothing but abstractions (in the Hegelian sense) from the true essence of society—man. The economists objectify, reify, set up in limited

71

and abstracted shape, as dead objects, what are vital human activities, activities that can only be grasped and correctly developed as part of the whole social man.[1]

It is because Marx rejects the conception of ethical criticism as being the application of 'ideal' standards and treats his ethico-logic as grounded in the way things occur, that he can insist that his criticism is purely empirical. 'My results have been gained through a wholly empirical analysis, founded on a conscientious critical study of political economy' (M I, 3, 33; cf. EPM 15–16). The first thing such a study reveals to Marx is the utter inadequacy of the abstract(ed) laws of political economy which fall into necessary contradictions and fail to grasp the fundamental principle that makes these contradictions necessary. The political economist says that originally and by its nature the entire product of labour belongs to the worker; at the same time he grants that in fact the worker receives nothing but the smallest and most unavoidable part of this product. He says that everything is bought with labour and that capital is nothing but accumulated labour; yet he grants that the labourer cannot buy everything but must sell himself and his human qualities. He says that labour is the only unchangeable value of things; yet nothing is more contingent than the value of labour; nothing is exposed to greater variations. The division of labour, according to the political economist, increases the productive power of labour and the wealth of society; yet it impoverishes the worker. According to their own nature, land rent and capital profit are deductions suffered by wages; in actual fact, wages are a deduction which land and capital permit to the worker. While the political economist claims that the interests of the worker are never in opposition to the interests of society, society stands constantly and necessarily opposed to the interests of the worker. (M I, 3, 43–5; EPM 28–9.)

By means of the political economist's own words, then, Marx has striven to show that labour, in so far as it increases work, is harmful. This is the paradoxical result of the abstracted laws of political economy. The worker sinks to the level of the most miserable commodity, his misery standing in inverse relationship to the size and power of his production. On the side of capital, the necessary result of competition is the accumulation of capital in a few hands, i.e., the frightful reimposition of monopoly. Thus the distinction between capitalist and

[1] Two years later, in the *Poverty of Philosophy*, Marx attacks Proudhon for not seeing this: 'The economist's material is the active, energetic life of man; M. Proudhon's material is the dogmas of the economist' (PP 117).

landed proprietor and between peasant and industrial worker finally disappears and the entire society must inevitably break apart into the two classes of property owners and propertyless workers. (M I, 3, 81; EPM 67.)

Here, then, we have the first version of what is undoubtedly Marx's best-known contribution to intellectual endeavour: his analysis of society based on private property in the stage of commodity–production. It is shot through with 'contradictions': the more the worker produces, the less he earns and enjoys; the more the capitalist competes, the more capitalists are ruined. At the very beginning of his venture into political economy, Marx has thus satisfied the requirements of his dialectical critique of society: he has shown to his own satisfaction that civil society (i.e., political economy)[1] is necessarily, by its very essence, self-contradictory, working by its own logic toward inevitable break-up and collapse. But Marx wants to go further than this. He wants to display the basic ground of the 'contradictions' in political economy. This ground cannot be displayed, or even understood, if we remain within the abstracted laws of political economy, if we follow the political economist in simply assuming the existence of private property and inventing fanciful primitive qualities, such as Adam Smith's tendency to barter, which simply assume what they are supposed to explain. But we can discover the basic ground of the whole movement of political economy if we begin, not with mythological prehistory, but with a contemporary fact:

The more riches the worker produces, the more his production increases in power and scope, the poorer he becomes. The more commodities a worker produces, the cheaper a commodity he becomes. The devaluation of the world of men proceeds in direct proportion to the exploitation[2] of the world of things. Labour not only produces commodities, but it turns itself and the worker into commodities and does so in proportion to the extent that it produces commodities in general.

(M I, 3, 82; EPM 69.)

This fact is the fundamental fact of political economy for Marx. It can be explained, explained in its very essence, as a necessary

---

[1] Like Hegel in the *Phenomenology*, Marx brings together the theory of a subject (here political economy) and the subject itself (here economic life or civil society), just as he had earlier identified the theory of the heavenly bodies and the bodies themselves.

[2] Marx is punning here on the words *Entwertung* (devaluation) and *Verwertung* (using, or gaining value from, a thing—i.e., exploiting it in the non-pejorative sense in which we speak of exploiting natural resources).

phenomenon, by careful logical analysis. If the worker is impoverished by producing riches, this can only be because production under the existing economic conditions takes away from the worker something that is part of him. This is what the fundamental fact of political economy expresses:

The object which labour produces, its product, confronts it as *something alien*, as a *power independent* of the producer. The product of labour is labour which has congealed in an object, which has become material; it is the objectification of work. The bringing of labour to reality (its realisation) is its objectification. Under the conditions of political economy, the realisation of labour, making it into a reality, appears as loss of reality by the worker, objectification appears as loss of the object, as bondage to it; appropriation appears as *estrangement*, as *alienation*.

(M I, 3, 83; EPM 69.)

Here, then, we have Marx's first detailed exposition of his theory of alienation in economic life. In the *Phenomenology of Mind*, Hegel had argued that mind or spirit passes historically through the stages of *Entäusserung* (externalising or projecting itself into objects) and *Entfremdung* (the estrangement or alienation that follows when mind treats its own externalisations as independent and even hostile objects confronting it). Feuerbach had strikingly applied the concept of alienation to religion, in which he saw man projecting his own powers into the blue mists of heaven and then falling on his knees to worship them as the powers of an alien, external being. Marx in the *Paris Manuscripts* pays strong tributes to the importance of Feuerbach's 'revolution in philosophy'; the historical background of Marx's thought and his debt to previous thinkers need not detain us here. The importance of alienation for Marx is that it can be used to show that the worker's misery is logically inescapable under the conditions of economic life as we have known it. Alienation is the fundamental fact of political economy. Political economists have been able to conceal this only by failing to examine the direct relationship between the worker (labour) and his product. Because of this alienation 'the more the worker produces, the less he has to consume, the more values he creates, the less value—the less dignity—he himself has; the better-shaped the product, the more misshapen the worker, the more civilised his product, the more barbaric the worker'. Thus, 'labour produces wonders for the rich, but strips the worker . . . It produces culture, but idiocy, cretinism for the worker.' (M I, 3, 84–5; EPM 71.)

So far, Marx has emphasised only the alienation of the worker's *product* from the worker, but this alienation is possible only because alienation is enshrined in the very *activity* of production, in the worker's labour itself. In what does this alienation within labour consist?

Firstly, in the fact that labour is *external* to the worker, *i.e.,* it does not belong to his essential being, in the fact that he therefore does not affirm himself in his work, but negates himself in it, that he does not feel content, but unhappy in it, that he develops no free physical and mental energy but mortifies his body and ruins his mind. Therefore the worker feels himself only outside his work, while in his work he feels outside himself. He is at home when he is not working and when he works he is not at home. His work, therefore, is not voluntary but coerced; it is *forced* labour. It is, therefore, not the satisfaction of a need but only a *means* for satisfying needs external to it. Its alien character emerges clearly in the fact that as soon as there is no physical or other compulsion, labour is avoided like the plague. External labour, labour in which man alienates himself, is labour of self-sacrifice, of mortification. Finally, the external character of labour for the worker appears in the fact that it is not his own but somebody else's, that in his labour he belongs not to himself, but to someone else . . . The worker's activity is not his own activity. It belongs to another, it is the loss of his self.

The result, therefore, is that man (the worker) no longer feels himself acting freely except in his animal functions, eating, drinking and procreating, or at most in his dwelling, ornaments, etc., while in his human functions he feels more and more like an animal. What is animal becomes human and what is human becomes animal.

Drinking, eating and procreating are admittedly also genuinely human functions. But in their abstraction, which separates them from the remaining range of human functions and turns them into sole and ultimate ends, they are animal.

(M I, 3, 85–6; EPM 72–3.)

We thus see alienation, says Marx, to have two aspects. Firstly, we have the worker's relationship to the product of his work, which is for him an alien object ruling over him. This alienation, according to Marx, is accompanied by a similar relationship to Nature, to 'the world of the senses'. Nature should be the stuff on which the worker's labour makes itself real, through which it is active. But in being alienated from the product of his work, the worker is also alienated from Nature. Secondly, we have the worker's alienation of his own activity and therefore of his personal life—'for what is life other than activity, than doing things' (M I, 3, 86). This, in other words, is the worker's *self-alienation*. Marx now wants to show that these two forms of alienation imply and create two further forms: man's alienation from his

75

own universal being as a man and from other men, which may be brought under one head by treating them as two aspects of man's alienation from his genus or species.

The actual argument is more than somewhat metaphysical. It depends upon a conception which Feuerbach expounds at the very beginning of his *Essence of Christianity* (pp. 1–5) and which we have already met, in slightly different form, in Marx's earliest works. Marx, as we have seen, took man's freedom and self-determined activity to be the specifically human characteristic that distinguishes man from the determined and conditioned beast. Feuerbach treats this freedom as *consciousness*, especially as consciousness of man's generic being. The animal has limited consciousness of itself as an individual, but that is all; its inner life is one with its outer life. Man, on the other hand, has both an inner and an outer life. 'The inner life of man', says Feuerbach, 'is the life which has relation to his species—to his general, as distinguished from his individual, nature.' It is on this consciousness of himself as a general, generic being that the functions of thought and speech depend when they are performed alone, without another being present. Marx, in the *Paris Manuscripts* makes this conception somewhat more concrete. Both men and animals live from inorganic nature. But the animal, according to Marx, 'is directly one with its life-activities. It does not distinguish itself from them. It is they.' To be sure, the animal, like man, is able to produce—a nest, a home, etc. But it produces only what it needs directly for itself or for its young. It produces only under the domination of direct physical needs. It produces only itself—in the sense that it can produce only according to the measure and the need of the species to which it belongs. Man, in contrast, 'makes his life-activities themselves an object of his willing and of his consciousness. He has conscious life-activities.' It is because of this and only because of this that his activity is free activity. When man produces, he can produce even in the absence of physical needs; indeed, he produces truly only in the absence of physical needs. In his production, man is not bound by the measure and need of his own species alone; he does not merely produce himself but reproduces the whole of Nature. He can create according to the measure of all species and knows how to fashion each object according to its own inherent measure; hence he creates according to the laws of beauty. But man's consciousness of himself as a generic being depends upon his being able to appropriate and dominate Nature and to see his own reflection in it:

It is precisely in working on the world of objects that man first genuinely proves himself to be a *generic being*. This production is his active generic life. Through it and because of it Nature appears as *his* work and his reality. The object of labour is therefore the *objectification of the generic life of man*, in so far as man duplicates himself not only intellectually, in consciousness, but practically and therefore recognises himself in a world which he himself has made. Hence, in so far as alienated labour tears from man the object of his production, it tears away from him his generic life, his real and actual objectification as a species, and transforms his advantage over the animal into the disadvantage that his inorganic body, Nature, has been taken away from him.

(M I, 3, 88–9; EPM 76.)

Marx's 'proof' that man's alienation from his species is *implied* by his alienation from the product of his labour (and not merely displayed in the *bellum omnium* of economic life) consists of nothing more solid than these metaphorical transitions, but he concludes emphatically:

Alienated labour therefore:
(3) turns *the generic being of man*, both Nature and the intellectual wealth of his species, into a being *alien* to him, into a means for his *individual existence*. It alienates his own body from man, it alienates from him both Nature outside him and his intellectual being, his *human* nature.
(4) A direct consequence of the fact that man is alienated from the product of his labour, from his life activity, from his generic being, is the *alienation of man from man* . . .

(M I, 3, 89; EPM 76–7.)

How then, Marx goes on to ask, does this concept of alienated labour express itself in real life? To whom do the worker's product and activity belong? They cannot belong to the gods; they can only belong to *another man*, a not-worker, to whom the worker's activity, a torment to the worker himself, is a delight and joy (M I, 3, 90). Even in religious alienation we find that alienation can appear only in a relationship among men, in the relationship between the layman and the priest, for only man can dominate over man. But the not-worker, the capitalist, is as subject to self-alienation as the worker, only he is not as conscious of *suffering* from it: 'Everything which appears in the worker as the *activity of alienation, of estrangement,* appears in the non-worker as the *condition or state of alienation, of estrangement.*'[1]
(M I, 3, 94.)

⸳   ⸳   ⸳   ⸳

[1] A year later, in *The Holy Family*, Marx was making the same point more clearly: 'The propertied class and the class of the proletariat present the same

We have seen how Marx in his article 'On the Jewish Question' already treated money as the power which turns man into a servile, dependent being, into a commodity. In the *Paris Manuscripts* he devotes a special section to money as the very essence of man's alienation. He quotes (M I, 3, 146) Mephistopheles in Goethe's *Faust:*

> Wenn ich sechs Hengste zahlen kann
> Sind ihre Kräfte nicht die meine?
> Ich renne zu und bin ein rechter Mann
> Als hätt ich vierundzwanzig Beine.[1]

and Shakespeare's Timon apostrophising gold:

> Thus much of this will make black, white; foul, fair;
> Wrong, right; base, noble; old, young; coward, valiant . . .
> Thou common whore of mankind, that putt'st odds
> Among the rout of nations.
>
> (*Timon of Athens,* Act IV, scene iii.)

Marx elaborates the same theme:

That which *money* can create for me, that for which I can pay (i.e., what money can buy)—that *I*, the possessor of the money, *am.* The extent of the power of money is the extent of my power. The properties of money are the properties and essential powers of me—its possessor. Thus what I *am* and what I *am capable of* is in no way determined by my individuality. I *am* ugly, but I can buy the *most beautiful* woman. Therefore I am not *ugly*, for the effect of *ugliness,* its power of repulsion, is destroyed by money. I— according to my individual nature—am lame, but money gives me twenty legs, therefore I am not lame. I am a wicked, dishonest, unscrupulous, stupid man; but people honour money, and therefore also its possessor. Money is the highest good, therefore its possessor is good. Besides, money saves me the trouble of being dishonest; therefore I am presumed to be honest; I am stupid, but money is the real mind of all things; how can its possessor lack mind?

(M I, 3, 147; cf. EPM 138–9.)

[1] . . . When to my car
My money yokes six spankers, are
Their limbs not my limbs . . .
Mine all the forces I combine —
The four-and-twenty legs are mine.
(John Anster's translation).

---

human self-alienation. But the former class finds in this self-alienation its confirmation and its good, its *own power*: it has in it a *semblance* of human existence. The class of the proletariat feels annihilated in its self-alienation; it sees in it its own powerlessness and the reality of an inhuman existence' (M I, 3, 206).

From Shakespeare, says Marx, we can see the two leading characteristics of money:

(1) It is the visible divinity, the transformation of all human and natural
properties into their contraries, the universal confounding and overturning
of things; it binds together impossibilities.
(2) It is the common whore, the universal pimp, of men and nations.
The confounding and overturning of all human and natural qualities, the
coupling of impossibilities—the *divine* power—achieved by money arise
out of its *essence* as the alienated, externalised generic being of man, which
has conveyed itself to another. It is the alienated *ability or wealth*[1] *of mankind.*

(M I, 3, 147–8; EPM 139.)

The analysis of economic conditions and of money then, according
to Marx, reveals the inadequacy of traditional political economy and
of the presuppositions of economic life. It reveals that the contradictions of political economy and of economic life are not accidental, but
necessary, results of the fundamental presupposition on which they
rest—that alienation of man's labour and man's products from man
which is expressed in private property. Until political economy grasps
its own essence as alienated human activity, and through the supercession of private property reunites man's activities and products with
man as an undivided social and generic being, these contradictions
cannot be resolved and overcome. Because of its failure to do this,
political economy, instead of being a science of man, ends by *negating*
man. It is based on a simple, inhuman, moral principle: eat less, drink
less, practise self-denial, give up as many human needs as possible and
save more. 'Its true ideal is the *ascetic* but *usurious* miser and the
ascetic but *productive* slave' (M I, 3, 130).

The fact that political economy rests on abstracted laws arising from
man's alienation comes out particularly clearly, for Marx, in its relation
to morality. It is a feature of systems based on alienation, he argues, that
each system has its own self-sufficient laws and falls into contradiction
with other systems. Each system studies a particular sphere of alienation; none studies the whole, undivided man. Thus, what is utter
depravity to morality is entirely consonant with the laws of political
economy:

If I ask the political economist: Am I obeying the laws of economics if I
draw money from selling and surrendering my body to another's lust? (The

---

[1] Marx, no doubt deliberately punning, uses the word *Vermögen*, which can
mean either ability or wealth.

factory workers in France call the prostitution of their wives and daughters the xth working hour, which is literally correct.)—Or am I acting contrary to political economy if I sell my friend to the Moroccans? . . . Then the political economist answers: You are not transgressing my laws, but see what Cousin Ethics and Cousin Religion have to say. My *political economic* ethics and religion have nothing to reproach you with, but—But whom am I to believe now, political economy or ethics?

(M I, 3, 131; EPM 120.)

It is thus, according to Marx, that political economy ignores the unemployed labourer, the man behind the work in so far as he is outside the relationship of labour. 'The thief, the swindler, the beggar, the unemployed, the starving, miserable and criminal working man—these are figures that do not exist for political economy, but only for other eyes: for the eyes of the doctor, the judge, the gravedigger and the bum-bailiff' (M I, 3, 97).[1]

This, then, is Marx's critique of economics and the doctrine of alienation in terms of which he seeks to explain the necessary contradictions of 'civil society' or economic life. The fact of alienation— the estrangement of nature and of such human functions as the political power or State from man—had already been postulated by Hegel in the *Phenomenology of Mind,* as Marx emphasises; but Hegel develops the concept of alienation only in the sphere of ideas, while Marx seeks to show its *practical* nature in the concrete social and economic life of man.

The metaphysical foundations and empirical ethical content of the concept of alienation we shall examine shortly, in Part III. The underlying conception of man's products as in some sense 'truly part of

[1] Marx concedes that there has been a partial revolution in the theory of political economy, an attempt to bring some human content back into the field. But the attempt was only partial, it failed to overcome the basic alienation on which political economy rests. It thus parallels the Lutheran revolution in religion. The Catholics, the fetish-worshippers of political economy, according to Marx, were the mercantilists, who worshipped private property in its material, symbolic, nonhuman, form—in the precious metals. Luther overcame the objective externalisation and estrangement of religion and made it subjective by bringing it, through the doctrine of faith, back into the heart of the layman. Similarly, Adam Smith overcame the external materialisation of wealth and incorporated private property into man himself by translating wealth into its subjective form, into labour. But to do this is not genuinely to overcome alienation. Private property is not reduced to its human content as a function of man —in taking private property into himself, man is himself reduced into a form of private property. Thus Ricardo, quite consistently with the nature of political economy, treats man as nothing more than a machine for consuming and producing and man's life as nothing more than a form of capital.

man', of nature as something which man 'appropriates', of consciousness as presupposing man's 'universal and generic being', of labour as
something that 'congeals' in the object it produces—all this, we shall
seek to show, must be rejected. Yet the concept of alienation, the
indictment of money, we shall suggest, has empirical content and
ethical relevance over and above its merely suggestive power (its
focusing of attention on the social background of economic operations,
its evocation of the interdependence of all social phenomena). But for
Marx himself the concept of alienation has a further significance, a
significance that gave it a fundamental role in his social dialectic. In
seeing alienation as the 'essence' of economic life in its 'political
economic' form, he had sought to reduce all the 'contradictions' of
economic life to a single fact: the human self-alienation expressed in
private property. If he is right, then the removal of that basic ground
—of human alienation and private property—will inevitably result in
the removal of all the contradictions that stem from it. It will, according to Marx, usher in the rational society of the complete, unalienated
man.

8. Communism and the Complete, Unalienated Man

ACCORDING to Marx, as we have seen, the laws of political economy and the facts of economic life rest on the uncriticised presupposition of private property, which conceals and accepts the fact of man's self-alienation. This alienation, Marx had sought to show, necessarily breaks out at every turn:

(1) The *product of man's work*, and ultimately the whole outer world of sense-experience, *all of nature*, are alienated from man and confront him as hostile, independent forces seeking to dominate him.

(2) *Man's own activity, the process of labour itself*, is alienated from him, made into an independent object, and similarly dominates man instead of being dominated by him.

(3) The alienation of nature from man means the alienation of man *from his own universal, generic social being*. His generic social existence, instead of representing his essential nature becomes a mere means for satisfying his narrow, individual demands.

(4) The alienation of man from his universal being means also his alienation *from other men*. Instead of being expressions of his own universal essence, they confront him as hostile beings.

Political economy cannot escape or resolve these contradictions because it does not criticise private property, because it does not see that the true basis of private property is human alienation. But in the *Paris Manuscripts*, at least, Marx insists on the logical priority of alienation: it is not enough merely to criticise or reject private property without recognising and resolving the human alienation that underlies it. Thus he emphasises (somewhat obscurely) that instead of asking 'What is the origin of private property?', we should ask 'How can we explain the alienation that broke out in the course of human development?'[1] (M I, 3, 93). Instead of studying laws of economic development from the abstracted standpoint of private property, from within alienation, we should ask: 'What is the relationship between the general nature of private property, as it has developed out of alienated labour, and *truly human* and *social property?*' Four years later, Marx (with Engels) was to attack scathingly in the *Communist Manifesto* this treatment of alienation as something distinct from and more basic than the economic facts supposed to follow from it:

It is well known how the monks wrote silly lives of Catholic Saints *over* the manuscripts on which the classical works of ancient heathendom had been written. The German *literati* reversed this process with the profane French literature. They wrote their philosophical nonsense beneath the French original. For instance, beneath the French criticism of the economic functions of money, they wrote 'Alienation of Humanity' and beneath the French criticism of the bourgeois State they wrote, 'Dethronement of the Category of the General', and so forth . . .

The French Socialist and Communist literature was thus completely emasculated. And, since it ceased in the hands of the German to express the struggle of one class with the other, he felt conscious of having overcome 'French one-sidedness' and of representing not true requirements, but the requirements of Truth; not the interests of the proletariat, but the interests of Human Nature, of Man in general, who belongs to no class, has no reality, who exists only in the misty realm of philosophical fantasy.

(SW I, 55.)

In 1844, without question, Marx still believed in the requirements of 'Human Nature, of Man in general', still insisted on alienation as something more than a series of economic facts. It is hardly surprising that the concrete value of his insistence that questions about private property should be converted into questions about alienation remains obscure. He does, however, in somewhat metaphysical form seek to derive one concrete point from it—a criticism of the 'crude Communism' which fails to see the alienation   behind private property.

---

[1] To substitute the latter question for the former, according to Marx, is already to advance a fair way toward the solution. But in point of fact he does not take this question any further in the *Paris Manuscripts*. His subsequent comments in the *Poverty of Philosophy* (p. 36) and in *Capital* (Book I, chapter 1) give no account of the *origin* of alienation but merely link it with commodity production and emphasise that the acute form of alienation is a product of modern capitalism. In the *German Ideology* alienation is traced beyond private property to the division of labour, seen as the common ground from which both alienation and private property arise. See *infra*, iv, 14.

Marx's point seems to be that if we regard private property purely as such we will think that the contradictions of political economy can be overcome by converting private property into public property, whereas in truth they can only be overcome by a thorough-going rejection and overcoming of all aspects of alienation, including the very concept of property and the very distinction between the 'individual' and 'society'.

Marx seeks to develop this theme by drawing a parallel between the successive stages through which alienation passes in establishing itself and the stages through which the overcoming of alienation must pass. He has already argued that the progress of man's self-alienation passes through an objective stage, when private property is worshipped in its material, non-human form, and a subjective stage when private property is seen as human labour, but still alienated from man. The overcoming of self-alienation, according to Marx, takes the same form. (What follows, however, reveals a fact often to be noted in Marx's later works; as he develops a position in detail, allegedly to illustrate an outline he has summarised, the detailed position does not quite match the architectonic with which he began.) Thus, in the first stage, the socialists, though recognising labour as the essence of property, still see private property only in its material and sectional form. They therefore seek only the overcoming of *capital* 'as such' (Proudhon) or ascribe the harmfulness of private property to some *special* form of work—agricultural labour being taken as at least the most important form of unfree labour in Fourier and the physiocrats, industrial labour in Saint-Simon. Communism takes us a stage further: it is the positive overcoming of private property. But Communism, too, has its stages. Unlike socialism, it sees private property in its *universality*, but in the first stage it seeks merely to *universalise* private property. This desire appears in a dual form: 'on the one hand Communism is so much under the sway of *material* property, that it wants to destroy everything which cannot be owned by everybody as *private property*; it wants *forcibly* to cut away talent, etc.' (M I, 3, 111–12). On the other hand, 'it regards direct physical ownership as the only aim of life and existence'; it thus continues the relationship of private property but stretches it to cover all men by converting it into the property of 'society'. The 'animal' expression of this emerges clearly in its treatment of women. To marriage (admittedly a form of exclusive private property), it contraposes the common ownership of women, which turns women into common, social property. This, indeed, shows us the particular secret 'of this still utterly crude and thoughtless Communism. Just as woman steps out of marriage into universal prostitution, so the entire world of riches, of the objectified being of man, steps from its exclusive marriage with private owners into the relationship of universal prostitution with society. This Communism, in its universal negation of the *personality* of man, is merely the consistent expression of private ownership, which is the negation of human personality. Universal *envy* constituting itself as power is only the hidden form in which *greed* reappears, satisfying itself in a *different* way . . . How little crude Communism's overcoming of private property is a genuine appropriation is shown by its abstract negation of the whole world of education and civilisation, by its return to the *unnatural* simplicity of the poor man without needs, who has not passed beyond private property but has rather not even reached it yet.' (M I, 3, 112.)

In the second stage, according to Marx, we have Communism still political in nature—whether democratic or despotic—or Communism already concerned with the dissolution of the State. In both forms, Marx claims (again somewhat obscurely) that Communism already recognises itself as standing for human re-integration, for the dissolution of alienation, but it still has not grasped the positive essence of private property or the *human* character of needs. Thirdly and finally we have:

Communism as the *positive* dissolution and transcendence of *private property*, of human self-alienation, and therefore as the real *appropriation of the human* essence by and for man; therefore as the complete and conscious return of man to himself as a *social* [*gesellschaftlichen*], i.e., human, man—a return fashioned with the whole wealth of his past development. This Communism is the consummated naturalism = humanism, the consummated humanism = naturalism, it is the genuine resolution of the conflict between man and Nature and between man and man—the true resolution of the strife between existence and true being [*Existenz und Wesen*], between objectification and self-confirmation, between freedom and necessity, between the individual and the species. Communism is the riddle of history solved; and it knows itself to be the solution.

(M I, 3, 114; EPM 102.)

The same point, Marx insists, applies to religion, family, State, jurisprudence, morality, science, etc.; they are all only particular forms of production and fall under the general laws governing the transcendence of alienation within production. The positive transcendence of private property 'through the appropriation of human life' is therefore the positive overcoming of all alienation, the return of man from religion, family, the State, etc., into his human (i.e., social) existence (M I, 3, 115). Society thus becomes the 'consummated unity in being of man and Nature, the true resurrection of Nature, the thorough-going naturalism of man and the thorough-going humanism of Nature (M I, 3, 116). Above all, we must avoid once more treating 'society' as an abstraction to be opposed to the 'individual'; the individual is the *social* being, under these conditions his individual life and his generic, social life become one, even if the existential form of individual life must necessarily remain a more particular or general form of the generic life.

Here then is the 'rational society' which Marx sees as the solution to the riddle of history. It is not merely the society in which private property has been abolished; it is above all not a society in which property has simply passed to the control of the State or to 'social' control. It is the society in which any opposition between individual and social demands has disappeared, in which wants and enjoyments lose their egoistic nature, in which utility becomes human, universal, social utility. Man *appropriates* Nature, makes it part of himself; his senses thus become true, truly human senses; man himself becomes the true, truly human, man.

PART THREE

Critical Résumé:
Ethics and the Young Marx

9. Ethics—Positive or Normative?

TO preach morality is easy, to give ethics a foundation is difficult. The difficulty stems from the contradiction that has lain at the heart of most traditional ethical theories and continues to lie at the heart of popular moralism. This contradiction is the uncritical mingling of science and advocacy in the illogical concept of a normative science, the attempt to give ethical judgments the objectivity of scientific descriptions and the imperative, exhortative force sought by prohibitions, recommendations and commands. The imperative side of ethical theory is essential to those who see ethics as a prescriptive theory of conduct and morality as the theory of obligation. The scientific, descriptive side is essential to those who want to save the objectivity of ethical judgments and to escape the conclusion that ethical disagreements are nothing more than the conflict of competing authorities, attitudes or demands.

The conflict between scientific and advocative conceptions of ethics is closely linked with the conflict between treating 'good' as a quality and treating it as a relation. The objectivity of ethical judgments can be most easily established if 'good' is a quality, an intrinsic character common to those things or activities we correctly call goods. The assertion that a thing or activity has a certain quality raises in logic a clear, unambiguous issue; the truth of the assertion is logically independent of any relations into which the thing or the activity or the assertor may enter. A table is either red or not red, painted or not painted; whereas it may be to the left of the bookshelf and to the right of the door. But whether the table stands to the left of the bookshelf or not, whether I like it or dislike it, has no logical bearing on the questions whether it is red or painted. Qualities do not logically depend on relations; nor do qualities by themselves imply relations. The assertion that this table is red does not, *by itself*, imply that I am attracted to it;

the assertion that X has the positive quality 'good' would not imply that I necessarily seek, commend or require it. To treat 'good' as a quality would be to open the way to making ethics a science and to clarifying the distinction between ethical and non-ethical fields; but it would also be to shear ethics of its advocative and its normative pretensions. It would be to investigate the common characters, the ways of working, of goods and the relations into which they are able to enter as a result of these characters;[1] but it would be to destroy the illusion that such goods logically *imply or require* support or pursuit. The question whether they are supported or pursued and by whom would be logically independent of their character and could be raised only *after* their common characters had been established.

The traditional moralist cannot afford to see 'good' as 'merely' a quality which some display or seek and others lack or reject. For him it must also be a relation, something demanded, pursued, required, which it is illogical—or 'wrong'—to reject. A vicious attempt to straddle the issue, to confuse and amalgamate quality and relation, reveals itself in the popular traditional conception of 'good' as *that whose nature it is to be demanded or pursued.* This is to treat a relation as *constituting* the character or quality of a thing. But things cannot be constituted by their relations: a thing must have characters before it can enter into a relation; it must be *some*thing before *it* can be commended, rejected or pursued. If we treat 'good' (or 'piety' in Euthyphro's case) as standing for a relation that *anything* may have, i.e., like the word 'burden', for instance, then, as the *Euthyphro* shows, our commendations would be entirely arbitrary, there would be nothing to prevent *anything* from being treated as 'good', or as pleasing the gods, just as there is nothing to prevent *anything* from becoming a burden.[2]

Normative conceptions of ethics *with positive, scientific pretensions,* then, require the confusion or the amalgamation of qualitative and relational treatments of good. This confusion is facilitated by the

[1] While a quality cannot by itself imply a relation, relations which are not purely spatio-temporal relations like 'down', 'before' or 'left' can and do imply qualities in the terms that enter into these relations. Thus marriage implies the sexual characteristics of the partners and only men can be uncles. But the fact that X is a man implies neither that he is a husband nor that he is an uncle.

[2] Cf. the seventeenth-century Cambridge Platonist Ralph Cudworth's 'Second Sermon': 'Virtues and holiness in creatures . . . are not therefore good because God loveth them, and will have them to be accounted such; but rather God therefore loveth them, because they are in themselves simply good' (cited in J. A. Passmore, *Ralph Cudworth,* pp. 83–4).

possibility of framing statements with *incomplete* relations as terms. 'John is taller', we say; 'Mary is much sought after'; 'Pork-eating is abhorrent'. In each case the sentence is logically incomplete. It does not raise a single unambiguous issue until we have filled in the additional term required by the relation: 'John is taller than Robert'; 'Mary is much sought after by those young people in her set who are interested in girls'; 'Pork-eating is abhorrent to pious Muslims and Jews.' In ordinary speech, we often save time by omitting the second term of the relation and relying on our hearer to fill it in for himself from the context in which we have uttered the phrase. Mostly this works satisfactorily; occasionally it leads to ambiguity and fruitless argument in which the contestants are not discussing the same issue and therefore not contradicting each other. 'Mary is popular' and the rejoinder 'No, she is not' are perfectly compatible with each other if the first speaker means 'popular with her friends' and the second speaker 'popular with her parents' friends'.

Relations, then, require *two* terms: the demander as well as the demanded, the pursuer as well as the pursued, the obligor as well as the obliged. What is made obligatory or demanded by one code, moral tradition or person may be forbidden or rejected by another. The concept of *absolute* obligation, of *unconditional* codes and duties, is thus revealed as a contradiction in terms, while the illusion of a single binding morality has to be replaced by the empirical recognition of competing 'principles' and 'authorities'—i.e., of competing demands and codes that cannot be brought before a common tribunal or under an 'ultimate' law. The conditional character of duties and obligations comes out, to some degree, in the terms 'right' and 'wrong'. Their relational character is evident; what is right in terms of one morality may be wrong in terms of another. But the moralist has an interest in preventing this recognition; he requires both the imperative force and the vagueness of terms like 'right' and 'wrong' and the suggestion of absolute, unconditional, qualitative distinctions conveyed by the terms 'good' and 'bad'.

The normative function of moralism, then, has partly depended on the adoption of a moral language particularly suited to obscuring the sources of the demands it makes by dealing in incomplete relations. 'You ought to do this', 'Stealing is wrong', 'Children must obey their elders' all suggest authority without specifying it: in many cases they thus successfully invoke the terrors of an anonymous authority, or of one filled in by the hearer himself, simply by leaving the relation incomplete. Ethical discussion and enquiry, on the other hand, require the completion of the relation and thus threaten the foundations of moral obedience much as a close acquaintance with officers and the general staff threatens the foundations of military obedience. It is here that the moralist is driven back on hierarchical, anti-empirical, conceptions of reality. If ethical propositions are to have prescriptive force, the *source* of moral demands must be elevated *above* 'the world' to which the demands are addressed. It is thus that the relational, prescriptive treatment of 'good' leads inevitably to a dualism of 'facts' and 'standards', 'actions' and 'principles', 'apparent interests' and 'true interests'. This is patently obvious where the source of moral obligation is treated as supra-empirical, as god, soul, or an unhistorical faculty of reason or conscience. It is equally true, however, where the source is allegedly 'natural'—human nature, human interests or social demands. These, too, have to be given a primacy in which moral advocacy masquerades as logical priority, and left imprecise to avoid conflict and incoherence. It is here that we find the reappearance of constitutive relations to protect the source of moral authority from criticism. Just as 'conscience' becomes that whose nature it is to approve of good, so 'principles' become that whose nature it is to be obeyed. For the empirical study of goods, or for the social and historical investigation of moral attitudes, we find substituted the attempt to bind conduct with seeming tautologies.

It is fashionable in certain circles these days to say that if one does abandon the claim to *absolute* moral obligation, or to 'objective' distinctions of 'right' and 'wrong', a coherent relational treatment of 'good' is possible. To say something is 'good', on this view, is to say nothing more than that it is commended, or commanded, or approved of, and while people may in fact share moral principles and attitudes, there is no logical way of resolving disagreements or of showing one set of attitudes or 'principles' 'better' than another. Commands and attitudes may conflict, but they do not contradict each other. Once we recognise that 'good' is not a quality,[1] there is not necessarily a

---

[1] The purely relational use of ethical terms might still invest them with a qualitative content implied by the context of their use, but such a content would be derivative and inconstant. It would vary with the context and source of the demand and would not itself distinguish the moral use of 'good' from non-moral, instrumental uses of the word. It is this derivative content which has been emphasised—against the 'crude' subjectivists—in C. L. Stevenson's *Ethics and Language* and R. M. Hare's *The Language of Morals*. When the village parson, as Hare puts it, calls Mary 'a good girl' we may be able to deduce some of Mary's

contradiction between your calling X good and my calling it not good.

If this view is sound, there can be no genuine study of the ethical content and contribution of Marx's thought. There can also be no ethical science. We might make some logical criticism of past illusions that there was an ethical science, we might consider whether any of these apply to Marx, and we would then draw up a list of the things Marx advocates, of the moral preferences he displays. About the soundness of his ethical views we could say nothing, for to us there would be no ethical field with which his views are concerned. But how then do we tell which are his *ethical* views, how do we distinguish his ethical demands from other demands? This is precisely what the ethical relativist cannot do. He cannot distinguish 'approval' from 'liking' except by a circular reference to goods; he cannot show how ethics, seen as a system of demands, is to be distinguished from economics, the science of demands in general;[1] he cannot explain how ethical distinctions came to be made or moral judgments came to maintain themselves. For if we pass ethical judgments, it is because we

[1] J. O. Urmson, taking this type of view in his paper 'On Grading', seeks to distinguish moral from non-moral uses of 'good' by arguing that moral grading 'affects the whole of one's life and social intercourse', while non-moral grading deals with 'dispensable' qualities (*Logic and Language*, Second Series, ed. A. G. N. Flew, p. 159 et seq., esp. p. 184). Apart from the fact that both ethical and psychological understanding would involve not 'judging a man as a whole', Urmson's criterion presupposes a moral distinction on the basis of which 'we' distinguish being a bad father from being a bad cricketer; his criterion follows from this distinction instead of creating it. Hare's attempt to distinguish moral principles from non-moral commands by arguing that commands are always particular and principles always universal is certainly more sophisticated, but it leads him into the well-known difficulty that any particular proposition can be converted into a universal one by limiting its subject and to the curious view that 'no person shall smoke in any train anywhere' is always a moral injunction and never a non-moral command.

intrinsic characteristics from our knowledge of the parson's moral preferences, just as we can deduce certain features of a motor-car from our friend's description of it as 'jolly good' *and* from our knowledge of his taste in motor-cars. Both Stevenson and Hare would reject the suggestion that underlying the moral uses, of 'good' is an implicit if obscure recognition of positive ethical qualities independent of one's attitudes to them. The main difficulty of such a position, apart from its utter neglect of the empirical material contained in traditional moral distinctions and traditional moral psychology, is how to distinguish ethical demands from non-ethical demands, approval from liking, moral 'principles' from commands.

suppose there are ethical facts; if there are no ethical facts, there is nothing to show that these judgments are ethical.

Anacharsis the Scythian, who came from the plains north of the Black Sea some two centuries before Plato, is reputed to have said:

Nature is almost always in opposition to the laws, because she labours for the happiness of the individual, without regard to other individuals who surround him, while the laws only direct their attention to the relations by which he is united to them, and because Nature infinitely diversifies our character and inclinations, while it is the object of the laws to bring them back to unity.

This tension between conflict and co-operation, discord and harmony, to which Anacharsis refers, has formed the underlying theme of most moral and political philosophy. Ethical and political theorists have portrayed it in different guises: as the struggle between egotism and altruism, self-love and love of the State, civil society and the political State, evil and good, chaos and harmony, Nature and civilisation or (alternatively) civilisation and Nature. The concrete empirical material here, however, has been obscured and distorted by a naive individualism (reflected in the false dichotomies of 'individual' and 'society', 'egotism' and 'altruism') and by the normative hopes and pretensions of moral and political theorists, leading them to the postulation of social and logical hierarchies.

The young Marx, as we have seen, also takes this struggle between discord and harmony, between necessary conflict and true co-operation, as the central theme of human history and social life. But he rejects flatly the attempt to *impose* harmony by appealing to supra-empirical powers, 'principles' or ideals. He sees that this would involve an insupportable dualism, that we could never connect these powers, 'principles' or ideals with empirical occurrences without robbing them of their supra-empirical pretensions and treating them as natural, historical events. He sees clearly that the supra-empirical can only be formulated and understood in terms of the empirical—that god, conscience and reason can have meaning only in so far as these words convey an empirical, historcal content. It is from historical experience that these conceptions arise; it is only in terms of historical experience that they can be understood. What hangs on the Cross, as Feuerbach said, is not God but man.

The dualism implicit in normative theories is not always a patent appeal to non-natural, supra-empirical powers. The logico-ethical hierarchy may be established seemingly within historical experience: 'true interests' may be singled out as having a more fundamental, *more real,* reality than 'apparent interests'; 'purposes' may be elevated above 'mere capricious desires' (especially if the purposes I strive for are confused with the question-begging notion of the purposes for which I exist); 'essential nature' may be contrasted with 'mere empirical nature'.

Marx was not a utilitarian. He recognised the incoherence and conflict of actual, existing human demands within existing societies, recognised that they sought no common end and could not be brought to a common market. He recognised—explicitly in his later work, tacitly in his earlier—that human demands are not ultimates: that we might as well judge a society by the demands it *creates* as by the demands it satisfies. But in his acceptance of the Hegelian view that history is working toward rationality, Marx was not able to come down unequivocally on the side of positive ethics against normative morality. He was not able to escape the dualism required by normative theories; he could not excise either individualism or the upholding of 'ends' from his thought. 'Reason,' we have seen Marx writing to Ruge (*supra* II, 6), 'has always existed, but not always in a rational form. The critic can therefore seize upon any form of the theoretical and practical consciousness and develop out of the special forms of existing reality the true reality of *that which ought to be*, of that *which is reality's final aim*' (my italics). The normative conception 'which ought to be' is linked, as always in normative theory, with the dualistic hierarchical conception of a 'true reality' opposed to a mere 'empirical reality'. 'What is the kernel of empirical evil?' we have seen Marx ask (*supra,* I, 4); 'That the individual locks himself into his empirical nature against his eternal nature.' Marx needs the distinction between 'eternal' and 'empirical' to lend the terms he sees as ethical a higher status, to elevate them as 'ends' towards which history is working. The dualism breaks out everywhere: between 'will' and 'caprice', between 'true law' and positive, empirical law, between *Wesen* and *Existenz*, Reason and Actuality. Characteristically, Marx's dualism leads inescapably to monism. The 'true reality' in which empirical conflict and discord are destined to disappear must finally absorb every distinction; it is thus that all differences, between State and society, law and morality, Nature and man, one man and other men, one social function and another, must all disappear. All become 'expressions' of the truly human, truly self-determined man. How we could distinguish one expression from another is something Marx could not coherently explain; the concrete content of 'the truly human', too, must be left vague lest the suppressed distinctions and conflicts break out once again.

These, then, are the inevitable results of Marx's failure to rid himself entirely of normative conceptions, the outcome of his attempt to mingle logic and ethics in a metaphysic of history. But it would be cavalier and to a significant extent false to regard the ethical distinctions he seeks to make as mere confused and unsupported advocacy of some metaphysical 'true reality' against empirical occurrences. As we have seen, he does link the distinction between good and evil with one of the traditional themes of moral and political philosophy—with the distinction between harmony and discord, freedom and dependence. It is not enough to say merely that these are 'advocative' terms; they may have an empirical content, they may point to real ethical distinctions. It would be surprising, at any rate, if these terms had maintained themselves so long without any objective empirical content.

Marx was a determinist. He recognised that there could be no question of distinguishing a realm of 'freedom' in the sense of indeterminacy from the realm of 'physical causation'. Human action and social events were as much determined, and determined in the same way, as all other events. It was primarily on this ground that he rejected the conception that ethics is concerned with 'guiding' human behaviour in those realms where human beings are 'free' to act in a number of possible ways. It is for this reason that he rejects the notion that morality is concerned with 'obligation'. A person cannot be 'obliged' to act contrary to the course his character and circumstances inevitably determine him to take, and there is no point in obliging him to act in accordance with this course, for he will do so in any case. Nor are the 'principles' of obligation themselves 'freely' established; their content and the time of their appearance is also strictly determined by human character and social circumstance. Any conflict between moral 'principles' and human actions will thus not be a conflict between 'what ought to be' and 'what is', but a conflict within human nature and social reality between different ways of working and different forms of striving. (The emancipation from moralism in the teeth of a moralistic upbringing and of a moralistic society takes time. In his earliest work, Marx was perhaps still prone to proclaim the 'principles' dictated by rational development and to see Law or the State as 'enforcing' them; at the least he seemed to see an irrational reality disintegrating when confronted by the 'principles' of reason. But this was even then a confusion—or possibly a concession to his journalistic aims—incompatible with his main view. By the end of 1843 he had certainly expunged this tendency from his work, and it was never to reappear. Few men have been as consistent as Marx in their refusal to attempt the binding of causality by confronting actions and habits with 'principles'. It is often argued, however, that the mere fact of Marx's political activism, his proclamation of party programmes and his appeals to the proletariat, themselves constitute a refutation of his thorough-going determinism. This seems to me false. Marx would have conceded that his own activities, his proclamations and his appeals, were as much determined as anyone else's. It would be as pointless to tell him not to engage in them as it would be to 'oblige' him to engage in them. As far as the influence of his appeals went, he would have insisted that they would be taken up only by those whose nature and circumstances determine them to do so. What Marx was inclined to overlook is that his appeals would be part of their circumstances. But while this would certainly raise difficulties for any economic reductionism implicit in Marxism, it raises no difficulties for Marx's determinism.)

What, then, can a determinist make of freedom? The young Marx, following a line laid down in Spinoza and Hegel, treats freedom as self-determination. To be free is to be determined by one's own nature. To be unfree is to be determined from without. Marx links this, as we have seen, with harmony and discord, co-operation and conflict. The self-determined activity, governed or determined by the rules of its own being, is necessarily harmonious; dependence is the result of conflict and leads to further conflict.

The difficulty here strikes at the very heart of Marx's position. The self-determined can have neither history nor environment. The passage from cause A to effect B is not some sort of physical concretisation of direct implication, by which A produces B from out of itself. The production of an effect, the occurrence of change, requires more than a single, preceding cause. It requires causal *action*, and the cause cannot act on itself. It is only in the action of one thing upon another, in the impact of a cause on a field,[1] that effects can be produced. To

[1] I adopt the terminology suggested by Professor John Anderson in his 'The Problem of Causality', *A.J.P.P.*, vol. XVI (1938), p. 127 et seq., where the

speak of the self-determined is to assert that the effect was its own cause; that is, to say that there has been no change.[1] The young Marx and Hegel, in seeing the rational both as the end or ultimate effect of history and as the original and ever-present cause of historical development, run squarely into this difficulty. Marx speaks of reason having always been present but not in 'a rational form'; it is difficult to see in this anything but an attempt to have it both ways, to assert that reason changes and is yet the same. The same difficulty arises for Marx regarding his conception of an essential human nature. If this nature is the determining cause of all historical development, he cannot show why there should be any development at all. If, on the other hand, history is a series of transactions between this essential human nature and its environment, then both will be affected in the process, then there is nothing more 'essential' about the human *Wesen* than about the occurrences on which it acts and which act upon it. Marx, indeed, in seeking to maintain the distinction between the human essence and empirical human interests, desires and 'caprices', is forced to disconnect the two entirely, till there is no significant sense in which the two are part of the same person or of the same development.

The attempt to establish the self-determined does not only imply that it can have no history. It also implies that it can have no environment. It must become, as Spinoza saw, the single, all-embracing substance. It is no accident that Marx is forced to take all social institutions, even non-human objects, into man himself, forced to reconcile Subject and Object by obliterating the distinction between them. But the distinction will not be obliterated and in his view that man will 'appropriate' nature, will determine it instead of being determined by it, Marx clearly reveals the anti-empirical, *anti-deterministic*, character of the belief in self-determination. His *anthropology*, his human reductionism, is the inescapable outcome of his metaphysical assumptions. In the name of determinism, of the continuity of human and non-human events, Marx has reduced everything to Man.

For the sake of self-determination, Marx had to destroy the distinc-

[1] A certain superficial plausibility is lent to the notion of self-determination by the observation of change and development *within* a system. But such change is not the result of the system acting upon itself, but of the interaction of the minor systems within the whole, acting upon each other externally. The changes in the relationship between the minor systems, of course, will always be dependent upon external exchanges with the environment of the entire system.

view of causality I am putting is more fully argued. The logical material in this section generally owes much to his work.

tion between the human and the non-human. For the sake of self-determination, he has also to destroy the distinction between one man and another. If man is to be truly self-determined, he cannot be determined by Nature, he also cannot be determined by other men. Marx requires a human community in which not only conflict, but even the very distinction, between one man and another has disappeared. This is the significance of his insistence that in the truly human society each man represents every other, that every activity carried out in this society is *my* activity. He bases this, as we have seen, on a seemingly metaphysical notion of the human essence as truly universal in a qualitative, intensional sense and not in a merely distributive sense.

As metaphysical doctrines, the belief in self-determination and in *a* universal which is yet not particular and resolves all particular differences will not do. But are we simply to dismiss them as Hegelian confusions that make the whole of the young Marx's position quite valueless, or can we find in them an empirical content, the significance of which can survive the rejection of Marx's false logical presuppositions?

There is a great deal of material in Marx's early work pointing to the conclusion that Marx's distinction between goods and evils, the self-determined and the dependent, the 'universal' and the 'particular' is connected with concrete distinctions in ways of working. Thus he argues that the free press is free, its activity is internally coherent, while censorship is necessarily incoherent and unstable, parasitic upon the press and unable to develop its presuppositions without inconsistency. Similarly, his whole distinction between the political spirit and civil society rests on this conception of goods as being able to work and co-operate coherently, while evils conflict not only with goods, but with each other. Now, this is a distinction which ethical theorists have repeatedly stumbled upon. We find traces of it in the great psychological studies underlying the theological imperativism of the Old Testament.[1] We find it clearly suggested—though subsequently obscured—by Socrates in Book I of the *Republic*. There are traces of

---

[1] Professor C. A. Simpson, in his article 'Old Testament Historiography' (*Hibbert Journal*, July 1958, pp. 319–32, esp. pp. 324–6), for instance, seeks to show that the story of David was in fact first told as a purely empirical study of the self-destructive character of evil motives, and that the attempt to ascribe his fate to God's intervention is a later accretion which ruins the whole point of the story.

it in the moral psychology of Aquinas; it emerges as the only empirical content of Kant's principle of universalisability and of Rousseau's universal and universalisable general will. We find it again in Schopenhauer's early, not very thorough-going, attempt to create a scientific ethics—his *Grundprobleme der Ethik,* where co-operating motives, however, are confused with motives that *aim* at co-operation, where love, for instance, is merged with altruism.

The divisiveness, the internal incoherence, of evils is vividly portrayed in Marx's analysis of the 'rights' of civil society and in his exposure of the 'contradictions' of political economy in the *Paris Manuscripts.* But his reductionism, his concern to treat divisiveness as temporary, prevents him from connecting it with the positive characters of the processes involved. He wants to see conflict as the result of 'external' determination. From this, as we have seen, nothing can escape. Alternatively, as in the *Paris Manuscripts,* he treats conflict and division as the result of 'abstraction', that is, of the fact that things have their own characters and are not all 'expressions' of a single underlying whole. But such 'abstraction' cannot be overcome; the reality of differences and distinctions cannot be made to disappear. Yet however much Marx's account of the reasons for incoherence may suffer from metaphysical confusions, the incoherence remains.

Goods co-operate and form a harmonious system; evils conflict not only with goods, but with each other. Much, perhaps most, of traditional ethical theory since the seventeenth century has concerned itself with the metaphysical constructions and the logical analysis forced on it by its normative form; but this was not always so. Where positive questions of ethical character have arisen, this distinction between co-operation and conflict, assistance and resistance, has been the leading empirical content of the distinction between goods and evils. An important subsidiary question, of course, has been whether ethical distinctions are to be made between motives or the things that motives aim at; but if we are to take assistance and resistance as central, we will hardly be able to work out a position unless we take as the material of ethical enquiry motives (and the social movements associated with motives) and not objectives or non-mental, non-social occurrences. Taking it that assistance means that a certain motive brings about circumstances in which another will act, and resistance that it brings about circumstances which prevent another from acting, we have the suggestion that assistance is the mark of good motives and resistance the mark of bad motives. With the qualification that Marx makes no reference to motives, but to human actitivies and social institution, this seems to be the position underlying much of his early work. It is also, as Anderson has pointed out in an article worth citing at length:

Substantially the view put forward by Socrates in *Republic*, I. He makes it clear, of course, that this distinction is not to be taken as a simple and final criterion, by pointing out that, while goods assist one another, they oppose bads; whereas bads oppose both goods and one another. There is no question then, of founding ethics on abstract attitudes of assistance and resistance (although, as Socrates develops the argument, this point is considerably obscured), any more than on abstract attitudes of altruism and egoism. The position may be expressed by saying that a good motive will always assist another of the same kind, so that that particular good can be communicated to an indefinite extent within the field of human activities. Love of truth, for example, will indefinitely communicate the spirit of discovery, and will assist the development and operation of that spirit wherever it appears and with whatever materials it may deal; a true investigator in any field will always encourage investigation in that or any other field. We do not, of course, *define* goodness by means of that relation, but if we decide, as I think we may, that it is common and peculiar to goods, then we can employ it as a criterion in particular cases. The same facts will show that a good motive will sustain itself in a particular mind by providing the materials for its continued operation, as one discovery leads on to another and the solution of one problem to the formulation of a new problem.

Bad motives, on the other hand, can never get rid of an element of resistance and repression, and, though they may co-operate to a certain limited extent, will eventually be found in opposition, and will always involve a certain friction. Hate, it may be said, breeds hate; but it also fights with hate and tries to destroy it, and in the individual it exhausts itself. So ignorance, though it may breed ignorance, fights with ignorance, and obscurantism defeats its own end. The degree of co-operation possible to motives which are not good is represented in the State sketched by Glaucon in *Republic*, II. Here the assistance is of an external or extrinsic sort, the utilization of common means to diverse ends, as contrasted with participation in common activities in which the distinction between means and ends is unimportant. We note in the compromise referred to (which is, of course, a fact of common experience) the absence of a common spirit and the recurrence of friction, and also, as Glaucon points out, the element of repression in that some demands are given up in order that others may have a *sure* satisfaction . . .

We may further illustrate the operation of assistance by reference to the process described by Freud as 'transference'. Freud is referring primarily to 'pathological' cases, but we may consider the matter more broadly. What occurs in transference is that one person, e.g., the patient, makes use of the powers of mind of another person, e.g., the analyst; 'identifies' himself with the latter, adopts his views and his ways of dealing with situations. In this way the patient's previously pent-up motives find outlet. But the same may take place within one person's mind, when a conflict is resolved and a new type of activity emerges by the aid of certain abiding motives or sentiments. This is the process of 'sublimation', where one motive finds for another a means of expression, provides it with a language, puts its own 'ideas' before it as objectives. This is also the process of education. It may be argued, then, that all good motives have this power of transference or conversion, whereby from hitherto dissociated material a new motive is formed which can co-operate with the good motive. Goodness is associative, evil is dissociative; goods have a common language, evils have not.[1]

On the basis of suggestions made by Anderson in this and other articles,[2] we can have an account of the distinction between freedom and compulsion—such as Marx requires—which would not come down to an anti-deterministic one, which would not end by putting ethical processes outside causality and the interaction it requires. Following Anderson, we might say that goods are those motives which are free or enterprising, which do not require internal repression or external protection or compulsion. They are activities which are disinterested, which do not fear knowledge or require error. Freedom would thus be seen as an ethical quality, bound up with the way in which goods work. It would not be seen as any metaphysical illusion of being undetermined or 'self-determined' or as the 'freedom from' external pressures. The point might be illustrated by considering what is a free love. It is not made free by the multiplicity of its objects, by its readiness to embrace every woman, or by the absence of *external* impediments. The free quality of a love lies in the fact that it does not require external restraints or internal illusions and repressions in order to continue as 'love'. Similarly, the fact that a man is externally 'free' to think, does not make his thinking free. The freedom of thought would lie in the fact that it does not itself strive to protect certain interests or support certain 'authorities', in that it does not subordinate itself to other ends. Further, as we have seen, goods communicate themselves with a spontaneity radically distinct from the enforced imitation enjoined by evils. (Compare the communication of knowledge with the inculcation of obedience. In the former case, the appeal

---

[1] 'Determinism and Ethics', *A.J.P.P.*, vol. VI (1927), pp. 251–3.

[2] Published in the *A.J.P.P.* from 1927 onwards. Besides the article already cited, see especially his 'Realism versus Relativism in Ethics', vol. XI (1933), p. 1 et seq., and 'The Meaning of Good', vol. XX (1942), p. 111 et seq., on which I draw in the account that follows.

is to the same motive, so that communication consists in producing a situation in which that motive is free to act; in the latter case, the appeal is to a different motive and its objective will be different. It is this which distinguishes the alliance, in a common activity, of genuine teacher and genuine pupil from the temporary submission of the pupil to an external 'authority'.) Goods co-operate with each other and display internal progress and development in a way that evils cannot co-operate and progress.[1] They have a certain 'universality', which Feuerbach and the young Marx dimly perceived when they distinguished man from the animal by reference to his ability to take anything for his object, to create consciously in all forms. This is the ability of goods to work under all conditions and take anything as their material: the universality of science, for example, lies in the fact that anything may be investigated scientifically.

Evils, on the other hand, though ineradicable, are parasitic upon goods. They conflict not only with goods but also with each other; they are interested as opposed to disinterested, repressive as opposed to free, consumptive as opposed to productive. Goods carry with them a characteristic devotion to movements 'transcending the individual', to ways of living in which he is 'caught up'; evils elevate the particular and produce such egoistic attitudes as hope, guilt and despair. The qualities characteristic of goods are displayed in love and courage, in the scientific, artistic and productive spirit, in the enquirer's and creator's honesty, detachment from self and immersion in his work. Goods require no censorship, no punishments, no protection as part

[1] Compare the history of science with the history of religion or tyranny. The conception of science, art or industry as progressive does not entail the vulgar conception that the scientific knowledge, the art or industrial production of any age is superior to that of the age preceding it; the conception means that science, art or industry are progressive in the sense that they can always build directly on previous achievements in their fields, can take up where a previous age left off, even if there have been intervening periods of ignorance or mediocrity. The suggestion that religions or tyrannies may progress, on the other hand, where it is not mere advocacy of the merits of a later tyranny over an earlier one, always resolves itself into the recognition of progress in the scientific, industrial or artistic material a religion or a tyranny may seek to appropriate, but which is intrinsically incompatible with it. Subjectivists, of course, may claim that they recognise 'progress' in tyrannies in the sense of increased efficiency—in which case any distinction between ethical and instrumental uses of 'good' ('this is a good poison') disappears completely. With it, however, there also disappears any possibility of accounting for the differences in the history of science and of tyrannies noted above.

of their ways of working. Evils, on the other hand, display their characteristics in obscurantism, superstition, the demand for censorship, luxury, commercialism, tyranny, leading to the 'sexual entanglements, cross-purposes, dissatisfactions, terrors [that] are an important feature of the hell of bourgeois existence'.[1] They require censorship, suppression, punishment and protection; they seek prior guarantees of security; they display a fundamental instability and incoherence.

Moralism itself, on this view, is the product of evil motives, of that search for security which is the characteristic of unfree activities. The necessary instabilities or moralistic theories which we have noted, and which Marx recognised, are typical of the instability of evils in general. Goods require no protection or commendation and do not seek it as part of their way of working; the question whether any person, movement or activity supports goods is irrelevant to their character. In actual fact, the extent to which men display goods and engage in good activities will depend not on exhortation, but on the goods they already have and their communication with other goods. Their support of goods—in so far as they do support them—is not something that precedes their pursuit of goods, but something that follows from the goods they have and display.

Ethical distinctions, on this view, occur among motives and the social activities with which these motives are connected. They do not occur characteristically among the *objectives* which motives or activities pursue. Traditional moral theorists have vacillated over the question whether ethical qualities should be ascribed to mental habits or to the things which these habits pursue: to the love of beauty, for example, or to beauty itself, to the love of truth or—whatever that may mean—to 'truth' itself. The issue has been much confused by the moralist's attempt to discover a realm of indeterminacy in order to 'justify' praise and blame. But in general, following Anderson again,[2] we might say that it is only through confusion with the goodness of the motives that pursue them that objectives come to be called positively and qualitatively good—a confusion that might often arise from the unjustified assumption that ends are superior to that which strives for these ends, that an objective must be better than the motive that pursues it.

Whatever the logical confusions on the opposing side, this question

---

[1] John Anderson: 'Art and Morality', *A.J.P.P.*, vol. XIX (1941), pp. 253 et seq., p. 264.

[2] 'Determinism and Ethics', loc. cit., p. 251.

and that of the nature of ethical distinctions and of the meaning of 'good' cannot be resolved by logic alone. It will be an empirical question whether we find distinctions in ways of working, differences in the manner of communication and forming alliances, in mental and social fields that we do not find in non-mental and non-social fields; it will also be an empirical question what these distinctions are and to what extent they provide the basis for a coherent science of ethics, divorced from its normative confusions. What I have striven to show is that certain of the traditional themes of moral philosophy can be given coherence and concrete empirical content if we treat goods in the way I have outlined. We can then also see why one feels a considerable strength in Marx's youthful doctrines despite the metaphysical confusions with which they are overlaid. But there can be no question of establishing ethical qualities by purely logical argument. At best, they can be exhibited for those who have felt them and seen them operate to recognise and recall, or offered as illuminating developments and distinctions that seemed obscure before. For if ethical qualities do exist, if they account for some of the alliances and discords, for the progress and regression in history and social life, then to neglect these qualities will be to fall seriously short in one's understanding of human history and social life. Without them, I would argue, we would see fully neither Marx's strength nor his weakness.

10. The Rejection of Moralism, of 'Rights' and of Normative Law

MARX'S rejection of moralism, of abstract rights and of normative law is commonly connected with his determinism. There is, as we have seen, some basis for this. He rightly insists that moral 'principles', constitutional rights and legal enactments are not rational and eternal 'norms' that logically precede society and determine its character from above. He sees correctly that principles, codes and rights follow from ways of living, from social activities and pursuits, and not *vice versa*, that it is to a specific function or movement, activity or class, that rights belong. As the character or social distribution of functions, classes and movements changes, the 'accepted' moral principles, constitutional rights and legal systems will also change.

The young Marx, however, is also concerned to make a more fundamental criticism of moralism, of the erection of rights and duties and of the compulsive application of law. This is an ethical criticism. Moralism, the postulation of rights and duties and the application of legal punishments and sanctions seek to bind men from outside. They are therefore forms of bondage and not of freedom. As such, they cannot produce freedom. This, we may remember, was his criticism of Hegel's conception of a coercive State that was nevertheless 'the rational form of freedom'. These things, in their coercion, are evils and cannot be productive of good.

The ethical theory outlined above enables us to make sense of this. Though Marx is content to rest on the confused opposition of 'self-determination' and coercion, his position depends on the implicit recognition of the distinction between spontaneous co-operation and communication characteristic of goods and the only apparent harmony, the eliciting of no more than external compliance, characteristic of the repression practised by evils. The position might be illustrated by means of Marx's distinction between coercive punishment and punishment under 'truly human' conditions—punishment passed by the criminal on himself (*supra*, I, 3). Marx is unable to put his view coherently precisely because he is still working with the conception of human self-determination and thus with the conception of the whole individual. But he is able to show that retributive punishment is radically different in its effects from the spontaneous co-operation elicited by goods—the state when the criminal sees 'in other men his natural saviours'. Thus goods operate by liberating the capacities that are themselves good within the criminal, placing before these the material required for their development. The 'regeneration' of the criminal would then be self-regeneration in the sense that it is the goods within him, strengthened by assistance and not by repression, which would have overcome the evils within him. While there would be no guarantee that the regeneration, the dominance of good motives, was permanent, no reason to suppose that evil motives could be entirely eliminated from any human mind, there would be an obvious sense in which the regeneration was true regeneration, was a genuine development of the goods within him. The regeneration practised by Sue, on the other hand, would be of a different character. Here, though the emphasis is still moral, still on producing certain mental habits within the criminal, the appeal is to evil motives. It is the longing for security, for comfort and consolation which Sue seeks to arouse and to utilise. But these motives will not establish genuine and lasting co-operation. They are by their very nature divisive; they rest on that elevation of the particular which is commonly called *egoism*. They must constantly be protected and sheltered from the operation of goods. Vitality, freedom and sincerity will be their enemies, knowledge and productive capacity will threaten them. It is, as Marx sees, no accident that the gangleader's eyes have to be gouged out so that he can learn to pray.

The same point, as Marx also saw, applies to the 'ethic' of Christianity. It, too, has to weaken goods in order to utilise evils. It has, in fact, no conception of the productive forces that operate within individuals, no conception of freedom, of spontaneous co-operation. It preaches the subordination of man to 'higher powers' and—ultimately—to egoistic ends.

Marx is wrong in thinking that vitality, freedom, sincerity and the capacities for production and spontaneous co-operation are somehow more truly human than the search for security, than avarice, the demand for protection, the longing for comfort and consolation. But he sees correctly that these evils are unable to overcome goods entirely and that they can neither form a coherent, stable system of their own or reach a stable and coherent accommodation with goods. It is thus that he can point to the contradictions in 'the rights of the citizen' and 'the rights of man' (*supra* II, 6). The accommodation of political State and civil society becomes a harmony of discord with harmony; the freedom of evils becomes their 'right' to seek to destroy each other. 'The human right of freedom is not based on the connexion of man with man, but rather on the separation of man from man . . . Man's right of private property . . . is the right of self-interest . . . It allows every man to find not the realisation, but the limitation, of his freedom . . . Security is the guarantee of egoism.' ('On the Jewish Question', *supra* II, 6.)

If we accept as the foundation of moral theory the utilitarian concern with ends and neglect the character of the motives and activities pursuing these ends, then—as Marx saw—we are necessarily driven into incoherence. Acquisitiveness conflicts with acquisitiveness, greed interferes with greed, security threatens security. Even if it were true that all persons display these demands, the fact that they are common to all still establishes no single common interest, no genuine basis for co-operation. This, I should argue, is the empirical content of Marx's distinction between mere numerical universality and a qualitative, intensional universality. For the utilitarian, with his elevation of divisive demands, 'society . . . appears as a frame external to individuals, as a limitation of their original independence. The sole thread that keeps them together is natural necessity, needs and private interest, the preservation of their property and of their egoistic person.' (*Supra,* II, 6.) Thus—though Marx did not go on to say this explicitly—the 'principles' of civil society and of the utilitarian elevation of individual ends cannot be formulated: the divisiveness of the ends accepted by the utilitarian is reflected in the incoherence of his principles. The 'right to liberty', for instance, cannot be proclaimed as such: it becomes the right 'to liberty that does not interfere with the liberty of others', and thus establishes as principle that I may not interfere with the liberty of others, but their liberties may interfere with mine. Subsidiary shifts have to be resorted to: we are exhorted to avoid *unneccessary* interference with people's liberty, where what is 'necessary' can never be established; we are told that the principle of liberty is after all not a principle, but a defeasible presumption, the operation of which is dependent on moral climate and political, legal and social policy. Whilst these devices might serve in the operation of a compromise legal code, helping to mitigate some conflicts and to make oppression more palatable, beside allowing the system to respond to changes in the balance of social forces, they establish neither a common interest nor a scientific foundation for ethics. Their very instability is a mark of the evils with which they seek compromise. The granting of 'liberty' to an activity, as Marx also saw, does not make it free.

Marx's contrast between the 'rational society' and the political structure of 'civil society', then, might be seen as a sound perception of the contrast between what we might call 'ethical justice' and 'political justice'. 'Political justice' is a compromise, a temporary working arrangement among hostile and divergent movements. Because these movements do diverge, because even the seeking of common ends does not imply the common, co-operative seeking of these ends, Marx has been able to show, the 'principles of political justice' cannot be developed coherently or established as permanent.

'Ethical justice', on the other hand, is rooted in the spontaneous co-operation of goods—a co-operation that we shall now turn to examine.

11. Ethics and the 'Truly Human' Society

MARX'S vision of the truly human society under Communism, it has been said, is the vision of a society of artists, engaged in creative production. The overcoming of alienation visualised by Marx, it is claimed, is an aesthetic conception, referring to the bond between the artist and the work. He shapes it and forms it and in doing so makes its materials his own. The roots of the conception may be found in the aesthetics of German romanticism, in the philosophy, for instance, of the young Schelling.

The parallel is apt, but to regard Marx's exposure of alienation and his postulation of activities in which it is overcome as the application of artistic or aesthetic 'criteria' is completely to miss the point. The parallel is apt because artists, *qua* artists, do habitually display freedom from alienation in their artistic activity. Their activity is not subordinated to ends outside the activity. In so far as their motives are artistic, they are not working for reward, or fame, or any other non-artistic end. They are working for the sake of the activity itself. They create, or seek to create, according to the laws of art, not according to laws dictated from outside the activity by non-artistic or anti-artistic motives and ends. There is no significant sense in which artistic activity overcomes—as Marx seems to think—the distinction between man and the objects on which he is working. The sculptor who creates a statue does not thereby obliterate the distinction between man and bronze. He may bruise his toe or break his neck on the statue the following morning. He may discover in it things he did not know were there; he may be influenced by it as the material was moulded by him. But it is true that in the process of production he and his material become part of a single process; that the exchanges between him and the material on which he is working come to him not as externally imposed means to a different end, but as part of the very activity which is his 'end'. The fact that this activity is not merely an activity 'governed' by aesthetic 'criteria', but is an activity displaying ethical qualities, an activity which is not merely artistic but also good, comes out in the relations it creates for him with other artists. In so far as he is an artist, he sees other artists not as hostile competitors, but as men whose work assists and inspires his work, whose artistic motives kindled and continue to strengthen his.

The fact that this relation, and the underlying quality of the activity, are not simply aesthetic is sufficiently illustrated by the occurrence of similar relations in other, non-artistic, activities. What has been said of artists is true, in every particular, of scientists and of anyone displaying the spirit of disinterested enquiry in general. It is true not only of the artistic producer, but of anyone seized with the productive spirit. The activities of other producers are to him a source of encouragement, not a threat of competition. He is stimulated by them; he is assisted by their methods and their discoveries; he seeks to emulate, and not to destroy or expropriate, their results.

A characteristic of goods, we have noted, is their rejection of *individual* ends and desires. They thus confer 'freedom' in another sense: they give the individual the capacity of transcending himself, of devoting himself to a movement of which he is merely a vehicle, which existed before him, exists in others beside him and will continue to exist after him. In so far as these goods exist within him, he feels no tension, no conflict, between him and others possessed by the same spirit. It is in this sense that Marx is rightly able to say that the opposition between individual and 'social' demands disappears, that wants and enjoyments lose their egoistic nature (see *supra*, II, 8).

In the working of evils we have a totally different situation. Here, as Marx himself suggests,[1] we find substituted for the creative, productive, enquiring interest the desire for possession. Here we find the elevation of 'ends' to which activities are subjected. Here we find the elevation of particular, individual satisfactions and the conflict of one demand with another. What co-operation exists is in the form of utilisation of common means to diverse ends. There is thus a gulf between the activity undertaken for an end and the end desired; the activity can become distasteful, unwanted, forced. Marx sees clearly this aspect

[1] *Paris Manuscripts*, M I, 3, 118: 'In place of all physical and intellectual senses has come the simple alienation of all these senses, the sense of *possession*.'

of labour under conditions where the work is performed merely for gain, that is, for an extrinsic object:

[Alienation consists] firstly, in the fact that labour is *external* to the worker, i.e., it does not belong to his essential being, in the fact that he therefore does not affirm himself in his work, but negates himself in it, that he does not feel content, but unhappy, in it, that he develops no free physical and mental energy, but mortifies his body and ruins his mind. Therefore the worker feels himself only outside his work, while in his work he feels outside himself. He is at home when he is not working, and when he works he is not at home. His work therefore is not voluntary but coerced, it is *forced labour*. It is, therefore, not the satisfaction of a need, but only a *means* for satisfying needs external to it. Its alien character emerges clearly in the fact that as soon as there is no physical or other compulsion, labour is avoided like the plague. External labour, labour in which man alienates himself, is labour of self-sacrifice, of mortification.

(M I, 3, 85–6; *supra*, II, 7.)

Marx's insistence that this alienation cannot be overcome by making the products of labour the property of the worker, or social property, but only by superseding the whole conception of property, shows how close he was to an appreciation of the true basis of alienation in the concern with ends, with consumption instead of production, characteristic of evils. And in his critique of political rights and legal justice we have seen his appreciation of the necessary conflict underlying the limited co-operation of evils.

The difference in the organisation and co-operation possible to goods and to evils may be brought out by considering the role of 'rules' in the two systems. Both goods and evils will, in the process of their working, formulate certain rules and policies. These may be called their respective moralities. Now, in the operation of goods we find that such rules are subsidiary to the activity itself; they are not required to protect the activity, as a social movement, from the inevitable conflict and dissension within it; they can be flexible and loose. Indeed, as Anderson has stressed,[1] a good—such as enquiry—'will be weakened unless it sits loosely to its rules and, for the most part, forgets about them. This, I think, would be admitted by many with regard to education, and it should not be hard for these people to admit it with regard to cultural communication in general. Policy, as we may put it, has to play second fiddle to spontaneity, and goods continue because of their own character—and emphatically *not* be-

[1] 'Ethics and Advocacy', *A.J.P.P.*, vol. XXII (1944), p. 184.

cause they are wanted.' Neither can they be made to continue by being *prescribed*. In the case of evils, on the other hand, the attempt to impose prescriptive norms and the resultant appeal to hierarchical conceptions of 'authority' is a necessary condition for the allaying of internal dissension and conflict—dissension and conflict which, in fact, can only be concealed but not suppressed. It is here that we find the subordination of activities to 'rules', the substitution of 'loyalty' to institutions and persons for 'loyalty' to movements and ways of life and the attempt to shelter rules, ends, institutions and persons from discussion or criticism.

Marx's vision of Communism, then, is in no sense an 'artistic' vision; it rests on his sound, if unworked-out, perception of the characteristic organisation and ways of working of goods; it rests, that is, on an ethical and not on an aesthetic distinction. The real reason his vision has been called artistic, it seems to me, is not because it embodies aesthetic conceptions, but because the society he portrays seems possible, to his critics, only as a society of artists. Immersion in activity, neglect of rewards, spontaneous co-operation and disinterested appreciation and emulation—the theory runs—are possible only to those engaged in the 'higher levels' of creative activity, in 'pure' science and art. This seems to me patently false. Artists, as people, can display hatred, envy and greed. They can be found subordinating their work to 'popular taste', to religious requirements or to the demands of the market; they can plagiarise, steal and intrigue. Soldiers, fishermen, farmers and artisans can be found exhibiting love or courage, displaying attachment to their activity for its own sake, co-operating spontaneously with their fellows and neglecting all thought of the 'rewards' of their work. The distinction between the morality of goods and the morality of evils is rather linked—as Georges Sorel suggests— with the distinction between the morality of the producer and the morality of the consumer. The producer emphasises activities, a way of life, a morality; he is stirred by production everywhere and brought together by the productive spirit with other producers. The consumer emphasises ends, things to be secured; he subordinates himself and his activity to these ends; his sentiments are not productive but proprietary and consumptive; his relations with other consumers involve friction, hypocrisy and envy.

The linking of ethical distinctions with productive and consumptive moralities in history does not imply that men can be classified into those who are producers and those who are consumers, or that the consumptive outlook can be eradicated from human life.[1] Just as the productive, the artistic and the enquiring spirit that enters into men cannot be accounted for by adding the motives of the participants, so it cannot be treated as seizing a 'whole' man. Devotion to enquiry can co-exist, in the one person, with proprietorial sentiments or the longing for security, for instance. The former sentiment cannot strengthen or be strengthened by the latter sentiments; the divisiveness of the latter will interfere with the co-operation and admirations spontaneously displayed by the former. But men do display internal conflicts; they are torn by the struggle of goods and evils *within* them; they recognise both as part of their nature. Nor is there anything in that nature to show that goods must triumph, that evil will be eradicated. If evils are divisive and unstable, goods can also be destroyed or weakened, either by the operation of natural conditions or by the force of evils.

There is no ground, then, for Marx's optimism, for his belief in the inevitable coming of a society completely given over to goods. He is able to maintain his optimism only by sliding into a confused individualism and an unempirical doctrine of ontological hierarchies. This is exemplified in his attempt to treat conflict and division as the result of society's 'abstraction' into the individual, in his failure to see conflict as the clash of social movements and ways of living, and in his belief that evils are the result of 'external' determination and incompatible with the 'truly human' essence of man. The motives Marx unwittingly strengthens in his conception of a society made safe for goods are evil motives: the desires for security and protection, for guarantees that the end striven for will be obtained. Yet these tendencies toward security-seeking, this desire for assurance of rewards and ultimate success, this withdrawal from the view that goods are *strengthened* in the continuous struggle with evils, are something that Marx helped to liberate in others. They are not something that he valued or needed himself. He himself lived the 'perilous, fighting life' (Croce) engaged in by goods; he himself despised the life of prudence and precaution as a base and mean existence.

* * *

The ethical position outlined above is sufficiently radical to cause considerable unease in the minds of most persons confronted by it for the first

[1] It does, however, mean rejecting Marx's claim (*Grundrisse*, pp. 11–16) that production and consumption are identical, or the even more naive claim that all production is for the sake of consumption.

time. In my own experience, the intelligent objections raised against it have tended to come down to a few basic arguments. A brief attempt to meet these arguments may help to clarify the position a little further.

Many modern philosophers would concede that 'good' cannot be both a quality and a relation and that the insistence that qualitative ethical distinction establish no obligations whatever meets most of their arguments against a qualitative treatment of 'good'. But to treat 'good' as a quality that carries no recommendations, they would say, is to fly presumptuously in the face of usage. 'Good' is an adjective of commendation; to treat it as anything else is to talk about something other than 'good'.

To this one can only reply that there is no coherent usage, and that the moral philosopher, in clearing up the confusions, will have to reject some usages and establish others. We are not confronted by one moral usage, but by many; these usages do not provide the 'ultimate facts' of moral theory, but embody the often mistaken conclusions of various moral theories. We can, of course, study the history and determining conditions of the normative conceptions and moral attitudes which people have often tried to express through ethical terms; to do this would be to do anthropology, history and sociology, but not ethics. Even such a study could hardly be carried out without having to consider—as a question independent of moral attitudes—whether ethical distinctions exist. If the insistence that 'good' is a quality results in the 'presumptuous' rejection of ethical 'norms', the insistence that 'good' is a relation results in the equally 'presumptuous' denial of the reality of ethical distinctions. Both the postulation of 'norms' and the belief in the reality of ethical distinctions have played an important role in the history of moral speculation; but we cannot consistently uphold both. The former, I have suggested, leads to incoherence and the subversion of any possibility of ethical science, the latter, it seems to me, not only provides a coherent basis for ethics but illuminates social and mental life.

A second objection is that the things I treat as goods or characteristics of goods—enquiry, immersion in an activity, neglect of reward—are not possible to all human beings, and come most easily in fact to those who through class position or occupation are freed from economic need. I have already suggested that I do not accept the view that disinterested enquiry or artistic production is possible only to those whose livelihood is assured. But even if this were in fact so, it would not be an argument against my position. 'Ought', says the moralist, 'implies can'. But I am not a moralist; I am not saying that goods 'ought' to be done. Certain natural or social conditions may militate against the emergence and communication of goods; this neither makes the conditions themselves of ethical relevance nor affects the character of ethical activities or motives when they do appear.

Two further arguments are more detailed. One argument claims that mutual co-operation, inspiration, etc., is not exclusive to goods while certain things that I treat as evils—the desire for money or recognition, for instance —are often necessary to produce scientific or artistic creation in a given individual, and may thus be found 'co-operating' with goods in a most intimate fashion. Champion billiard players, orchid growers, etc., I have been told, display all the characteristics I claim for artists and scientists: their developments of technique assist one another, they themselves keep in touch with each other, exchange hints, inspire each other. 'Yet this does not seem to be of any ethical interest.' I should argue, on the contrary, that it is of ethical interest; the orchid grower and billiard player who exchange information freely with others in their fields, who are inspired by advances in them, are displaying ethical qualities that assimilate their activities to those of the scientist and the artist and the producer in general and radically distinguish them from those fellow-exponents of their craft who are concerned with fame, with profit, with 'getting one over' the men whom they see as hostile competitors.

The allied suggestion that scientific and artistic production of a high order frequently display an extraordinary intertwining of motives—of intellectual interest with unusual egotism, ambition or the desire for self-assertion— raises more serious issues. It is true that a person's immersion in good activities may be intensified by evil motives: a man's scientific work may be goaded on by his desire for wealth, honour and the love of women, as Freud puts it. Nevertheless, it seems to me that such an alliance between good and evil motives can only be of the 'extrinsic' kind outlined above. The length of time for which such motives can co-operate without overt friction will depend upon purely fortuitous circumstances. At the same time, the assistance which evils can render goods in specific circumstances seems to me akin to the assistance which non-mental occurrences—earthquakes, epidemics or poverty—can render goods and not at all akin to the assistance goods render each other. In general, I should be inclined to suggest that evils, where they assist goods, do so only by inhibiting other evils. A man's love of money will prevent him from seeking luxury at a particular moment or from showing his envy of his colleagues if he has reason to believe that his reputation and work as a disinterested scientist will get him greater money in the end. But the love of money cannot give him the conception of disinterestedness or the capacity to display it on those occasions that he does display it.

The second and last of the detailed arguments concerns the distinction between goods as involving immersion in an activity in which the distinction between means and ends is unimportant, and bads as involving the elevation of ends. It has been objected that the pursuit of ends need not be the pursuit of possessions, that a man's end may be the promotion of a good activity, the securing of conditions in which the activity can go forward. This kind of position is often put, with considerable sincerity, by Vice-Chancellors of

Universities and heads of scientific and educational institutions. Yet the very difficulties in which such people repeatedly find themselves seem to me to expose their claim. The 'protection' of education or culture, the securing of guarantees and conditions as an aim preceding the activity itself, invariably threatens to end in the subordination of education or culture to the non-educational and non-cultural forces whose protection and guarantees it seeks. There can be a consistent and coherent educational, scientific or artistic policy; there cannot be a consistent and coherent policy for securing education, science and art their 'rightful' (i.e., protected and guaranteed) place in a society of competing interests and ways of life.

This is not to say that any particular person or institution or movement can escape the problems of practice, of allocating insufficient resources, struggling and at times compromising with inimical movements and concentrating on one thing rather than another. It is to deny both that ethics is in any sense a handbook or a set of principles for such practical accommodations and that any such handbook could be composed. It is to insist, on the contrary, that accommodations are between existing movements, that policies follow and do not precede activities and ways of life. Goods are not constituted by what they aim at, but by what they are.

PART FOUR

Ethics and the Mature Marx

12. The New Edifice: Historical Materialism and the Rejection of 'Philosophy'

MARX, we have seen, began his political activity as a philosopher. His tools were primarily logical; the core of his belief was a philosophical, indeed, metaphysical, conception of the necessary dialectical development of man, through alienation and the inevitable conflicts resulting from alienation, toward the truly universal and truly self-determined. He did display, from the very beginning, a strong anti-transcendental strain, an increasingly confident rejection of anything divorced from empirical reality. Between 1841 and the end of 1844, Marx's views became steadily more social in content: the Communist society replaced the Hegelian Absolute, the dialectical conflict in history became a conflict of movements and institutions rather than of categories and ideas, the 'party of the concept' was replaced by the proletariat. But in the second Hegel critique published in February 1844, his insistence on seeking the positive social content of all human beliefs is still no more than the insistence that all knowledge is empirical, that the supra-terrestrial can always be reduced to the terrestrial. Toward the end of the *Paris Manuscripts* (M I, 3, 115) Marx argues that the laws of alienation which dominate political economy also apply to religion, the family, the State, jurisprudence, morality, science and art. But this is so because all these are, like industry, forms of human production and alienation evinces itself within all human production. There is nothing in his work yet to suggest that economic production must dominate and determine, at all times, all other forms of production and of social life. There is nothing in his work to call into question the precise status or content of the logico-ethical categories—

dependence, alienation, self-determination, 'the truly human'—with which he is working.

By the middle of 1845, however, these questions do move into the forefront of his work. In that year, after completing the *Paris Manuscripts* of 1844, Marx discovered or proclaimed his materialist interpretation of history[1]—his insistence that economic production dominates and determines all social institutions and beliefs. In the *German Ideology* he writes:

Already here we see how this civil society is the *true source and theatre of all history*, and how nonsensical is the conception of history held hitherto, which neglects the real relationships and confines itself to high-sounding dramas of princes and States. Civil society embraces the whole material intercourse of individuals within a definite stage of development of productive forces. It embraces the whole commercial and industrial life of this stage and, in so far, transcends the State and nation, though, on the other hand again, it must assert itself towards foreign peoples as nationality, and inwardly must organise itself as State . . . Civil society as such only develops with the bourgeoisie; the social organisation evolving directly out of production and commerce, *which in all ages forms the basis of the State and of the rest of the idealistic superstructure*, has, however, always been designated by the same name.

(M I, 5, 25–6. Italics mine.)

In the letter to P. V. Annenkov of December 28, 1846, written soon after the completion of the *German Ideology*, Marx develops the same point:

What is society, whatever its form may be? The product of men's reciprocal activity. Are men free to choose this or that form of society for themselves? By no means. Assume a particular state of development in the productive forces of man and you will get a particular form of commerce and consumption. Assume particular stages of development in production, commerce and consumption and you will have a corresponding social order, a corresponding organisation of the family and of the ranks and classes. Presuppose a particular civil society and you will get particular political conditions which are only the official expression of civil society . . . the social

[1] See Engels' well-known statement in his preface to Marx's *Revelations Concerning the Communist Trial in Cologne*: 'When I visited Marx in Paris in the summer of 1844, our complete agreement on all theoretical questions became clear . . . When we met again in the spring of 1845 in Brussels, Marx had already developed out of these foundations the main lines of his materialist theory of history.'

history of men is never anything but the history of their individual development, whether they are conscious of it or not. Their material relations are
the bases of all their relations. These material relations are only the necessary
forms in which their material and individual activity is realised.

(SC 7–8.)

It is on this basis that Marx can turn viciously[1] on his own earlier
conception 'of Human Nature, of Man in general, who belongs to no
class, has no reality, who exists only in the misty realm of philosophical
fantasy'. There is, he insists in the *German Ideology*, no essential Man
apart from real man and real men are shaped by economic forces:

This sum of productive forces, forms of capital and social forms of intercourse, which every individual and generation finds in existence as something
given, is the real basis of what the philosophers have conceived as 'substance'
and 'essence of man'.

(M I, 5, 28.)

'All history', he reminds Proudhon,[2] 'is nothing but the continuous
transformation of human nature.' Thus, finally, he can replace philosophy by the economico-historical science of society:

Where speculation ends—in real life—there real, positive science begins; the
depiction of the practical activity, of the practical process of development,
of men. Empty talk about consciousness ceases, and real knowledge has to
take its place. With the depiction of reality, philosophy as an independent
branch of activity loses its medium of existence. At best, its place can only
be taken by a summing up of the most general results which can be abstracted
from observation of the historical development of men. In themselves,
viewed apart from real history, these abstractions have no value whatever.
They can only serve to facilitate the arrangement of the materials of history,
to indicate the sequence of the separate stata. But by no means do they afford
a recipe or schema, as does philosophy, for neatly trimming the epochs of
history. On the contrary, our difficulties begin only when we set about the
observation and arrangement—the real depiction—of our historical material,
whether of a past epoch or of the present. The removal of these difficulties is
governed by premises which it is quite impossible to state here, but which
only the study of the actual life-processes and activity of the individuals of
each epoch will make evident.

(M I, 5, 16–17.)

Morality—at least in the sense of normative 'principles', which Marx
had already rejected in his earlier work—went just as definitely:

[1] In *The Communist Manifesto*, SW I, 55; *supra* II, 8.
[2] *The Poverty of Philosophy*, p. 165.

Communists preach no morality at all . . . They do not put to people the moral demand: Love one another, be not egoists, etc.; on the contrary, they know very well that egoism, like sacrifice, is under certain conditions the necessary form of the individual's struggle for survival.

(Op. cit., p. 227.)

Communists know very well, too, that 'conscience is related to the knowledge and whole way of life of a man. A Republican has a different conscience from Royalist, a propertied man has a different conscience from one who is propertyless, a thoughtful man a different one from a man without thought.'[1] What applies to conscience, according to Marx and Engels, applies to all human ideas and conceptions:

Does it require deep intuition to comprehend that man's ideas, views and conceptions, in a word, man's consciousness, changes with every change in the conditions of his material existence, in his social relations and in his social life? What else does the history of ideas prove, than that intellectual production changes its character in proportion as material production is changed? The ruling ideas of each age have ever been the ideas of its ruling class.

When people speak of ideas that revolutionise society, they do but express the fact that within the old society the elements of the new one have been created, and that the dissolution of the old ideas keeps even pace with the dissolution of the old conditions of existence.

(*The Communist Manifesto*, SW I, 49.)

If conceptions of religion, morality, law and ideals of freedom and justice have been common to all past stages of society, this is merely because

one fact is common to all past ages, viz., the exploitation of one part of society by the other. No wonder, then, that the social consciousness of past ages, despite all the multiplicity and variety it displays, moves within certain common forms, or general ideas, which cannot completely vanish except with the total disappearance of class antagonisms.

(Op. cit., p. 50.)

This, at any rate, is one side of what Marx began saying from 1845 onward and continued to say till the end of his life in 1883. It was on these conceptions that Engels erected his 'scientific socialism' and subsequent Marxists their materialist dogmas. How far they correctly represent his mature thought and how far they constitute a repudiation

---

[1] Marx, in his article 'The Trial of Gottschalk and Others', published in the *Neue Rheinische Zeitung* of December 22, 1848 (M I, 7, 501).

of his earlier philosophical and ethical beliefs we shall have the opportunity of judging.

A preliminary difficulty for the criticism and elucidation of Marx's mature position concerns the 'status' of any assertion that may be made about Marxism or any other subject. His mature thought is often interpreted—by Marxists at least—as implying that there can be no question of 'objective' truth or 'objective' knowledge and that any criticism or elucidation of Marxism in terms of 'fixed concepts', such as he displayed in his earlier work, is therefore completely pointless and inadmissible.

There are two main sources for this interpretation. One is the eleven *Theses on Feuerbach*, jotted down by Marx in his notebooks in the spring of 1845 and first published by Engels (in a version not wholly true to the original) in the appendix to the separate edition of his *Ludwig Feuerbach* in 1888. The second is the specific pronouncements on truth by Engels in his *Ludwig Feuerbach* and his *Anti-Dühring*. The position suggested by Marx and the line taken by Engels are not the same.

'The chief defect of all hitherto existing materialism (including that of Feuerbach),' Marx writes in the first thesis, 'is that the thing, reality, sensibility, is conceived only under the form of the *object* or of *contemplation*, but not as *human sensory activity, practice* [*Praxis*], not subjectively' (M I, 5, 533; cf. SW II, 363). The point is developed in the second thesis:

The question whether objective truth can be attributed to human thinking is not a question of theory but is a *practical* question. In practice man must prove the truth, i.e., the reality and power, the this-sidedness of his thinking. The dispute over the reality or non-reality of thinking which is isolated from practice is a purely *scholastic* question.

(M I, 5, 534; cf. SW II, 365.)

That this implies a pragmatic theory of truth—the position that true beliefs are those which work or aid the solution of 'tasks'—is taken to be confirmed by the famous eleventh thesis:

Philosophers have only *interpreted* the world differently; the point, however, is to change it.

(M I, 5, 535; SW II, 367.)

Now, in so far as the *Theses* are an attack on the Cartesian *cogito*, on the doctrine of the passive mind merely confronted by the 'external' object, Marx's position is perfectly sound. He is insisting that the mental activity and the object interact in a single process and that mental activities do not passively cognise an object, but actively strive toward it. It is this recognition that the mental and the non-mental belong to the same historical, spatio-temporal reality, that they interact on a single plane, and not any doctrine of the primacy of the 'substantial', which is the valuable part of Marx's *materialism*.

The quotations given, however, reveal far more questionable material. If idealism enabled Marx to reject the dualism of mind and matter and to see the mind as active, knowing as a form of striving, it also led him into the false view that terms which are part of a single process become the same term. It is this false amalgamation of the knower and the known, the denial of any final distinction between them, which seems to bring him to the view that knowledge is possible only to those who actually *participate* in the movement of things.[1]

That Marx's position is false is brought out sufficiently by the admissions implicit in the eleventh thesis. If knower and known are the same process, if knowledge consists of 'moving' with the known, then the idle speculation and interpretation which Marx decries would simply be impossible. Neither could we make any sense of the demand that the knower must change 'the world'. If he and 'the world' are one, if his knowing it consists of moving with it, then he cannot at the same time act on it from the outside or produce changes within it. (The same incoherence comes out in the Marxist slogan, formulated by Engels, that 'freedom is the insight into necessity'. If the development is truly necessary, then the knower's insight or lack of insight into it is totally irrelevant. The process *must* continue in the way set down; if the observer himself is treated as part of the process, then the observer, too, must be carried along in its development. But whether he is treated as part of the necessary development or not, he must be powerless to affect it and his insight must therefore be irrelevant. Else the development is not necessary.)

A faint suggestion of cruder instrumentalism—of pragmatism in its true sense—lies in Marx's association of truth with reality *and power*.

[1] Cf. John Anderson: Critical Notice of H. B. Acton's *The Illusion of the Epoch*, *A.J.P.*, vol. 37 (1959), p. 156 et seq., at p. 158: 'The general position of the *Theses* is that to have true knowledge is to be moving with the movement of thing, which is a revolutionary movement; it is only the revolutionary, participating in that movement, who really understands it—who has a "dialectic" understanding (i.e., precisely *participatory*, going beyond himself) as contrasted with the idle speculation of the non-participant.'

If Marx is saying that true beliefs are proved—or more accurately, confirmed—in practice, in our dealing and grappling with the objects of these beliefs, then this is perfectly sound: though it again implies that knower and known can be distinguished as distinct processes. If Marx is saying—as some pragmatists have said—that ' "all X are Y" is true' means nothing but ' "all X are Y" works in practice', he is faced with the obvious difficulty that the latter proposition still has to be treated as true in the ordinary, and not in the pragmatic, sense. Otherwise the proposition '("all X are Y" works in practice) is true' would have to mean '("all X are Y" works in practice) works in practice' and so on to a vicious infinite regress. At some stage we should have to be able to say 'Does it work in practice or not?' and this could only be made a significant question by treating the truth of a proposition as the issue 'Is it so or not?' and not as a pragmatic question of its consequences.

The position suggested by Engels has not the merit of confusedly drawing attention to important issues. It is simply the most naive proclamation that all truth is relative, accompanied by material that makes it clear that Engels himself has confused different issues and hardly knows what his statement means. Since Hegel, he says in his *Ludwig Feuerbach*:

One cannot be imposed upon any longer by the inflated insubstantial anti-theses of the older metaphysics of true and false, good and evil, identical and differentiated, necessary and accidental; one knows that these antitheses have only a relative significance, that that which is recognised as true now, has its concealed and later-developing false side, just as that which is recognised as false, its true side, by virtue of which it can later on prevail as the truth . . .

(SW II, 351, amended according to the superior translation in the Kerr edition.)

In *Anti-Dühring*, Engels proclaims the same relativism and takes it to be proven by the spectacle of human disagreement and human error:

That twice two make four, that birds have beaks, and similar statements, are proclaimed as eternal truths only by those who aim at deducing, from the existence of eternal truths in general, the conclusion that there are also eternal truths in the sphere of human history—eternal morality, eternal justice, and so on—which claim a validity and scope equal to those of the truths and deductions of mathematics. And then we can confidently rely on this same friend of humanity taking the first opportunity to assure us that all previous fabricators of eternal truths have been to a greater or lesser degree asses and charlatans, that they have all fallen into error and made mistakes; but that *their* error and *their* fallibility have been in accordance

127

with natural law, and prove the existence of truth and accuracy in *his* case; and that he, the prophet who has now arisen, has in his bag final and ultimate truth, eternal morality and eternal justice. This has all happened so many hundred and thousands of times that we can only feel astonished that there should still be people credulous enough to believe this, not of others, but of themselves.

(AD 104-5.)

The central weakness of such relativism has been exposed by Plato in the *Theaetetus*. The relativist, in claiming that all truth is relative, does not put his own claims forward as relative but claims for them 'absolute', i.e., unambiguous, truth. There is in fact no other way of conveying an issue: to say all truth is relative, however much the issue may be confused by reference to what is 'true for me' is simply to say that X both is and is not Y and thus to make discourse impossible. That Engels has no real wish to do so is made sufficiently evident by his shirking of the issue over mathematical truths and his admission, in *Anti-Dühring*, that certain 'trivial' propositions—'twice two make four', 'birds have beaks', etc.—are unambiguously and not relatively true. His position, indeed, depends entirely on the consideration of more 'complicated' theories and assertions which, he claims, may be true to a relative extent but not absolutely. He illustrates this by citing Regnault's discovery that Boyle's law does not apply *in certain cases*— a proof, according to Engels, that Boyle's law is untrue and yet not false. But the actual position, of course, is that Boyle's law—the assertion that *all* gases have property X—is positively and not relatively false, while a *different* assertion—that all A-gases have property X—is positively and not relatively true.[1] If neither assertion were unambiguously true or false, there would be no way of choosing between them.

What Engels is really saying is that men are more prone to error in general statements than in particular ones and in social and historical fields than in natural sciences. This, far from implying the relativity of all truth, requires the recognition of unambiguous truth, of a positive and definite distinction between truth and error. Thus, when Engels writes in *Anti-Dühring* (p. 101) that 'the knowledge which has unconditional claim to truth is realised in a series of relative errors . . . through an endless eternity of human existence,' it is clear that the word 'relative' has no meaning here. It should simply be dropped. The movement described by Engels is not a movement from relative to

[1] For a fuller discussion of this particular example, and of Engels' theory of truth in general, from the realist standpoint I myself adopt, see John Anderson: 'Marxist Philosophy', *A.J.P.P.*, vol. XIII (1935), p. 24 et seq., esp. pp. 26–32.

absolute truth, but a quantitative movement from the knowledge of some facts to the knowledge of more facts. But what we know and what we can know is irrelevant to the objective issue of what is, or is not, the case. (Neither, of course, is there any ground for Engels' vulgar optimistic doctrine that knowledge constantly progresses, that there are no regressions, no recrudescences of error. The suggestion that every theory contains 'more truth' than the theory which preceded it is patently false.) The point, however, is that if all truth were relative, we could not speak of a movement, of discovery, at all—we could not distinguish true beliefs from error. What Engels has patently done is to confuse 'absolute' truth in the sense of *total* knowledge, knowledge of all that is to be known, with 'absolute' truth in the sense of conveying an unambiguous issue, of being either true or false and not both. His correct assertion that there can be no total knowledge in no way implies that any single issue is not unambiguous or even that it cannot be known correctly. If everything had to be known before knowledge could begin or error discovered, knowledge could not begin and error could not be discovered.

A third attack on the very basis of criticism, on the positive treatment of philosophical or ethical issues, rests on the 'materialist' reduction of ideologies to the material foundations of society, to the material position of a class or (more ineptly) to the material 'interests' of a class. We have seen this view in the citation from the *Communist Manifesto* a few pages back; it is to be found, in different forms and with varying degrees of ambiguity, in most of Marx's mature work. What is proclaimed as truth, these statements are read to imply, is what any particular man is necessitated into thinking by the social situation of which he is part: since no man can escape this determination, there can be no question of 'objective' truth; since social situations constantly change, there can be no question of permanent truth. Thus Marx insists that the sensory world is itself a historical product, indeed, a product of activity in the world of industry and trade:

Even the objects of the simplest 'sensory certainty' are given through social development, industry and commercial relations. The cherry tree, like almost all fruit trees, was transplanted to our zone, as is well known, through *commerce*; it was only by *virtue of* this action of a determinate society at a determinate time that it was given to 'the sensory certainty' of Feuerbach.

(M I, 5, 32–3.)

The bearing of this on the *truth* of any proposition, such as the belief that cherry trees blossom in spring, need hardly be taken seriously. While Marx's attempt to socialise the whole of reality, to suggest that all non-human things are products of human material activity, is obviously false, he is quite right in suggesting that knowledge has conditions and that these conditions are historical, that they change. It may even be true that what people know is what they—or some motives within them—wish to know: we know that which satisfies some desires or eases some tension. This is very different from insisting that a man's belief in what is true, or even his errors, are determined by his class position, or that the ruling ideas of any age are the ideas of the ruling class. These propositions are obviously empirically false. But in any case, all these assertions concern only *how* a man comes to know; they have nothing to do with the truth of what he believes. To the question whether cherry trees blossom in spring, the origin of cherry trees and the manner in which I came to know them, are entirely irrelevant. Marxists, as well as Marx himself, do confuse questions about the origin of a thing with questions about the actual nature of the thing; but their confusions have to be brought out and firmly rejected. They themselves, as we have seen, cannot talk, cannot make any assertions at all, without assuming that the truth of an assertion is a positive and definite issue, and that a thing can be distinguished from the conditions which produced it.

Philosophy 'as an independent branch of activity', we have seen Marx suggest, 'loses its medium of existence' once positive historical science begins. Does this, then, make logical or philosophical criticism of Marx's work 'inappropriate'?

There is a great deal in Marx's writing—early and late—to suggest that he would reject completely any conception of philosophy as a 'meta-science' concerned purely with methodology, axioms or principles that logically precede the possibility of any science whatever. There are, Marx would have insisted, no 'principles' preceding empirical knowledge or independent of it; there can be no question of 'applying' 'principles' to 'facts'. There is, as he says in the *German Ideology*, no 'fruitness' apart from real fruits, no 'humanity' apart from real men. Universal propositions can have significance, according to Marx, only in so far as they isolate the common characters of existing events.[1] This position of Marx's, I should argue, is unexceptionable.

Marx's Hegelianism, however, drove him further. Nothing could be

[1] 'All epochs of production have certain distinguishing features in common, have common characters. *Production in general* is an abstraction, but an intelligible

understood in itself, as having positive and unambiguous characters; everything was a 'moment' in the history of its development toward a final end; it could be understood only in terms of its total situation and the total process of which it was part.[1] This position is not unexceptionable—it seems to me, in fact, entirely untenable. It requires Marx, as we have seen, to destroy or 'overcome' all positive distinctions. It forced him to treat 'Nature' as a social product that will finally be taken into man. It now also forces him—since his new underlying reality is to be society and no longer Man—to minimise[2] any specific human characteristics and to treat men as no more than a reflection or product of social relations. It is this totalism which accounts for the tendency in Marx to treat his historical materialism as a form of economic reductionism and to treat the products of social forces as mere 'reflections' of them. But if all things are to be part of one process, determined by 'it', they cannot have their own characters, their own ways of acting.

This appears to be the upshot of Marx's 'materialist' or economic interpretation of history—a theory we shall now turn to examine more closely.

[1] 'All stages of production have common characters, which thought establishes as universal; but the so-called *universal characters* of all production are nothing but these abstract moments, with which no actual historical stage of production can be understood.' (*Grundrisse*, p. 10).

[2] Passages in the *German Ideology*, the *Poverty of Philosophy*, *The Communist Manifesto* and the *Theses on Feuerbach* suggest that the mature Marx does not merely minimise the importance of permanent human appetites, attitudes and drives, but actually denies their existence. Yet in a draft passage written for the *German Ideology* and dropped before publication, he specifically distinguishes *permanent* human appetites, which are modified by changing historical conditions but are not produced by them, from *relative* appetites 'which owe their origin to a specific form of society, production or exchange' (M I, 5, 596). Again, arguing against Bentham in the first volume of *Capital*, Marx reminds us that before deciding what is useful for man, we would have to consider first 'human nature in general' and then that human nature 'which history modifies in every epoch' (K I, 640; C I, 668). Both passages are yet another reminder of the dangers of deducing a Marxian 'system' from those of his pronouncements that have become well-known because of their seeming simplicity and general scope.

abstraction in so far as it really brings out, fixes, the common and therefore saves us repetition', Marx wrote in his notebook in 1857 (*Grundrisse*, p. 7).

13. The Materialist Interpretation of History and Marx's Critique of Moralities

THE basis of the 'materialist interpretation of history', according to Marx and also to Engels, is a simple proposition both were to reiterate time and time again—the proposition that 'the mode of production in material life determines the general character of the social, political and spiritual processes of life' (CPE 11). 'Material life' is what the eighteenth-century philosophers and Marx himself used to call 'civil society'; Marx now refers to it more frequently as 'the material foundation' or 'the world of industry and trade'. On this, he believes, everything else is in some (not always clear) sense dependent.

Marx, and Engels after him, distinguish within the material life of men two separate, if related, factors: productive forces and relations of production. The productive forces are the skills, knowledge and tools (all of them social products) existing at any given period of society. The relations of production are the ways in which different factors of production are appropriated and secure their returns—in other words, what Marx calls the class structure of society. While both Marx and Engels are generally loose in their references to the economic or productive foundation by which all social life is allegedly determined, Marx does make it clear that, on his theory, 'the relations of production correspond to a definite stage of development of their [men's] material powers of production' (CPE 11). The fact that it is these forces of production that are taken as the basic determinants of social change is confirmed by his insistence that social change takes place—always violently—when the relations of production come into conflict with the productive forces. For while the productive forces are constantly developing, the relations of production in any given period are comparatively fixed and resist change. It is thus that the relations of production which began by 'expressing' (serving the needs of) the development in the forces of production, end by becoming 'fetters' upon this development. It is then that a new class, called into being by the new developments in the productive forces, emerges into the arena of history and bursts the old class structure asunder. Inevitably and repeatedly the constantly developing forces of production triumph over the lagging productive relations. Only with the supercession of all classes and the emergence of 'rational and intelligible relations' among men does the tension between productive forces and productive relationships and the violent change from one social form to another disappear from the historical stage.

Engels, most of Marx's followers and most of his critics took and have taken Marx's position to imply an underlying technological determinism. On the basis of some of Marx's statements and many of Engels', including the latter's discovery of primitive communism,[1] the theory has been elaborated thus:[2]

The study of history shows that there have been four stages of technological development, each of them producing a corresponding stage of the relations of production. First, there was an era of stone tools, to which corresponds a primitive communism in the means of production and the distribution of products. With the advent of metal tools, society split apart into masters and slaves—the first form of the class society. Then came feudalism, which, as Marx suggests in the *Poverty of Philosophy*,[3] was based on the hand-mill and finally industrial capitalism, based on the steam-mill or power-driven machinery in general (though there was an earlier form of mercantile capitalism preceding the industrial revolution). The highly elaborate forces that result from the increasing application of modern science to industry will bring about the next stage, that of socialism merging into Communism, where the division of labour will be replaced by the organisation of production (cf. *Grundrisse*, pp. 88–9), where control and planning will be by the community as a whole.

[1] In a footnote to the 1888 English edition of the *Communist Manifesto* (SW I, 33), Engels explains that he and Marx were not aware of the existence of primitive communism when they wrote the *Manifesto* in 1847, but that its existence had become evident from recent researches by Haxthausen, Maurer and Morgan.

[2] Cf. the summary by H. B. Acton: *The Illusion of the Epoch*, p. 135.

[3] 'The hand-mill gives you society with the feudal lord; the steam mill society with the industrial capitalist.' (M I, 6, 179; PP 122.)

The technological interpretation of Marx's materialist doctrine cannot treat it as a theory of direct and unmediated technological determinism. Marx insists that the history of society is the history of social struggles, that the key to political and ideological forms lies in the class structure of all past societies. The determinism exercised by the productive forces must therefore be mediated by the productive relationships that result from these forces—else all classes would share the same ideology. The theory thus becomes that productive forces determine productive relations and that these, *in turn*, determine the social superstructure: the legal and political forms of the society and the philosophical, ethical, legal, aesthetic and economic theories or ideologies to be found in that society.

Marx's materialist interpretation of history has been discussed often and at length, both as a fundamental 'principle' belonging to the philosophy of history and as a summary of detailed historical studies to be confirmed or disproved by actual historical events. Some critics have denied the possibility of framing any general law of historical development; others have striven to prove, as a matter of fact, the independence and power of ideological forces in history. But the argument has constantly been bedevilled by doubts: precisely what is Marx's position, exactly what is he claiming?

It does not follow from the fact that Marx has a position that he himself would have been able to provide satisfactory answers to these questions. In the *German Ideology,* it is true, he and Engels write confidently:

Morality, religion, metaphysics, all the rest of ideology and their corresponding forms of consciousness thus no longer retain the semblance of independence. They have no history, no development; but men, developing their material production and their material intercourse alter—along with these— their real existence and their thinking and the products of their thinking.

(M I, 5, 16; GI 14–15.)

But before examining the sweeping propositions contained in this passage in themselves, let us see what they come down to—in Marx's own hands—in practice. Consider first Marx's handling of a problem in aesthetics—is it shown to have no 'semblance of independence', to be completely reducible to men's material production and intercourse? In his notebook Marx writes:

Known—that Greek mythology is not only the arsenal of Greek art but its foundation. Is the view of nature and of social relations which lies at the basis of Greek imagination and therefore of Greek mythology possible with self-actors and railways and locomotives and electric telegraphs? What becomes of Vulcan faced with Roberts et Co., Jupiter faced with the lightning-conductor, Hermes faced with the *Crédit mobilier?* All mythology overcomes and dominates and moulds natural forces through the imagination and in the imagination, disappears therefore with actual domination over these [forces]. What happens to Fama next to Printing House Square? Greek art presupposes Greek mythology, i.e., Nature and social forms already worked over by folk imagination in an unconsciously artistic form. That is its material. Not any mythology you care to choose, i.e., not any unconsciously artistic fashioning of Nature (hereby everything objective, therefore society, included). Egyptian mythology could never be the foundation or maternal lap of Greek art. . . . But in any case, *a* mythology. Hence in no circumstances a social development which excludes any mythological relationship to Nature . . .

From another side: is Achilles possible with powder and shot? Or the Iliad, altogether, with the printing press and the steam press even . . .

But the difficulty does not lie in understanding that Greek art and Greek epic poetry are tied to specific forms of social development. The difficulty is that they still give us artistic satisfaction and in certain respects remain as norms and unattainable models.

A man cannot become a child again, or he becomes childish. But is he not pleased by the naiveté of the child and must he not again strive to reproduce its truth on a higher level? Does not the nature of the child reveal to each epoch its own character in its elemental truth? Why should the historical childhood of mankind, where it blossoms most beautifully, not exercise eternal charm as a stage that can never reappear? One finds bad-mannered children and children old before their time. Most of the ancient peoples belong in these categories. The Greeks were normal children. The charm of their art for us is not inconsistent with the fact that their art grew from an undeveloped stage of society. [The charm] is rather the result of this and is rather indissolubly linked with the fact that the unripe social conditions under which this art developed, and only under which it could develop, can never come back.

(*Grundrisse*, pp. 30–1.)

Consider this passage carefully. First, we note that Greek mythology and art are not here presented as passive reflections or passive effects of Greek social organisation. The existence of Greek social organisation and the absence of later social organisations and knowledge are *necessary* for Greek art and mythology, but *not sufficient*. To become mythology, Greek nature and social forms must be 'worked over by folk imagination in *an unconsciously artistic form*'. To become art, one gathers by implication, they must be worked over in a consciously artistic form. (How this would enable us to distinguish a myth from a short story without inspecting the author is not clear, but that is not our present point.) Artistic form, then, is also necessary for something to become mythology or art, and this artistic form, clearly, is not something that reflects the social organisation, but something additional to it.

Secondly, consider Marx's attempt to account for the charm that Greek mythology still exercises on us. This is not an attempt to account for the artistic form of Greek art or mythology; the form is presupposed as an intrinsic characteristic independent of our attraction to what has the form. But Marx is not willing to say that its charm lies in the form. He wants an economic account. But again, the account breaks down. The parallel with childhood is forced; the 'elemental truth' which Greece reveals to us remains obscure. But in any case, the appeal of childhood and of such elemental truth is presented as an eternal verity, a truth of human psychology in no way linked with the social organisation under which we—the appreciators—live. Once again, Marx has shown at best—and this time, quite unconvincingly— that the economic organisation of Ancient Greece (its infantile character) is a necessary condition for its fascination over us; it is not a sufficient condition because it requires also our interest in the infantile —an interest which remains unrelated to economic factors altogether. At the same time, Marx seems also to concede that not all children exercise fascination for us—it is only (in the first reference) beautiful children or (in the second, more explicit reference) normal children. In any case, it is clearly not the children that reflect our economic structure, satisfy our economic needs or serve the interests of our class. In such an analysis, it is hardly surprising that Marx should speak of Greek art and mythology being '*tied to*' specific forms of social development instead of saying they are *determined* by them.

Nor is this bringing in of factors which are not on the face of it economic at all confined to Marx's rough and possibly ill-considered notes. We find it repeatedly in his long, concrete and considered account of capitalist development in the first volume of *Capital.* 'The forcible process of expropriating the mass of the people in the sixteenth century gained new and terrible momentum from the Reformation and the colossal theft of church property which followed it,' he writes (K I, 759; C I, 792). 'Church property constituted the religious bulwark of the traditional relationships in landed property. With its fall these could no longer be maintained' (K I, 761; C I, 793–4). Again, discussing the methods of primitive accumulation in general: 'These methods rest partly on the most brutal might, e.g., the colonial system. But all of them use the *might of the State*, the concentrated and organised might of society, in order to accelerate the process of transforming the feudal into the capitalist mode of production and to shorten the transitions. *Might is the midwife of every old society pregnant with a new one. It is itself an economic power.*' (K I, 791; C I, 823–4—Marx's italics.)

In Marx's brief discussion of aesthetics, his economic account eschews—as we have noted—such central issues as the characteristics of 'artistic form' and the nature of beauty. The same is true of his far more frequent comments on law. In general terms, Marx insists in the *German Ideology*, in the *Poverty of Philosophy* and in *Capital* itself on the secondary character of law, its dependence on economic factors and its service in the interests of the ruling class. At no stage, apart from a few vague remarks about law being based on property, does Marx try to analyse the fundamental categories and principles of English law, or of its various branches, and show that they are determined by the economic structure of English society. He noticeably avoids any consideration of the large and important part of the criminal law concerned with offences against the person; nowhere does he discuss the tremendous changes in the substantive content and procedural rules of the civil law, changes that were taking place and arousing widespread attention before his very eyes. Instead, he shows, with considerable and generally convincing supporting detail, the capitalist bias of contemporary European Factory Acts, the shameless protecting of their own interests by mill-owners sitting as justices of the peace, and the way in which legal procedure was used to discriminate against workers, e.g., by prosecuting workers for breach of contract, while similar causes of action against masters were confined to the civil courts.[1] It is significant that all this material shows economic interests

---

[1] See especially his chapters, in the first volume of *Capital*, headed 'The Working Day' (K I, 239–317; C I, 255–330) and 'Machinery and Large-scale Industry' (K I, 387–532, esp. pp. 505–29; C I, 405–556, esp. 526–52). Marx implicitly concedes the devotion and independence of view of many of the factory inspectors appointed under the Acts, and their attempts to expose the intolerable nature of factory conditions and some of the worst legal abuses in the *Reports*, from which Marx draws much of his material. Marx, and Engels in his *addenda* to subsequent editions, note that some of the abuses (including the discrimination against workers over breach of contract) have been, or are being, remedied. Of course, this would not in itself show that all the features of the capitalist

at work in the actions of individuals or in Parliamentary legislation; Marx never attempts to show the same economic interests enshrined in the very structure of the common law.[1]

Nowhere does Marx show in detail that the structure or content of any ideology is wholly determined by the economic conditions or social structure of the group or society that gave it birth. But neither does he show precisely *what* it is that would, on his view, determine the content of the ideology. This difficulty emerges even in the scant references that the mature Marx makes to morality. What does a morality 'reflect'? The general character of productive relations in the society? This seems to be the suggestion Marx is making when he insists on the conflict of rights and duties as 'reflecting' the conflicts and incoherence of 'civil society'. But how, then, is one morality to be distinguished from its remaining contemporaries? Here Marx falls back on a different determinant: the social situation *seen from the standpoint of a specific class*. Thus he reduces Kant's doctrine of the good will not directly to the productive relations in eighteenth-century Germany, but to the *political impotence* of the German bourgeoisie coupled with its *aping of the French model*. How is the standpoint of one class to be distinguished from that of another? Here Marx falls back on a doctrine of class 'interests' (seen, no doubt, as themselves economically determined). The proletarian, Marx and Engels write in the *Communist Manifesto* (SW I, 42), sees law, morality and religion as 'so many bourgeois prejudices, behind which lurk in ambush just as many bourgeois interests.' This, in very crude terms, is the line popularised by Engels in *Anti-Dühring*:

We maintain . . . that all former moral theories are the product, in the last analysis, of the economic stage which society had reached at that particular epoch. And as society has hitherto moved in class antagonisms, morality was always a class morality; it has either justified the domination and the interests

[1] Modern Soviet legal theorists, further embarrassed by their inability to discover fundamental differences in content between Soviet and 'bourgeois' law similarly concentrate on showing how the judicial process can be *distorted* by economic interests, rather than how it is shaped by them. Thus, Vyshinsky's discussion of the concrete working of 'bourgeois' law (*The Law of the Soviet State*, pp. 501–3) is taken up almost entirely with an account of the Dreyfus, Beilis and Sacco-Vanzetti trials.

factory system which Marx exposes are merely temporary—but the interaction of many factors in factory legislation, which Marx has to admit implicitly, raises difficulties for his whole theory of economic determination with which he never tries to cope.

of the ruling class, or, as soon as the oppressed class has become powerful enough, it has represented the revolt against this domination and the future interests of the oppressed.

(AD 109.)

Thus Engels distinguishes in modern times the Christian-feudal morality of the feudal aristocracy, the modern bourgeois morality and the proletarian morality. Kautsky, following the Engels line in his *Ethics and the Materialist Conception of History*, argues that in the ancient world the ethical question first emerged clearly as a result of the class tensions that followed the Persian wars. These wars placed the Greeks at the centre of widespread commercial activity and produced three leading types of morality: the Epicurean, representing those connected with private production; the Platonic and Neo-Platonic, representing the section of the aristocracy not engaged in personal control of production; the Stoic, representing several of the remaining classes and acting as a mediating ethical theory.[1]

All this has its origin in a subtler and rather more intelligent treatment of historical moral codes by Marx and Engels in the *German Ideology*. The interpretation given there does not lay itself open to a voluntaristic 'conspiracy' theory of morality, by which moralities come to be seen as consciously-fashioned tools in the struggle for domination. In the *German Ideology* Marx and Engels consistently take morality as aiming to express the common interests of a society. In the rational society of Communism such interests will be truly harmonious and universalisable; a perfectly coherent morality, in which private and social interest will be completely fused, will therefore arise. In the class society, the common interest is an illusion, an ideal which alienates man's social functions from man and sets them up to oppose him. The moralities of class society are therefore necessarily fraudulent and incoherent. They represent not the common interest of the whole society, but only of a class; its particular economic interests disguised as general social interests. The result is on the one hand a constant changing of moralities as the social initiative passes from one class to another, on the other a tension between the specific interests of the class and its claim to represent society as a whole:

[1] Most contemporary Soviet ethical philosophers, such as Sharia and Shishkin, take the same line that each morality represents the economic interests and attitudes of a class, though unlike Kautsky, they make no serious attempt to link the fundamental ethical structure of a theory with its alleged class background. They are satisfied instead with an occasional example of obvious 'class' prejudice in a moral philosopher, e.g., Aristotle's contempt for slaves.

Each new class which puts itself in the place of the one ruling before it, is compelled, merely in order to carry through its aim, to represent its interests as the common interest of all the members of the society, put in an ideal form; it will give its ideas the form of universality, and represent them as the only rational, universally valid ones.

(GI 40–1; M I, 5, 37.)

This procedure, according to Marx and Engels is not, in the initial stages of the new class struggles, entirely Machiavellian.

The class making a revolution appears from the start, merely because it is opposed to a class, not as a class but as the representative of the whole society; it appears as the whole mass of society confronting the one ruling class. It can do this because, to start with, its interest really is more connected with the common interest of all other non-ruling classes, because under the pressure of conditions its interest has not yet been able to develop as the particular interest of a particular class.

(GI 41; M I, 5, 37.)

The situation described here, Marx and Engels seem to assume, provides evidence for their view that history displays a moral advance toward true universality. After describing how the victory of the French bourgeoisie over the aristocracy enabled many proletarians to raise themselves into the ranks of the bourgeoisie, they conclude:

Every new class, therefore, achieves its hegemony only on a broader basis than that of the class ruling previously . . .

(GI 41; M I, 5, 37.)

These are the most explicit and detailed comments on morality to be found in the work of Marx the Communist, and the most sensible to be found in the work of Engels. They are not enough. They tell us nothing about the vexed question of interests; they eschew any consideration of the truth or falsity of moral claims; they give no account of the issues that have dominated the history or moral theory and ethical controversy. They give us no basis for distinguishing between the political programme and the ethical convictions of a class, nor do they make any attempt to see whether there are constant themes in the history of ethics and, if so, how they could be accounted for. Moralists, after all, have condemned other things beside theft.

We are now in a better position, perhaps, to return to a general consideration of the content and force of the materialist interpretation of history. It comes out, even in Marx's work, as a theory that is formulated loosely, ambiguously, without proper care; it is never demonstrated in detail in even a single case; it is frequently ignored and virtually subverted in the discussion of concrete social developments. Its most concrete point seemed to be that economic conditions determine ideology and never *vice versa*, yet even this had to be modified the moment it was seriously questioned. In his letter to Conrad Schmidt of October 27, 1890, Engels made a host of concessions:

Where there is division of labour on a social scale there is also mutual independence among the different sections of work. In the last instance, production is the decisive factor. But when the trade in products becomes independent of production itself, it follows a movement of its own which, while it is governed as a whole by production, still in particular cases and within this general dependence follows particular laws contained in the nature of this new factor; this movement has phases of its own and in its turn reacts on the movement of production . . .

It is similar with law. As soon as the new division of labour which creates professional lawyers becomes necessary, another new and independent sphere is opened up which, for all its general dependence on production and trade, still has its own capacity for reacting upon these spheres as well. In a modern State, law must not only correspond to the general economic position and be its expression, but must also be an expression which is *consistent in itself*, and which does not, owing to inner contradictions, look glaringly inconsistent. And in order to achieve this, the faithful reflection of economic conditions is more and more infringed upon. All the more so, the more rarely it appears that a code of law is the blunt, unmitigated, unadulterated expression of the domination of a class—this in itself would already offend the 'conception of justice' . . . Thus to a great extent the course of the 'development of law' only consists: first in the attempt to do away with the contradictions arising from the direct translation of economic relations into legal principles, and to establish a harmonious system of law, and then in the repeated breaches made in this system by the influence and pressure of further economic development, which involves it in further contradictions (I am only speaking here of civil law for the moment).

The reflection of economic relations as legal principles is necessarily also a topsy-turvy one: it happens without the person who is acting being conscious of it; the jurist imagines he is operating with *a priori* principles, whereas they are really only economic reflexes; so everything is upside down. And it seems to me obvious that this inversion, which, so long as it remains unrecognised, forms what we call *ideological conception,* reacts in its turn upon the economic basis and may, within certain limits, modify it. The basis of the law of inheritance—assuming the stages reached in the development of the family are equal—is an economic one. But it would be difficult to prove, for instance, that the absolute liberty of the testator in England and the severe restrictions imposed upon him in France are only due in every detail to economic causes. Both react back, however, on the economic sphere to a very considerable extent, because they influence the division of property.

(SC 478, 481–2.)

Here, again, we have all the usual ambiguities. Law now reflects economic relations and not class interests; though precisely how an economic reflex or an economic relation becomes a normative legal principle is not clear. Nor is it readily apparent why the translation of economic reflexes into legal principles should lead to contradictions, or how a materialist interpretation of history would account either for the interest in harmony and consistency or for our conception of justice. But what is clear is that Engels has conceded that ideologies are *not* purely passive, and even that they may affect the economic base 'to a very considerable extent'. There is no force after this in Engels' attempt to save the situation by insisting that 'in the last instance, production is the decisive factor.' If production is affected by ideology, then the production that proves decisive is not the production that formed the economic base. Once we grant even 'relative' independence and multiple interaction in social events, once we recognise that law may react back on economic forces and economic relationships, we have to admit that history is not a single-factor story, that social action does not move in only one direction, and that there is no way of setting necessary limits to the possible social effects of social movements, activities and beliefs.

What accounts for much of the confusion surrounding the material-ist interpretation of history is Marx's inadequate view of causality—his consistent tendency to think of causality in general as the produc-tion of an effect by a *single cause* which is by itself both necessary and sufficient for the effect. This view, I have suggested earlier, is unsound: it is only by acting on a *field* that a cause will produce anything, and the cause which is necessary and sufficient to produce effect E in field A may not be necessary or sufficient to produce effect E in field B. The steam mill may produce capitalism in certain social situations; it will not do so in others. Precisely because Marx does not distinguish between the cause and the field on which it acts, we find him and Engels so frequently amalgamating the two and treating as the social determinant what amounts simply to the entire social situation. Again, because the false picture of causal action as a direct passage from cause to effect so readily suggests logical implication, Marxists consistently think they have saved economic determinism by arguing that patently non-economic causal factors acquire honorary economic status because they were themselves at an earlier stage economically determined.

With all these—fatal—weaknesses, the materialist interpretation of history still carries with it a suggestion of saying something very important. Why? It is not only that emphasis on economic factors, social pervasiveness and social situations is infinitely preferable to the naive individualism and emphasis on the directing rôle of moral ideals which Marx's theory largely displaced and discredited. It is rather that Marx *is* saying something positive, which was only obscured by his causal formulation of the materialist interpretation of history and can be salvaged from it. His real point is the point he had made as a young man against Hegel: Hegel reverses a true and important relationship by treating the State as the subject and society as its predicate. For Marx, society remained the subject. From 1845 onward he came to recognise the central and continuous role of production in social life. He recognised that what distinguished the social from the non-social was its being a *productive organisation* and that men were not the subjects to which this productive process belonged, but were themselves part of it. A coherent development of this insight would not lie in treating needs, interests, rights and moral and legal rules as causal products of a system of production, as effects following it in time. The rights, etc., as many critics of Marx have pointed out, would be part of the system of production. The point is rather, as Anderson puts it,[1] 'that it is to a given factor in production that "rights" belong, that it is their "subject", that through which alone their character and history can be grasped, just as the productive process in general is the "subject" of the whole system or distribution of "rights".' It is in the internal function and external conflict of social provinces that laws and sanctions are required; it is forms of activity, and not 'individuals', that have needs and formulate 'rights'.

The important insight underlying the materialist interpretation of history has been obscured by the causal formulation Marx tended to give his doctrine; it has been weakened even more seriously by Marx's inability to free himself from individualism, from seeing moralities as serving human ends and human interests. He thus opened himself up to the individualistic caricature of his work by Engels and made it possible for a subsequent generation of Communists to erect—in his name—a preceptual morality and a coercive system of law.

[1] 'Crit. Notice of Acton's *Illusion of the Epoch*', *A.J.P.*, vol. 37 (1959), p. 163.

14. Historical Materialism and the Overcoming of Alienation

THE distinction between freedom and alienation, we have seen, was the ethical *leitmotif* of Marx's philosophical and political development. What Hegel and Feuerbach had seen in the history of human *thinking*, Marx saw in the history of human production and social life. It was alienation that Marx discovered in the facts, as well as the theory, of political economy; it was the tension and instability resulting from alienation which would inevitably end in its collapse and the inauguration of a new, unalienated, economic and social life. Yet in the economic *magnum opus* of his mature period—*Das Kapital*—he does not rely on the term 'alienation' at all. Was it, then, one of the casualties of his tendency toward economic reductionism? Had it been dropped as a 'philosophic' or 'ethical' concept having no place in his new objective and scientific historical materialism?

The answer is no. The positive content which Marx gave to the term 'alienation' remains central to the position he is expounding in *Capital*. The mental process of objectifying one's own product and allowing it to dominate one Marx now calls the *fetishism* of commodities (K I, 76–89; C I, 4); it remains the same process. Man's loss of control over his labour power Marx calls his *dehumanisation;* it, too, is the same process—a process which for Marx remains of central importance to the understanding of capitalism. Man's loss of control over the product of his work Marx now calls *exploitation;* a term which does not mean that Marx thinks the capitalist is getting too much—more than is '*reasonable*', but which underlines his insistence that what belongs to one man, or to men in general, is being appropriated by others, or by some men in particular. Exploitation is made possible by the creation of surplus value; but its basic ground for Marx remains the alienation of man from his labour power, the fact that man's activity becomes a commodity. In the *German Ideology* and in Marx's economic notes and drafts made between 1850 and 1859 the connexion of all this with the term 'alienation' is made specific (cf., e.g., G I, 64–7; M I, 5, 56–9; *Grundrisse*, 73–82, 88–90, 151–62, 504–8). But we do not need to have the connexion made specific, to have the actual term flourished in the text, to see precisely the same theme in *Wage Labour and Capital*, the *Critique of Political Economy* and *Capital* itself. 'Marx's condemnation of capitalism', writes Karl Popper,[1] a critic not at all interested in alienation, 'is fundamentally a moral condemnation. The *system is condemned*, for the cruel injustice inherent in it which is combined with full 'formal' justice and righteousness. The system is condemned, because by forcing the exploiter to enslave the exploited it robs both of their freedom. Marx did not combat wealth, nor did he praise poverty. He hated capitalism, not for its accumulation of wealth, but for its oligarchical character; he hated it because in this system wealth means political power in the sense of power over men. Labour power is made a commodity; that means that men must sell themselves on the market. Marx hated the system because it resembled slavery.'

Marx, of course, is not *confronting* capitalism with a moral *principle* established independently of his enquiries and *condemning* it for not being 'what it ought to be'. Whatever the logical weaknesses Marx's account of the distinction between dependence and freedom may have, the distinction rests, as we have seen, on an empirical basis. If Marx and his readers are drawn toward freedom and repelled by dependence and alienation, this is not because he has striven to show that they 'ought to be'. It is rather because some goods, at least, operate in Marx and in many of his readers, so that the morality of freedom, the sympathies and antipathies of goods themselves, are something he and they can also feel. Marx, of course, in his mature work as much as in his earlier work, wants to go somewhat further than this. He wants to show that history is inevitably working toward freedom, toward the Communist society where men's production will no longer enslave them, but will become part of them, where tools will cease to be men's masters and become their servants. But however unfounded this view may be, it, too, is not—in Marx's sense—a moral view. It neither presupposes nor establishes a new moral *obligation* in place of those which Marx exposed.

[1] *The Open Society and Its Enemies*, vol. II, p. 199.

In his mature work, then, Marx describes the same process and predicts the same goal as he described and predicted in the *Paris Manuscripts*. Much of the seeming gulf between the 'philosophical' terminology of these *Manuscripts* and the empirical descriptive terminology aimed at in *Capital* has been bridged for us with the publication of the *Grundrisse*. These notes and drafts reveal clearly the extent to which Marx remained a philosopher, thinking in philosophical categories and *then* seeking for their empirical content. This is what he did with 'alienation' and—less successfully—with 'freedom'. The results of his quest did not, it seemed to him, destroy these concepts: on the contrary, they gave these concepts richer content and confirmed their value.

There is, of course, one obvious distinction between Marx's conception of alienation in the *Paris Manuscripts* and his later conception. In the *Manuscripts*, he still sees man as alienated from a generic, social being which is at once the universal nature common to all men and the essential nature underlying man's empirical development. In the *Theses on Feuerbach*, the *German Ideology* and the *Communist Manifesto* he rejects this conception specifically. There is no eternal or essential human nature from which man has become alienated, no 'Man in general, who belongs to no class, has no reality, who exists only in the misty realm of philosophical fantasy' (*Communist Manifesto*, SW I, 55, *supra*, II, 8, III, 12). 'Human nature [*Wesen*],' he now writes (in the sixth thesis on Feuerbach), 'is no abstraction inherent in each separate individual. In its reality it is the ensemble of social relationships.' (M I, 5, 535.) But the metaphysical conception of an essential human nature, however much Marx may need it for his conception of Communism, is certainly not necessary for the portrayal of alienation under capitalism, even in the form in which Marx depicts it in the *Paris Manuscripts*. He has no difficulty in exhibiting the same alienation, and the same features of it, in his later work. 'The exercise of labour power is the worker's own life-activity,' he writes in *Wage Labour and Capital*[1] (SW I, 77; M I, 6, 475), 'the manifestation of his own life. And this *life-activity* he sells to another person in order to

---

[1] The series of articles published by him in the *Neue Rheinische Zeitung* in April, 1849. They were based on lectures he had given to the workers' Club (*Arbeiterverein*) in Brussels in 1847 and formed only part of a larger manuscript the publication of which was interrupted by the February Revolution. (See Marx's note in *Capital*, K I, 607; C I, 633.) The complete manuscript has been lost.

secure the necessary *means of subsistence.* Thus his life-activity is for him only a means to enable him to exist. He works in order to live. He does not even reckon labour as part of his life, it is rather a sacrifice of his life.' (Marx's italics.) This is the alienation of the worker from his own activity which Marx noted in the *Paris Manuscripts.* It implies, Marx had argued in the *Manuscripts,* the worker's alienation from his product. This, too, is reaffirmed in *Wage Labour and Capital:*

What [the worker] produces for himself is not the silk he weaves, not the gold he draws from the mine, not the palace he builds. What he produces for himself is *wages,* and silk, gold, palace resolve themselves for him into a definite quantity of the means of subsistence, perhaps into a cotton jacket, some copper coins and a lodging in a cellar.

(Loc. cit.)

The worker's alienation from his activity and from his product: these conceptions are not merely reaffirmed in *Capital,* they form one of the major themes running through the entire work.

There was a third aspect of alienation noted in the *Paris Manuscripts*—man's alienation from other men and therefore from society and social powers. The same alienation is stressed in the first and third volumes of *Capital,* e.g.:

Since the instruments of labour [under capitalism] confront the labourer as independent, economy in their use also appears as a special operation which has nothing to do with him and which is therefore separated from the methods which raise his personal productivity.

(K I, 340; C I, 357.)

Finally, as we saw earlier, in actuality the worker treats the social character of his work, its combination with the work of others for a common purpose, as a power alien to him; the instruments necessary to bring this combination into being are alien property to him, to the waste of which he would be quite indifferent if he were not forced to treat them economically.

(K III, 105; C III, 102.)

This alienation between man and the social character of his activity can be seen in every sphere of capitalist society: it is presupposed by the existence of law, religion, etc. But only under capitalism does this alienation appear in all its nakedness. In feudalism, as we have seen Marx stressing in his earlier work, man is dependent but not yet divided; in capitalism his dependence is intensified in practice and his division is accomplished in theory (K I, 82–7; C I, 88–96). The slave sold his person, the serf sold part of his labour power, the worker under capitalism sells all of his labour power, but he sells it piecemeal. His alienation is therefore more thorough-going, more complete, than that of the slave and of the serf who preceded him in the arena of history. (Cf. *The German Ideology,* M I, 5, 56–9, GI, 64–8; *Grundrisse,* 73–82; *Capital,* K I, 76–89, C I, 81–95.)

The final aspect of alienation brought out in the *Paris Manuscripts* is man's alienation from nature. Instead of controlling it, making it part of his being, he is dominated by it, becomes part of its being. In the *Grundrisse* and *Capital* the reference is more frequently to *production,* but the concept remains the same. Instead of making production *his* activity, controlling its laws, man becomes a mere tool of production and develops according to its laws. In this sense, the capitalist is as dependent as the worker. Both are shaped and determined, in their character, their activity and their beliefs, by the inexorable laws of the economic process. *Thus the very epitome of the laws of historical development in the class society that forms the pre-history of mankind—the materialist interpretation of history—is for Marx the ultimate and fundamental expression of human alienation: it recognises as law man's subjugation by powers that should be and once were his own.* The coming of Communism, the supercession of alienation, means that man ceases to be the product and slave of production, and becomes its master.

There is no basis, then, for seeing Marx's rejection of a 'metaphysical' human nature as radically affecting his use of alienation in the economic and social contexts in which he had always thought its value to lie. It is true—as the Institute of Marxism-Leninism of the Central Committee of the C.P.S.U. puts it—that 'by "estrangement" or "alienation", Marx means the forced labour of the labourer for the capitalist, the appropriation by the capitalist of the product of a worker's labour and the separation of the labourer from the means of production which, being in the capitalist's possession, confront the labourer as an alien, enslaving power'. (EPM, Introduction, p. 8.) But this is not all he means. Dependence is not confined to capitalism: it began with the division of labour and private property, capitalism is only its most virulent and pervasive form. Economic dependence necessarily produces human dependence in all other fields—in religion, morality, law. The fact that Marx no longer uses the general term 'alienation' in *Capital* to sum up all these ramifications of economic dependence, does not prevent him from taking every opportunity in the same work to emphasise or display the pervasive dependence and dehumanisation on which capitalism rests and which it constantly extends and intensifies.

The distinction between freedom and alienation, I have argued, cannot be understood without recognising that Marx has grasped, however instinctively, the positive distinction between the operation of goods and of evils, between the morality of freedom associated with the productive spirit and the linked motives of domination and submission that emerged in the consumer's morality, in the subordination of activity to 'ends'. It is because the history of artistic and scientific production displays the producer's morality more clearly, more unequivocally, than industrial production—and only because of this— that there is a certain superficial plausibility in connecting Marx's vision of man in Communist society with the creative work of an artist living in a society of artists. Nothing in Marx's mature work repudiates or alters this conception of the distinction between free and alienated living. Not only that, but Marx himself brings out, in the *Grundrisse*, the positive ground of his distinction and its intimate connexion with the character of artistic and scientific activity:

In the sweat of thy face shalt thou labour! was Jehovah's curse, which he gave to Adam. And it is thus as curse that A[dam] Smith regards labour. 'Rest' appears as the adequate condition, as identical with 'freedom' and 'happiness'. A. Smith seems far from seeing that the individual, 'in his normal condition of health, strength, activity, capacity and skill,' has also the need for a normal portion of work, for an end to rest. It is true that the amount of labour is itself determined externally, by the purpose sought and the obstacles to the attainment of that purpose which must be overcome through labour. But A. Smith has just as little conception of the fact that this overcoming of obstacles is itself the activity of freedom—of the further fact that the appearance of merely external natural necessity is stripped off from external purposes and that these purposes are revealed as purposes which the individual sets himself—of the fact, therefore, that the overcoming of obstacles is self-realisation, objectification of the subject, therefore concrete freedom, whose action is precisely work. He is right, however, in seeing that in its historical forms as slavery, feudal services and wage labour, labour always appears as something repulsive, as *external forced labour*, and that not working appears in relation to this as 'freedom and happiness'. This is doubly true: it is true of this contrasted labour, of the labour which has not yet created the subjective and objective conditions . . . to make it *travail attractif*, self-realisation of the individual, which does not mean that it becomes mere fun, mere amusement, as Fourier thinks with all the naiveté of a *grisette*. Truly free labour, e.g., composition, is damned serious at the same time, it is the most intensive exertion. The work of material production can acquire this character only by (1) having its social character affirmed (2) having a scientific character and being universal labour, the exertion of a man not as a tamed natural force, but as a subject which appears in the process of production not only in its natural form and development as part of nature, but as an activity regulating all natural forces.

(*Grundrisse,* 504–5.)

These notes were not meant for publication. But this is how Marx reacts, this is how he saw dependence and freedom.

In the years between 1844 and the publication of the first volume of *Capital* in 1867 Marx read and appropriated into his thinking an enormous mass of economic material. As an economist he was not shallow: he was not merely a Ricardian glibly seizing upon the labour theory of value as a convenient tool for bringing out the alienation, dehumanisation, exploitation inherent in capitalism. He was also, in economics, a very learned and a very perceptive man. He became engrossed in all the technical and professional details of his subject: monetary theory, accumulation, constant and variable capital, prices, absolute and relative surplus value, trade cycles, labour conditions and factory organisation. What is amazing in view of this is not how much new material came in as the *Paris Manuscripts* grew into the three volumes of *Capital,* but how much of the old material and of the old thought remained. Nowhere is Marx's conception of the appropriation of things external to man exemplified more clearly than in his own intellectual work. He took materials from everywhere, but he subsumed them to his own purposes, moulded them into his system, strove to weld everything into a single coherent structure whose fundamental plan retained its original purpose and thrust.

Marx, we have seen, did come to reject any conception of an essential and eternal human nature preceding and underlying the process of production which has come to dominate man. The importance of this rejection as a radical *break* in his development should not be over-rated. Already in the *Paris Manuscripts,* for all his alleged Young Hegelianism, Marx had insisted that it is only in 'working on the world of objects', in production, that man proves himself to be a generic or social being. (M I, 3, 88, *supra,* II, 7). But there he still thought of the generic being as somehow part of the 'essence' of man—*proved* rather than *created* by production. Now, in his mature work, he combines the belief in a universal, social, generic being of man with his historical materialism by seeing this being as the *result* of production, which socialises man, brings him into union with his fellow-men, and lays the technological foundations which enable man to become the master and not the slave of Nature. This is the dialectic of capitalism: the 'contradiction' between its *socialisation* of man and his labour, its creation of ever-increasing organisation and interdependence, and its separation of men into classes, its alienation of one man from another, even within the same class.

By sympathy, Marx always remained a philosopher. Throughout twenty years of intensive labour in the economic field, he despised economics. His correspondence with Engels in the later years of his life is studded with gross and contemptuous references to the subject. He resented the fact that it prevented him from turning to other fields that interested him: law, morality, aesthetics. But he knew economics to be fundamental to his position: the back-breaking labour could not be avoided. His extraordinary achievement had been to take the onto-logical concept of alienation and invest it—quite early in his thought—with concrete social and economic content. It was because alienation and freedom remained central to his thought that the argument had to be followed to the bitter end.

The final flowering of alienation was capitalism. The collapse of capitalism had therefore to be shown inevitable, not by moral criticism but from the logic of its own development. This occupied much, perhaps most, of Marx's attention. The doctrine of surplus value, the analysis of competition, the attempt to prove the inevitable pauperisa-tion of the working masses and the 'simplification' of social classes are vital to Marx for this purpose. They showed, he thought, that the alienated society could not survive and could not be destroyed without radically eliminating all of its presuppositions. These presuppositions, according to Marx, are the division of labour, private property and production for monetary return—all of them essential for the appear-ance of alienation. Marx invests his analysis of the history of produc-tion with a tremendous mass of detailed material, but the basic outline of the preconditions and development of alienation is quite simple. The division of labour begins in the family and gradually extends throughout the society:

The division of labour implies from the outset the division of the conditions of labour, of tools and materials, and thus the splitting up of accumulated capital among different owners, and thus, also, the division between capital and labour, and the different forms of property itself. The more the division of labour develops and accumulation grows, the sharper are the forms that this process of differentiation assumes.

(M I, 5, 56, G I, 64; cf. K I, 368ff., C I, 385ff.)

What makes this division and separation possible is that with the extended division of labour, production is no longer for use, but for money, for exchange value.

The social division of labour makes the labour [of the goods-possessor] just as one-sided as it makes his needs many-sided. For this reason his product can serve him only as an *exchange value*. It can acquire universal, socially accepted forms of equivalence through money, and the money is in someone else's pocket.

(K I, 111; C I, 119.)

Since money does not disclose what has been transformed into it, everything whether a commodity or not, is convertible into gold. Everything becomes saleable and purchasable. Circulation is the great social retort into which everything is thrown and out of which everything is recovered as crystallised money. Not even the bones of the saints are able to withstand this alchemy; and still less able to withstand it are more delicate *res sacrosanctae extra commercium hominum*. Just as all the qualitative differences between commodities are effaced in money, so money on its side, a radical leveller, effaces all distinctions. But money is itself a commodity, an external object, capable of becoming the private property of any individual. Thus social power becomes a private power in the hands of a private person.

(K I, 137–8; C I, 148–9.)

The division of labour, private property and money: these three (the latter two made inevitable by the first) in turn make inevitable the alienation, the dependence and separation that pervades the whole of capitalist society. They create the division of town and country, of worker and master, of 'individual' and 'society', of man and his labour. They alienate man from other men, from his work, from his product, from his society.

How, then, is this alienation to be overcome? By the inevitable logic of the development of the productive process, which will end by destroying private property and with it the division of labour and the production for monetary gain. This is the point of Marx's detailed analysis of the capitalist economy: it shows, Marx believed, that capitalism will be destroyed, and it shows this from 'simple', quite unphilosophical, economic facts.

What Marx thought to be the basic outlines of the Communist society of freedom are clear. The distinction between classes, resting on their relationship to property, would disappear with the super-cession of property. So would the division of labour, the distinction between urban and rural interests, between mental and physical labour. Production and social intercourse will be stripped, for the first time, of their independent character and subjugated 'to the power of individuals united' (G I, 70; M I, 5, 60).[1] The material process of production will become 'a process carried on by a free association of producers, under their conscious purposive control'; the relations between human beings in their practical everyday life will 'have assumed the aspect of perfectly intelligible and reasonable relations between man and man, and between man and Nature' (K I, 85; C I, 92).

Engels had attempted to set out what this means in concrete terms in an early draft for the *Communist Manifesto*—his *Fundamental Principles of Communism*, a revolutionary catechism written in October, 1847:

Question 20—*What will be the consequences of the final abolition of private property?*

Answer—Society, by taking out of the hands of the private capitalist the utilisation of the various productive forces and means of intercourse, as well as the exchange and distribution of goods, and controlling them according to a plan based on the available means and needs of the whole whole society, will above all abolish all those harmful effects which at present are still connected with the operation of big industry. Crises will disappear; increased production, which is over-production for the present social order and a powerful cause of misery, will then not even prove sufficient and will have to be increased far more. Instead of bringing misery in its wake, over-production will reach beyond the immediate needs of society to the satisfaction of everybody's needs; it will create new needs and at the same time create the means for their satisfaction. It will be the cause and determining condition of new advances; it will bring about these ad-vances without throwing the social order into confusion, as has always been the case in the past. Big industry, free of the pressure of private ownership, will develop at an increased rate compared with which its present form will

[1] 'This is not possible without the community. Only in community with others has each individual the means of cultivating his gifts in all directions; only in community, therefore, is personal freedom possible . . . The illusory com-munity, in which individuals have up till now combined, always took on an independent existence in relation to them, and was at the same time, since it was the combination of one class against another, not only a completely illusory community, but a new fetter as well. In the real community the individuals obtain their freedom in and through their association' (G I, 74–5: M I, 5, 63–4).

seem as small as commodity manufacture seems compared with the big industry of our days. This development of industry will provide our society with a sufficient mass of products to satisfy the needs of all. Similarly, agriculture, also prevented by the pressure of private ownership and the division into lots from utilising the improvements and scientific developments already at hand, will gain new life and provide society with a mass of products fully ample for all. Thus society will produce enough goods to arrange distribution in such a way that the needs of all its members will be satisfied. The division of society into separate classes opposed to one another will become superfluous. Not only will it be superfluous, it will even be incompatible with the new social order. The existence of classes arose out of the division of labour, and the division of labour in the form it has had hitherto disappears completely. For mechanical and chemical aids are not sufficient to bring industrial and agricultural production to the heights depicted above by themselves; the capacities of the men who utilise these aids must be developed correspondingly. Just as the peasants and artisans of the last century altered their whole way of life and became quite different people when they were caught up in large industry, so the common control of production by the whole society and the resultant new development of production will both need and create totally new men. The communal control of production cannot be carried out by men like those of today, each of whom is subordinate to a single branch of production, is chained to it and exploited by it, each of whom has developed only one of his capacities at the expense of all the rest, each of whom knows only one branch, or only one branch of a branch, of the whole of production. Even industry today has increasingly less use for such people. Industry controlled in common in a planned way by the whole of society presupposes men whose capacities are developed in all directions, who are able to review the entire system of production. The division of labour, which makes one man into a peasant, another a cobbler, a third into a factory-hand and a fourth into a stock exchange speculator, is already undermined by machinery; it will disappear completely. Education will enable young people to go rapidly through the whole system of production, it will enable them to go in rotation from one branch of production to another, as the needs of society or their own inclinations may direct. It will therefore deprive them of that one-sided character, which the present division of labour stamps on every individual. In this way society organised in Communist fashion will enable its members to utilise their many-sided talents in many fields. This, however, necessarily results in the disappearance of separate classes. So Communist society on the one hand is incompatible with the continuation of classes; on the other hand the creation of this society itself provides the means for dissolving class differences.

It follows from this, that the contrast between town and country will also disappear. Wholly material causes already make the pursuit of agriculture and industry by the same men, instead of by two separate classes, a necessary condition of the Communist order. The dissemination of the peasant population on the land, compared with the crowding together of the industrial population in the large towns, is a condition which corresponds only to an as yet undeveloped stage of agriculture and industry, a barrier to all further development which can already be felt strongly in the present time.

The universal association of all members of society for the common planned exploitation of the forces of production, the increase of production at a rate that will enable it to satisfy the needs of all, the end of a state of affairs in which the needs of one are satisfied at the expense of others, the total destruction of classes and their contradictions, the development of the capacities of all members of society in all directions through the abolition of the division of labour as known hitherto, through industrial education, through the rotation of jobs, through the participation of all in the satisfactions created by all, through the fusion of town and country—these are the main results of the abolition of private property.

(M I, 6, 516–19.)

Marx was an infinitely abler, subtler and theoretically more perceptive man than Engels. Where Engels puts thing concretely, simply and often naively, Marx tends to put them philosophically, subtly and sometimes abstrusely. He would have liked to believe what Engels believed—it is just possible that he did. Certainly, Marx, too, refers to the disappearance of the distinction between mental and physical labour (*Critique of the Gotha Programme*, SW II, 23), to the shortening of the working day (K III, 873–4; C III, 954–5), to the combination of productive labour and education 'as a method not only increasing social production but as the only method of producing human beings developed in all their aspects' (K I, 509; C I, 530). But he is certainly less emphatic about the social unity of Communism resting on the fact that technology will be able to satisfy all of men's needs. He speaks, in the *Critique of the Gotha Programme* (loc. cit.) of the ultimate period when 'the productive forces have also increased with the all-round development of the individual and all the springs of co-operative wealth flow *more* abundantly' (my italics); 'the realm of freedom', he insists, 'begins in actuality only when labour which is determined by need and external utility ceases' (K III, 873; C III, 954); but he does not see this as flowing from the satisfaction of all needs. Marx was simply not the utilitarian that Engels was; he was not concerned with *how much* a man had, but with the way in which he acquired what he had, with the conditions under which he worked. The essential thing for Marx that makes production truly social is the abolition of money as a circulating exchange value (K III, 932; C III), the fact that the individual is no longer an abstract buyer and seller of commodities, but a *participant* in the social business of production and of consumption. In truly communal production

> its communal nature is taken as the foundation of production. The labour of the individual is taken from the start as social labour. Therefore whatever the specific material form of the product which he creates or helps to create may be, that which he has bought with his labour is not a special specific product, but a specific share of the communal production. For this reason he has no special product that he has to exchange. His product is *not an exchange value*. The product does not have to be translated into a specific character form in order to acquire a universal character for the individual. Instead of a division of labour, necessarily ending in the exchange of exchange value, we would have an organisation of labour, which results in the participation of the individual in communal consumption.
>
> (*Grundrisse*, 88–9.)

What does this passage mean? It means, I think, that Marx was both far less and far more naive than Engels about production under Communism. He foresaw tremendous improvements in working conditions, a considerable decrease in the amount of labour needed from each man as a result of technological advance and the abolition of any need for labour-discipline of the capitalist type (K III, 103; C III, 100). In its stead, there would be social determination, by the community, of the working day and of the distribution of labour (K III, 213, 907; C III, 221, 992) and, naturally, increased but more centralised book-keeping. That resources would still need to be husbanded, and allocated among alternative uses, Marx understands quite well;[1] that people would have to do extra work on behalf of those in the community who cannot work he himself mentions (K III, 932; C III, 1021–2). He is simply not concerned to portray Communism as the society of plenty; he is concerned to portray it as a society of human dignity: a society in which labour

---

[1] 'If we think of society as not being capitalist, but Communist, then money-capital disappears entirely and with it, therefore, the disguises that it carries into transactions. The matter simply becomes that society must calculate beforehand how much labour, how many instruments of production and provisions can be expended, without upset, on branches of activity which, like the building of railways, for instance, will produce neither instruments of production nor food nor any useful effects for a length of time, a year or more, but which will draw away labour, tools and provisions from the total production for the year.' (K II, 314; C II, 361–2.)

acquires dignity and becomes free because it is carried out by full and conscious participants in a community given over to co-operation and common aims. The model of a co-operative, productive community of artists or scientists (which Engels never understood) is again apposite: its members may hunger, undertake enormous exertions, spend hours on tasks not interesting in themselves—but they know what they are doing and why they want to do it. In that lies their freedom and their dignity. It is for these reasons, because Marx himself has the productive morality, that he is more concerned with time than he is with plenty:

Assuming communal production, the determination of time remains important. The less time society needs to produce wheat, cattle, etc., the more time it has for other production, whether material or intellectual. As in the case of the single individual, the universality of its development, of its satisfaction and its activity, depends on saving time. Economy of time is what all economics finally comes down to. Society must thus divide its time usefully in order to arrive at a measure of production suitable to its total needs; just as the individual must divide his time properly to gain knowledge in suitable proportion or to satisfy the different demands on his activity.   (*Grundrisse*, 89.)

Marx's vision of Communism, then, is not the vision of a society of plenty, in which conflicting interests have disappeared because everyone has everything he wants, or, at least, needs. But is he relying on an economic reductionism, on the view that all alienation and conflict stem from private property, and will therefore disappear when private property is abolished? There is much in Marx's work to suggest this view. Yet fundamentally, I believe, he felt a certain uneasiness about it. His vision of the coming of Communism, as we have seen, retained much that was metaphysical about it. The inevitability of the complete supercession of property depends on nothing more concrete than the claim that the proletariat, being divorced from all property, must make the abolition of property its 'principle'—it is here that Marx has made the least advance on the views he held in 1843 and 1844. *Capital* gives the impression that he is desperately looking for specific, concrete connexions that will show the actual truly free, truly communal form of the society that succeeds capitalism inevitable. This is why he is anxious to stress the co-operation and socialisation developing within capitalism. He sees the seeds of Communism in the limited company, 'the dissolution of the capitalist mode of production within the capitalist mode of production itself' (K III, 479; C III, 519); he sees them also in the co-operative factories of workers themselves (K III, 481; C III, 521). He is anxious to show that even under capitalism the truly human quality of the worker can appear, especially when he is freed from the crippling effects of the detailed division of labour.[1] But Marx is not willing to stake too much on these examples; the character of Communism as the society in which property is completely overcome and production controlled by the free association of producers is assumed throughout *Capital* and never demonstrated in detail.

Within a few years, the glibness of Marx's vision was being questioned, especially by men of anarchist tendencies who insisted that Marx had grossly underrated the despotism imposed by technology itself, by the very nature of factory production. Engels, with his hard-headed 'realism' and no understanding whatever of the subtleties of Marx's conception of freedom, was in no position to resist their arguments. To question the nature of authority in a factory, he argued in a polemic with some Italian anarchists, is plainly utopian:

At least with regard to the hours of work one may write upon the portals of these factories: *Lasciate ogni autonomia, voi che entrate!* [leave, ye that enter in, all autonomy behind!] If man, by dint of his knowledge and inventive genius, has subdued the forces of Nature, the latter avenge themselves upon him by subjecting him, in so far as he employs them, to a veritable despotism, independent of all social organisation. Wanting to abolish authority in large-scale industry is tantamount to wanting to abolish industry itself, to destroy the power loom in order to return to the spinning wheel.

(*Basic Writings on Politics and Philosophy*, ed. L. S. Feuer, p. 483.)

Marx, I think, would have replied quite differently. The authority in a factory would have seemed quite different to him from external dependence or capitalist labour discipline *once the social nature and*

---

[1] Marx quotes approvingly an account given by a French workman after returning from San Francisco: 'I never could have believed that I was capable of working at the various occupations I was employed on in California. I was firmly convinced that I was fit for nothing but letter press printing . . . Once in the midst of this world of adventurers, who change their occupation as often as they do their shirt, by my faith, I did as the others. As mining did not turn out remunerative enough, I left it for the town, where in succession I became typographer, slater, plumber, etc. In consequence of thus finding out that I am fit for any sort of work, I feel less of a mollusc and more of a man' (K I, 513; C I, 534).

control of production had been presupposed. Why? Marx could not quite say this in terms of his historical materialism, but obviously his answer is: because the individual's attitudes to authority will be quite different. The force of the authority will not flow from an external structure imposed upon him, but from the nature of the activities in which he is engaging freely and consciously. Those who have authority will be fellow-producers, seeking the same productivity as he seeks: their 'authority' will rest on competence and experience he himself recognises and admires.

In concrete human terms, this situation is again not entirely utopian. Such voluntary acceptance of guidance and of the rules necessary for the continuation of an activity can be found in institutions and teams seized with the productive spirit. How such guidance and such rules appear to any individual in the institution will, in fact, depend upon his 'attitude', i.e., on the extent to which he himself is seized by the productive spirit. This is not to say that conflicts of views or competing interests will not break out in an organisation given over to production; but in so far as the productive spirit is strong within the organisation such conflicts will be subordinated to the needs and rules of the productive activity itself.

What is utopian in Marx's vision is his constant reliance on the productive spirit, on the operation of goods in individuals, without paying any attention to their character, to the conditions in which they arise in any given individual and spread through a society, and to the character of the forces opposing them. It is here that the 'human essence' is still assumed in Marx's mature work. Co-operation and production are taken as the 'normal' way of working of the individual freed from the pressures of external determination; a view for which Marx provides no evidence and could provide no evidence. Above all, he fails to consider the view—which his own concrete examples of free activity suggest—that productive organisation can only result from an already existing productive spirit: not merely from the interdependence created by capitalism, but from what Sorel calls 'the heroic values' of enterprise, immersion in productive activity and indifference to reward.

Here is the central weakness of Marx's vision. Unlike Engels, Marx was not a utilitarian; he was not trying to build a society of the future on the enlightened self-interest of the individual, on the promise of peace and plenty. The freedom and dignity he proclaimed as the goal of history were not entirely a utopian vision: such freedom and such dignity have been displayed by men and women in their life and work. But only those who have such dignity and such freedom can bring it about. Marx would have liked to believe that the industrial proletariat was evolving such freedom, such enterprise, even under capitalism. But he was not prepared to stake much on the conception. History seemed a more powerful ally. The proletariat remained for him fundamentally a vehicle of history: not a class displaying enterprise, production and co-operation, but a class denied enterprise, production and co-operation, not a class that has freed itself from the shackles of property, but a class denied property, a class whose whole character consisted of nothing more than its exclusion from property, than its suffering. In not seeing the proletariat as the bearers of enterprise, as the class of free men, Marx may have been right; but if he was right his vision was doomed. In fact, the proletariat proved more thoroughly the child of capitalism than Marx had ever dreamt possible: the movement he founded helped to destroy the vision he worked for.

PART FIVE

Communism and Ethics

15. Ethics and the Communist Party

THE fundamental weakness of Marx's thought, then, lies in his failure to work out a theory of classes and organisations, and of freedom and servility, in *positive* terms, in terms of the *character* of the processes and movements involved. What things *are* is prior to their possible adjustments and their aims; it is in the struggle of specific movements and organisations that adjustments arise and aims are formulated. It is only because Marx glosses over the positive character of social movements and ways of living that he is able to believe in a classless society, in a society in which the *conflict* of movements and way of living has disappeared. The *transition* to socialism thus becomes something he simply cannot afford to examine seriously: the precise character of the dictatorship of the proletariat, the 'values' and ways of living represented by the people in whose hands it would lie, have to be left out of account. Here he is driven back on a crude economic reductionism: the abolition of private property destroys the foundation on which competing interests rest.

Socialism, on Marx's view, would be born out of capitalism. But it would be the society of true freedom and enterprise, in which the capitalist morality had been entirely destroyed. He was right in the first proposition and wrong in the second. Socialism was born of capitalism. But it was not the result of the catastrophic collapse of capitalism. On the contrary, it sprang from the very ideology fostered by capitalism: the concern with economic ends over ways of living, the belief in the universal exchangeability of all things, in the possibility of rational control of all things seen as mere means to a commercial end. The socialist's vision of society, as Rosa Luxemburg once said of Lenin, is the capitalist's vision of a factory, run by an overseer. The conception of economic planning, Schumpeter has pointed out, is a capitalist conception: the capitalism manager is the prototype of the socialist administrator. Both depend in their ideology on the commercial morality of utilitarianism: on the conception that all things can be treated and assessed as means to ends and that ends can be reduced to a common measure.

Marx had a strong desire to believe that the proletariat, in its misery, yearned for initiative, enterprise and freedom, that it rejected servility, careerism and the concern with security as Marx himself had rejected them. It would not be bought off with ameliorated conditions, prospects of greater rewards, or of 'opportunities' for the individual to 'better' himself. But Marx was not prepared to make such a claim part of his theory, to see socialism as the extension and culmination of the freedom and enterprise already displayed by the worker. Essentially, he stuck to his negative view of the proletariat as the *most suffering class*; a class whose future was determined not by its character, but by its conditions. This prevented him from paying serious attention to freedom and enterprise as historic traditions, operating in any society, strengthened and not necessarily weakened in the struggle against adversity. It prevented him from seeing the importance of other forms of production and of other manifestations of the productive spirit in social life: of artistic and scientific production as continuing traditions capable of supporting and strengthening the productive spirit in industry. Instead, Marx chose to rely on 'history', to hold out to the proletariat the vision of a classless society *made safe* for goods, where enterprise and freedom would be *guaranteed* by the economic foundations of society itself, where freedom would not lie in struggle, but follow from mere existence. The servile character of such a conception, its appeal to the demands for safety and for security, for certain returns, has been noted already. Its servile character was even further strengthened by the fact that it was Engels, with his blindness for alienation, with his crude evolutionism, his utilitarian concern with economic *satisfaction,* who became the 'ideologue'—the propagandist and populariser—of Marxism.

There can be no question that the labour movement, and even the socialist movement, was at no stage wholly given over to enterprise. The search for security, for welfare and economic sufficiency, was always a powerful motive within it. But there can also be no question that propaganda of a Marxist colour, with its insistence on ends and aims, its elevation of consumer's demands, did much to destroy what enterprise there was. In their controversies with anarchists and syndicalists Marxists may have been able to expose much that was utopian in both movements. But against the anarcho-syndicalist elevation of the free and enterprising character of the existing working-class, Marxists were upholding a servile and unfree morality.

Partly as a result of Marx's failure to deal positively with ethical questions, to highlight ways of life and of organisation, ethical distinctions did not play a central part in the splits and controversies that racked Marxism. The revisionists in the 1890's, it is true, made much ado about their Kantian ethics, and Bernstein proclaimed his seemingly sound slogan: 'The movement is everything, the goal is nothing.' But Bernstein, for all this, preached security and sufficiency all his life. The real issue confronting Marxists was not ethics, but the consequences of their neglect of ethics. Marx had been wrong in forecasting the imminent collapse of capitalism and the growing pauperisation of the worker; no longer driven by needs, the workers were displaying their character, their preference for rewards and security over freedom and struggle. If one wanted to follow the worker, the Marxist vision of a radically new society born of struggle had to be dropped. Socialism became a matter of negotiation and demand for improved conditions and greater security *within existing conditions*. This was the path of reformism. Notably, the Marxist neglect of ethics prevented them from attacking reformism for its elevation of rewards and security; the orthodox Marxists had to argue instead—quite implausibly—that the reformists were bound to fail, that increased rewards and greater security could not last under capitalism.

Orthodox Marxists, clinging to the vision, had to find a substitute for the proletariat. Lenin, drawing on Russian Populism, found it in the revolutionary intelligentsia and the centralised hierarchical party, acting as the 'vanguard' of the working-class, driving it beyond the bread-and-butter politics at which the working-class by itself would always remain. Enterprise was not to be won by the worker but for him.

The bringing of freedom and enterprise to somebody is not a free but a despotic conception. Yet Marx, too, had seen freedom as something that would be brought to the worker by 'history'. His work laid no foundations for exposing the course the Communist Party was soon to follow. Indeed, his failure to see freedom as a force within history, his treatment of it as merely a final end, made it possible to erect despotism in his name. The point is Marx's refusal to consider the qualities of movements and institutions themselves, his idealist insistence that to do so is to treat them 'abstractly'. It is their role in history, not their character, that matters to Marx. Social movements and relationships are not good or bad, but progressive or reactionary, doing 'the work of history' or frustrating it. There is no point in judging in isolation, especially when the path of history is not one of slow steady improvement, but one of inevitable conflicts, necessary miseries, and later resolutions.

'Reason,' Hegel had said in one of the most famous passages in his *Encyclopedia,* 'is as cunning as it is powerful. Cunning may be said to lie in the inter-mediative action, which, while it permits the objects to follow their own bent and act upon one another till they waste away, and does not itself directly interfere in this process, is nevertheless only working out the execution of its aims. With this explanation, Divine Providence may be said to stand to the world and its process in the capacity of absolute cunning. God lets men direct their particular passions and interests as they please; but the result is the accomplishment of—not their plans, but His, and these differ directly from the ends primarily sought by those whom He employs.' (Wallace translation, Section 209.) In the *Communist Manifesto* especially, Marx also emphasised this disparity between the character of men's actions and intentions and the results that inevitably followed from them. The exploitation of slaves made inevitable the agricultural development of feudalism; the greed of the capitalist merchant built industrialism; the increasing misery of the proletarian was the indispensable precondition of the rational society of the future. In the face of the ethical qualities of the end, the ethical qualities of the preceding stages, if they could be spoken of at all, were irrelevant. If history proceeds inevitably toward the truly rational, then, indeed, one can say with Hegel—*Die Weltge-schichte ist das Weltgericht.*

For the Communist Party, as 'the party of history', the principle was of inestimable value in imposing iron discipline and unquestioning obedience in a period of militant struggle accompanied by the opportunism of constantly shifting tactics. Reinforced by Marxist essentialism, by the conception that each stage of history requires the solution of a dominant 'task', the victory of the proletariat under the leadership of the Communist Party became the only relevant moral criterion in the period of struggle under capitalism. (Stealing from capitalist employers used to be denounced in party catechisms on the simple ground that it would discredit the party in the eyes of the public.) Lenin, claiming that there is no shred of ethics in Marxism from beginning to end, repeatedly emphasised the moral primacy of proletarian victory.

Trotsky, in his *Their Morals and Ours*, took the same line. A gun in itself is neither good nor evil; it becomes good in the hands of a proletarian fighting for the classless society and evil in the hands of a capitalist fighting for oppression and exploitation. At the same time, within the party and within the Soviet Union the principle could always be used to justify those who actually gained and kept power.[1] History was on their side. It is this which plants the first seeds of doubt in the mind of the anti-Stalinist Rubashov sitting in his prison cell in Arthur Koestler's *Darkness at Noon*; within Marxism he can find no answer.

[1] Quite typical is this attempt by Mehring's translator, Edward Fitzgerald, to defend Marx (in an addendum) against Mehring's moral strictures over the Bakunin episode: 'Any discussion of "the moral qualities" of the methods used in the fractional struggles between Marx and Bakunin and their followers can be of only very subordinate interest to day. Marx and Engels were not "innocent lambs", but Bakunin and his friends were also not and they waged the fractional struggle by no means in strict accordance with the categorical imperative. In any case, all this is of very subsidiary importance. In the struggle between Bakunin and his followers on the one hand and Marx and Engels on the other, fundamental principles and history were on the side of Marx and Marxism and therefore, we may assume, "moral" justification also.' (Mehring: *Karl Marx*, p. 556.)

16. Law and Morality in Soviet Society

THE Soviet Union is not a society of artists co-operating freely and consciously in tasks that require no coercive discipline but that express the community's mastery over the process of production. In their forty-four years of existence, Soviet law, Soviet morality and Soviet legal theory have trailed meekly in the wake of economic and political requirements dictated from the top—requirements that frequently suffered abrupt change and which even more frequently flowed from practical aims quite inconsistent with Marx's theory. But throughout, there has been the wish to portray Soviet society as constantly nearing the free, co-operative community envisaged by Marx: the community in which law and the very conception of moral rights and duties will have withered away.

For the Soviet legal theorist, the problem did not become acute until the 1936 Stalin Constitution ushered in a period in which law was for the first time openly proclaimed as an intimate and not highly temporary part of the socialist society. In the period of 'War Communism' from 1917 to 1921, Communist leaders had taken the opposite view. Convinced of the imminence of world-wide socialism, they strove to rid their country of every vestige of capitalism. They abolished private ownership of land and of the means of production; prohibited private trade in consumers' goods, did away with inheritance, paid wages partially in kind, conducted moneyless transaction between State business houses, and predicted the speedy coming of true Communism, under which money, class and State authority would disappear. Law was therefore regarded as strictly transitional and as still representing class interests—as a set of rules designed for the suppression of the 'class enemies' which would become unnecessary once the liquidation of these enemies had been accomplished. Thus, even the criminal law was seen as a pure class measure dictated by the economic interests of the proletariat. The *Leading Principles of Criminal Law*, enacted by the People's Commissariat of Justice in 1919, expresses this attitude bluntly:

In the interests of economising forces and harmonising and centralising diverse acts, the proletariat ought to work out rules of repressing its class enemies, ought to create a method of struggle with its enemies and learn to dominate them. And first of all this ought to relate to criminal law, which has as its task the struggle against the breakers of the new conditions of common life in the transitional period of the dictatorship of the proletariat. Only with the final smashing of the opposing overthrown bourgeois and intermediate classes and with the realisation of the Communist social order will the proletariat annihilate both the State as an organisation of coercion, and law as a function of the State.[1]

The New Economic Policy of 1921–28, it is true, saw a drastic reversal of this trend. With the reappearance of money, private trade, *kulaks,* and private business managers operating under State licences, a detailed system of law and legal procedure quickly emerged.[2] But it set no basic problem for Soviet legal theory. The New Economic Policy was an open, though partial and strictly controlled, restoration of the capitalist market—the laws required, therefore, were not socialist laws, but temporary laws on the capitalist model, which would disappear when the concessions to capitalism were once more eliminated. The new Codes were frankly based on those of the non-socialist world—on the Codes of Germany, Switzerland, Imperial Russia and France. Legal capacity, persons, corporations, legal transactions, Statute of Limitations, property, mortgages, landlord and tenant, contracts and torts, unjust enrichment and inheritance, as Berman remarks,[3] were dealt with in traditional terms. In so far as one can speak of any specifically socialist conception of law in this period, it rests not on the legal concepts or principles exemplified in the Codes, but on their subordination, in the last resort, to the alleged economic interests of

---

[1] Quoted by Harold J. Berman: *Justice in Russia*, pp. 23–4, from *Sobranie uzakonenii i rasporiazhenii RSFSR (Collection of Laws and Orders of the RSFSR)*, 1919, no. 66, Art. 590.

[2] 'In 1922 and 1923, there appeared a Judiciary Act, a Civil Code, a Code of Civil Procedure, a Criminal Code, a Code of Criminal Procedure, a Land Code and a New Labour Code'—Berman, op. cit., p. 25.

[3] Ibid., p. 26.

the proletariat. The famous Article 1 of the Civil Code states this over-riding principle of the NEP conception of law: 'Civil rights shall be protected by law except in instances when they are exercised in contra-diction with their social-economic purpose.'[1] There is no suggestion that these social-economic purposes themselves lay the foundation for a positive system of distinctively socialist law.

This became absolutely clear in 1928, when the NEP compromise was abandoned and replaced by the two Five-Year Plans, designed to turn Soviet Russia, independently of world revolution, into a socialist society as quickly as possible.

Now, for the first time, positive content was given to the Marxist idea of the disappearance of State and Law under socialism. It was thought that Law, an instrument of the class-dominated State, would be replaced by Plan, the manifestation of the will of a class-less society. Through the Plan all the characteristics of the original Marxist dream would be realised. Planning would eliminate exploitation; money would be transformed into a mere unit of account; private property and private right generally would be swallowed up in collectivism; the family would disappear as a legal entity, with husbands and wives bound only by ties of affection and children owing their allegiance and their upbringing to the whole society; crime would be exceptional and would be treated as mental illness; the coercive machinery of the State would become superfluous. The Plan would give unity and harmony to all relations. The Plan itself would differ from Law, since it would be an instrument neither of compulsion nor of formality but simply an expression of rational foresight on the part of the planners, with the whole people participating and assenting spontaneously. Society would be regu-lated, administered—much as traffic at an intersection is regulated by traffic lights and by rules of the road; but in a society without class conflict there would be few collisions and to deal with them it would be unnecessary to have a system of 'justice'. Social-economic expediency would be the ultimate criterion; disputes would be resolved on the spot.[2]

In this period, under the leadership of E. B. Pashukanis, N. Krylenko and P. J. Stuchka, Soviet legal philosophy was unquestionably at its best. Pashukanis and Stuchka were theorists, genuinely concerned to

[1] Lenin put this forcefully in his letter to Kursky preceding the enactment of the 1922 Civil Code: 'We do not recognise any "private" thing; with us, in the field of economics, there is only public, and no private law. The only capitalism we allow is that of the State . . . for this reason, we have to widen the sphere of State-interference with "private" agreements. Not the *corpus juris Romani*, but our revolutionary consciousness of Justice, ought to be applied to "Civil law relations".' Quoted by R. Schlesinger: *Soviet Legal Theory*, p. 150.

[2] Berman, op. cit., pp. 30–1.

work out a coherent Marxist account of law. This, they knew, no one had yet done properly. They wanted to show, as they thought Marx showed, and as Soviet leaders had so far agreed (though Lenin had a genius for ambiguity), that socialist law was a contradiction in terms. Law, they held with Marx, was a reflection of economic antagonisms; with the eradication of these antagonisms it would necessarily disappear. A Marxist theory of law, says Pashukanis, cannot claim to seek the general concept of a proletarian law. 'The dying out of the categories of bourgeois law will . . . signify the dying out of law in general: that is to say, the gradual disappearance of the juridic element in human relations.'[1] Pashukanis saw, however, that this view needed far more support in the field of law than Marx, Engels and Lenin had ever given it. He saw, above all, that it was necessary to show—as we have seen Marx never showed—that bourgeois law is not merely influenced and distorted by economic interests, but that its basic structure, concepts and principles are the reflections of economic categories of bourgeois society that make no sense without it. Pashukanis, in fact, goes further and insists that law itself is essentially bourgeois, that it rests on conceptions necessarily linked with commodity exchange, and that law can therefore only attain its consummation in bourgeois society. All law, Pashukanis argues, is private law. There can be no true public law establishing the relationship between the State and private individuals because the State is by its very nature above and outside the law. Law is built on the contractual relationships required in the process of exchanging commodities on a free market—its corner-stone is the abstract individual of capitalist economic life, 'the right- and duty-bearing unit.'[2] This contractual conception dominates every sphere of law—tort, family and marriage law, labour law, constitutional law (based on a 'social contract') and even criminal law, in which Pashukanis sees the *ius talionis* giving way, after an intermediate stage of money composition, to the commercial idea that a crime must be paid for *ex post facto*. With the overcoming of the bourgeois abstraction of the individual, the abolition of commercial relations and the establishment of the social interest and the social man, the whole structure of law necessarily loses meaning and collapses.

---

[1] Quoted in Hans Kelsen: *The Communist Theory of Law*, p. 106. Pashukanis concedes, of course, that in the transitional dictatorship of the proletariat 'the proletariat must necessarily utilise in its interest these forms which have been inherited from bourgeois society and thereby exhaust them completely.'

[2] Berman, op. cit., p. 19.

Then, in 1936, a major theoretical upheaval began. Socialist society, it was formally announced, had finally been achieved. The first stage of the classless society, it contained three strata—the workers, the peasants, the intelligentsia. These, however, were friendly and mutually supporting sections of the population, not the hostile economic groupings of the societies of class antagonism. Yet the conclusions that would have followed from this announcement on earlier Marxist theory were categorically denied. The State was not to wither away, law was not to begin disappearing. On the contrary, the allegedly successful completion of the foundations of stable socialist society was to permit the unflowering of a truly socialist State and a truly socialist law as an intimate part of Soviet society.

Formally, the theoretical backing for this radical change in theory lay in the doctrine of 'socialism in one country'. Soviet theoreticians have at no stage denied, and do not deny even now, that State and law will ultimately wither away.[1] But from 1936 onward, the building of socialism in one country was taken to make the earlier confidence in the speedy withering away of the State inapplicable. Surrounded by a hostile capitalist world, the theory ran, Soviet society needed the protection of a strong State, and such a State inevitably needed law.

The theory itself was far from consistent, of course. Even if one granted—and many Marxists did not—the possibility of a Marxist theory of socialism in one country, the compulsive powers of a State based purely on the threat of a surrounding capitalist world should be confined to matters connected with that threat and to its occasional intrusions, through spies or saboteurs, into Soviet society. It does not lay the foundations for a coercive socialist law of marriage, family and civil relations, non-political crime and so on. Yet it was precisely in these fields that a mounting change was making itself most strongly felt. The cause was not primarily theoretical but practical. By 1934 and 1935, a major crisis in the social relations of Soviet life was becoming more and more evident. Soviet leaders were becoming increasingly conscious of the failure of the more radical Marxist theory to command the support of the common people or to cope with such widespread problems as juvenile delinquency and the instability of Soviet family life. They responded with a wholesale abandonment of radicalism.

[1] Vyshinsky, laying the foundations of the new Soviet view in his *Law of the Soviet State* (1938) states specifically that law and the State will disappear, but only 'after the victory of Communism in the whole world' (p. 52). Shishkin, op. cit., p. 38, takes the same view in 1955.

'Free love' was denounced,[1] abortion controlled, patriotism verging on Russian chauvinism strongly encouraged. There were major concessions to religion. 'Soviet legality' was suddenly proclaimed a fundamental basis of Soviet social life. What Soviet leaders had realised—but could never say—was that the new economic basis of Soviet life in no way dissolved the traditional non-economic conflicts of social and family life. Not Plan, but Law, was needed to deal with these.

The first task was to sweep away the theories of Pashukanis and Stuchka, with their emphasis that law, in treating men as abstracted individuals, was necessarily capitalist in nature. Both men were denounced as wreckers and traitors, seeking to sabotage Soviet socialist development. The reaction was begun by P. Yudin's article *Socialism and Law*,[2] which rather unably re-emphasised the normative functions of law as a class weapon, even in the socialist State.[3] It was consummated with a far more vicious but equally unable attack by the then Procurator of the U.S.S.R., A. Y. Vyshinsky, in his *The Law of the Soviet State*.

Ironically, Vyshinsky begins with a typical lack of theoretical farsightedness to launch an attack which is quite sound but the implication of which is to destroy the whole foundations of Marxist theory in so far as they depend on economic reductionism. Law, he insists, cannot be reduced to economics. 'Stuchka's fundamental perversion in this question is that he reduced Soviet civil law to the sphere of production and barter. What then is to be done with the part of law which regulates marriage and family relationships? Or must these likewise be regulated from the view-point of "socialist planning"? Clearly civil

---

[1] Great emphasis has been placed ever since on denouncing 'free love' as a form of social and personal irresponsibility. (See, e.g., Sharia, op. cit., p. 99, Shishkin, op. cit., pp. 260-2, Shishkin, *Iz istorii eticheskikh uchenii* (*From the History of Ethical Doctrines*), pp. 235-8, 320-8.) The critics have little difficulty in showing that love does not become free by constantly feeding on new objects; but their emphasis on 'discipline' in love certainly suggests an implicit awareness and fear that sexual protest supports and encourages other forms of protest. There is indeed much evidence that freedom in love is a necessary, though not a sufficient condition, of all other freedoms.

[2] A full English translation of the article (which originally appeared in *Bolshevik*, No. 17 of September 1, 1937) may be found in the collection by Hazard *et al.*, *Soviet Legal Philosophy*, pp. 281-301.

[3] Pashukanis, of course, had largely obscured Marx's notion of law as a normative weapon in the class struggle, and treated it instead in a positive, rather passive, fashion as reflecting the structure of the commodities-producing society as a whole.

law embraces a sphere of relationship broader than those of barter only (as Pashukanis asserts) or even those of production and barter only (Stuchka).'[1] 'Reducing law to economics, as Stuchka did, asserting that law coincides with the relations of production, these gentlemen slid into the bog of economic materialism.' 'Stuchka and his followers liquidated law as a specific social category, drowned law in economics, deprived it of its active, creative role.'[2]

Vyshinsky wants to save law as a specific social category. But while his hard-headed realism—spurred on, no doubt, by political calculation—enables him to see the obvious difficulties of economic reductionism, he cannot throw enough of it overboard to give an account of this category himself. Economics and politics, he has to concede, determine law. But the effect, he argues, is not the same as the cause. Law has a specific nature of its own, in socialist society at least.

What, then, is the specific nature of law? Here Marxism drives Vyshinsky into nothing but contradictions. 'Law,' he says boldly, 'is the totality (a) of the rules of conduct, expressing the will of the dominant class and established in legal order, and (b) of customs and rules of community life sanctioned by State authority—their application being guaranteed by the compulsive force of the State in order to guard, secure and develop social relationships and social orders advantageous and agreeable to the dominant class.'[3] In other words, law again is the expression of class interest, and though Vyshinsky avoids characterising class interests as economic, it is clear that what is specifically legal has still not appeared.

What is specifically legal never does appear in Vyshinsky's work. He does, with the naiveté of Communist utopianism, assert that in Soviet society the will of the toilers has become the will of the whole people. The single general guiding principle for all Soviet law in all its branches is socialism.[4]

For all his heroic criticism of reductionism, then, Vyshinsky has

---

[1] *The Law of the Soviet State*, p. 54.

[2] Quoted by Berman, op. cit., p. 46. What especially worried Vyshinsky, as Berman's quotations show, is the undermining of the absolute authoritativeness of law by reducing it to economics or politics. 'Reducing law to politics,' Vyshinsky writes indignantly about the Soviet 'wreckers' of the past, 'these gentlemen depersonalised law as the totality of legal rules, undermining their stability and their authoritativeness, introducing the false concept that in a socialist State the application of a statute is determined not by the force and authority of Soviet law, but by political considerations.'

[3] Vyshinsky, op. cit., p. 50.   [4] Loc. cit., p. 77.

nothing positive to offer. Uneasily conscious of the fact that actual Soviet law—especially in what Vyshinsky takes to be the obviously legal spheres of family and social relationships—is surprisingly like bourgeois law in content, he yet wants to deny that there are universal legal categories or forms underlying all legal systems. Bourgeois law, to Vyshinsky, is indeed simply an expression of economic interests, only socialist law is truly legal law. Why? Not because it has certain specifically legal qualities lacking in bourgeois law, but because it has come to express the will of the entire people. In which case, as Marx and earlier Marxists saw, there should simply be no need for law.[1]

The conflict between the theories of Pashukanis and those of Vyshinsky begins as a conflict of emphasis. Pashukanis leans heavily on the anti-authoritarian strain in Marx's work. He takes as his starting-point Marx's insistence that law expresses man's alienation from other men and society—in law, these confront him as hostile forces. Conditions of freedom, therefore, will make law impossible. Vyshinsky claims to agree with this. In conditions of true freedom, the social and the individual interest will be finally merged; law *will* disappear. But Pashukanis himself had conceded that in the transitional stage the proletariat, having captured control of society, must still use law and force in suppressing its class enemies. This, we have seen, is the conception of socialist law with which Vyshinsky begins. He, too, leans heavily on certain ideas in Marx's work: the conception of the dictatorship of the proletariat, from which the path to Communism must commence,[2] and Marx's treatment of law and political power

---

[1] I have drawn heavily in the preceding pages on Section III of Alice Ehr-Soon Tay and Eugene Kamenka: 'Karl Marx's Analysis of Law', loc. cit., pp. 30–8.

[2] Marx and Engels proclaim this clearly at the end of Section II of the *Communist Manifesto* (M I, 6, 545–6), where the proletarian seizure of state power is treated as the inauguration of a dictatorship which will make despotic inroads into the old order until it sweeps away by force the old conditions of production and with them the conditions of class antagonism. Then shall arise 'an association in which the free development of each is the condition for the free development of all'. In other words, the proletariat must constitute itself as a ruling class and exercise despotic political power in its class interest before it can destroy all classes, including itself, and its own supremacy. In Marx's three articles on 'The Class Struggles in France' (1850) this conception is still strong, though soon to be combined with the 'permanent revolution' that we find in 'The Eighteenth Brumaire of Louis Bonaparte' (1852). Marx's references to the dictatorship of the proletariat certainly do not suggest that he saw the transitional period as a lengthy one which would produce a full-blown social form of its own. A certain

generally as 'merely the organised power of one class for oppressing another' (*The Communist Manifesto*, M I, 6, 5 46). The initial distinction between Pashukanis and Vyshinsky thus seems to be merely that one emphasises the imminence of true freedom under Communism while the other emphasises the necessity of coercive law in the transitional period of the dictatorship of the proletariat, in which class distinctions and their consequences have not yet entirely disappeared from social life.

Such differences in emphasis need not, on the face of it, be incompatible. Marx does emphasise in several works that there is a certain lag between developments in the economic structure of society and resultant changes in the political and ideological superstructure. His view seems to be that the abolition of property does not immediately eliminate the psychological attitudes born of property: these disappear slowly in the ensuing generations which have lost even the memories of class society. Where Vyshinsky would have appeared to Pashukanis and earlier Communists to be going well beyond what can be justified from Marx is in his emphasis that Soviet law as a normative weapon still has 'a creative role' to play and in his insistence that there are social spheres to be regulated from points of view other than that of socialist planning. Here, then, once more was the superstructure playing an active and not merely passive role.

We have seen already that Marx himself was far from taking seriously his own doctrine of 'reflection' and always treating factors in the superstructure as purely passive. Might, he recognised, could become an economic force; and his whole conception of the proletariat transforming production *through the exercise of despotic political power* rests on this non-reductionist assumption. Marx himself attempted to

---

tension between the centralising motive in his thought (which came to the fore again in his 'Critique of the Gotha Programme' in 1875) and his concern with the free society appears in his *The Civil War in France* (1871). The impression which the anarcho-federalist ideas of the Paris Commune, inspired by Proudhon, made on him is quite evident. 'The new Commune . . . breaks the modern State power . . . The Communal Constitution would have restored to the social body all the forces hitherto absorbed by the State parasite feeding upon, and clogging the free movement of, society. By this one act it would have initiated the regeneration of France.' (CWF 42.) After Marx's death Engels showed a decided tendency to minimise the earlier emphasis on violent revolution and to see Communism coming through parliamentary action. (Cf. his introduction to the new German edition of 'The Class Struggles in France' in 1895.) For Engels' earlier view of the dictatorship of the proletariat see his letter to Bebel of March 18–28, 1875 (SC 336–7).

avoid any open conflict in his theory by treating the proletariat's political action as itself economically determined. Vyshinsky and his followers have wanted to go further than this, to invest socialist law with all the majesty of conscious rationality, to see freedom enshrined *within* the very dependence proclaimed by (their) law. This required more than a grudging admission of a certain amount of interaction between the superstructure and the base. It required a new and totally un-Marxist conception of ideologies and legal and political institutions as vital, creative and conscious forces moulding society; it required the administrator's delusion that policies determine society. Stalin, indeed, came close to it:

The superstructure is born of the base, but this does not at all mean that it only reflects the base, that it is passive, neutral, that it is indifferent to the fate of its base, to the future of classes, to the character of the [social] structure. On the contrary, having come into the world, it becomes a mighty active force, actively helping its base to develop and grow stronger, taking all measures to help the new order to ruin and liquidate, the old economic base and the old classes.[1]

Marx's economic reductionism, as we have seen, closed off the positive study of ethics just as Marx himself was beginning to lay foundations on which it might be developed. To the revolutionary socialist this was not so obvious while his primary struggle was against social slavery in the form of political bondage or utter economic dependence. Marx's reductionism, with all its incoherencies, had enabled Marx to emphasise the disparity between 'formal' and actual justice in the societies of class domination, to show the emptiness of 'rights to do' that were not accompanied by the actual capacity to do. In some societies, such as Victorian England, which occupied a favourable position in the world economy of their day, in which the standard of living was rising rapidly and where the pressure of competition was not particularly severe, the Marxist analysis made no great ethical or political impact. It was natural for leaders of all sections of the community to confuse the benefits of a period of increasing prosperity with the benefits that might accrue from morality. In nineteenth-century Russia there was no such rapid rise in prosperity, and no corresponding faith in the efficacy of conventional moral principles, orderly political negotiation and legal 'rights'. 'Legal rights

[1] *Marksizm i voprosy yazykoznaniia* (*Marxism and Questions of Linguistics*), 1950, pp. 4–5.

have no value for a man unless he possesses the material means to benefit by them,' wrote the Russian revolutionary N. G. Chernyshevskii at the time that Marx was writing *Das Kapital*.[1] 'Man is not an abstract legal person, but a living creature . . . A man who is dependent for his material means of existence cannot be an independent human being in fact, even though his independence is proclaimed by the letter of the law.' Subsequent Marxists in Russia had little difficulty in taking up this thread in both Chernyshevskii and Marx and making it,— together with the materialist rejection of supra-empirical norms—their main criticism of the 'class' moralities of the past. The insistence that there is no common or social interest above other interests in the class society, the rejection of unhistorical 'norms' and of the abstract 'individual' and the exposure of contradictions between formal 'rights' and actual social situations is the one steady and reasonably respectable theme running through Marxist and Soviet ethical writing.

In the pre-Revolutionary period and in the early days of the Revolution there was also considerable emphasis on Communist morality as the morality of freedom—but it came more from intellectuals captivated by the vision of a new society than from the professional and disciplined revolutionaries whom Lenin saw as the true bearers of Communism. Thus both P. B. Struve and N. A. Berdyaev, during their brief Marxian period in the last decade of the nineteenth century, emphasised the Kantian dictum that the individual person must always be treated as an end and never as a means, while rejecting Kant's ethical formalism and his concern with 'abstract obligation'. Communism, to them, as to Marx in his more individualist moments, was the universal kingdom of ends. By 1903, when both Struve and Berdyaev had turned from Marxism, four other young Russian Marxists were proclaiming Communism as the true dawn of the individual. They were A. V. Lunacharsky (1875–1933), later to become People's Commissar for Culture under Lenin; Stanislav Volsky (pseudonym of A. V. Sokolov, 1880–1936?); A. A. Bogdanov (pseudonym of A. A. Malinovsky, 1873–1928); and V. A. Bazarov (pseudonym of V. A. Rudnev, 1874–1936?). Lunacharsky and Volsky, as G. L. Kline points out,[2] drew heavily on the work and ideals of Nietzsche,

[1] *Sochineniia (Works)*, vol. IV, p. 740. Marx said later that Chernyshevskii's writings 'brought true honour' to Russia (ME *Soch.*, XIII, i, 354).

[2] 'Changing attitudes Toward the Individual', in C. E. Black (ed): *The Transformation of Russian Society*, pp. 606–25, at pp. 618–23. I have relied on a number of Dr. Kline's interesting citations from works not easy to obtain in the West.

explicitly rejecting any conception of moral obligation and upholding the individual as a free creator of values and ideals. Moral indoctrination, Lunacharsky writes,[1] can generate nothing but slaves. The new social order will emancipate man completely, establish the individual's right to be guided in his life solely by his own desires. Admittedly, social and individual interests may clash; but the species has no existence apart from its individual members. 'What is a living powerful species if not an aggregate of living, powerful individuals?' In 'the splendid future', under the new social order, the interests of the individuals and those of society will be in complete harmony. Volsky takes the same line, hardly less passionately but somewhat more coherently. Obligatory norms will disappear with the defeat of capitalism. The bourgeoisie had freed the individual in the hour of revolution only to enslave him in the hour of triumph; the proletariat will command the individual in the hour of revolution only to free him in the hour of triumph. 'The class sees in itself something to be eliminated, the individual something to be asserted.'[2]

Bogdanov and Bazarov are also concerned to free the individual from coercive norms, but they do not see the socialist collective as an aggregate of powerful, self-driven individuals. The individual, rather, will become fused into the collective—as 'in ecstatic moments . . . when it seems to us that our tiny being disappears, is fused with the infinite.'[3] Individualism, both Bogdanov and Bazarov insist, was a liberating movement in its conflict with authoritarianism, but becomes reactionary in its struggle against the socialist future (Kline, pp. 621, 622). In the new society, emphasis will fall upon *sobornost* (organic togetherness), upon 'objective, immediately social creativity, in which the very notion of 'the individual' and his interests will be extinguished.'[4]

The upholding of individualism, we have suggested above, is not a satisfactory answer to Marxism: there is some truth in Bazarov's suggestion that a free society will not be 'walled off into the miserable little cells of self-sufficient individualities.' The intimacy of lovers, he

[1] *Osnovy positivnoi estetiki* (*Foundations of a Positive Aesthetic*) in *Ocherki realisticheskogo mirovozzreniia* (*Outlines of a Realist Weltanschauung*), St. Petersburg, 1905, cited by Kline, loc. cit., p. 619.

[2] *Filosofiia borby: opyt postroeniia etiki marksizma* (*The Philosophy of Struggle: An Attempt at Building a Marxist Ethic*), Moscow, 1909; Kline, p. 620.

[3] *Tseli i normy zhizni* (*The Goals and Norms of Life*), written in 1905, and republished in *Novyi mir* (1920), p. 64; cf. Kline, p. 621.

[4] Cited by Kline, pp. 622–3.

writes, gives only 'a faint hint of that fusion of all human souls which will be the inevitable result of the Communist order.'[1] Similarly, when Bogdanov insists[2] that Goethe did not produce *Faust* or Darwin the theory of evolution, but that both men put the finishing touches to a collective effort, there is more truth in this than Kline, say, is willing to stress. Bogdanov has perceived, as Bazarov also perceived, something of the mutually supporting character of artistic creation, love and enquiry, the way in which they can 'transcend' the individual and appropriate freely materials furnished by others. Recognising this however, does not require us to minimise the role that any particular person—Goethe or Darwin—might play in shaping the finished product of theory, whereas Bogdanov and Bazarov do patently wish to minimise this role. The new society, Bazarov writes, will favour not 'artists of disorderly individual searching, but artists in schools which move by plan toward their goal.'[3] Here we have more than the correct recognition that free activities are mutually co-operative activities. Here we have the reimposition of servility, the elevation of goals and plans over the spontaneous workings of the free and creative life.

When Bogdanov and Bazarov turn to attack not Kant's abstract will but his elevation of man as an *end*, and themselves substitute other ends, the servile character of their doctrine is finally confirmed. 'The free man not only regards his neighbour as a means; he demands that his neighbour should see in him only a means . . . for the neighbour's own ends.'[4] 'The recognition of the 'individual person' as an absolute principle has always been, and will always be, alien to the proletariat.'[5] By 1920, the point of all this had become painfully evident. Leon Trotsky, in his *Terrorizm i kommunizm* (p. 61), repudiates scornfully the 'Kantian-clerical, vegetarian-Quaker chatter about the "sanctity of human life".' The doctrine that individuals are ends in themselves is a metaphysical, bourgeois doctrine; the proletarian and the revolutionary know that where necessary (for the Revolution) the individual is and should be treated only as a means. The prominent party theorist

[1] *Na dva fronta (Toward Two Fronts)*, St. Petersburg, 1910, p. 140; Kline, p. 623.

[2] *Padenie velikogo fetishizma (The Fall of the Great Fetishism)*, Moscow, 1910, p. 46; Kline, p. 623.

[3] Op. cit., p. 164; Kline, p. 623.

[4] Bazarov: '*Avtoritarnaia metafizika i avtonomnaia lichnost*' ('Authoritarian Metaphysics and the Autonomous Personality'), in *Ocherki realisticheskogo mirovozzreniia*, p. 271; Kline, p. 623.

[5] Bazarov: *Na dva fronta*, p. 141; ibid.

A. B. Zalkind put the position bluntly five years later: 'For the proletariat, human life does not have a metaphysical, self-sufficient value. The proletariat recognises only the interests of the . . . revolution.'[1]

The struggle between individualists and collectivists was resolved emphatically by the régime that followed the October Revolution. Lunacharsky's period of grace was short-lived; the poet Blok died and the poet Yesenin committed suicide; the primacy of the proletarian revolution, of the party, of collective discipline and individual subordination and obedience were established with increasing firmness. Ethical speculation was discouraged; intellectuals were treated with suspicion as 'individualists' and possible dissenters. The principle of collective criminal responsibility was used to crush the peasantry and the principle of guilt by class-origin or kinship was used to crush the *intelligentsia*. Everything, it is true, was done in the name of freedom, seen as a goal soon to be achieved; but the immediate content of moral conceptions was the primacy of the victory of Communism and of the rules of the Party. Then came the period of the Stalinist dictatorship and of the 'great purges' and ethical theory reached its nadir.

The change in ethical theory, as in law, came with the new Stalin Constitution in 1936. The new concern was with social stability, with reinforcing the family, the love of country and the security of 'ordinary life'. Moral radicalism, which had failed to capture the masses, was largely abandoned. The exigencies of war produced heavy emphasis on cònventional moral slogans and normative exhortation; they also led to increased stress on 'socialist humanism', the respect for man which 'progressives' had displayed in all ages and shared in all countries even today in their struggle against the 'fascist beasts'. Forthright attacks on the importance of the individual disappeared from Soviet writing. Communism means the 'true flowering of the individual', but such flowering 'is only possible on the basis of the leading role of social interest.''[2]

The vital and creative role of Soviet law had been stressed by Vyshinsky—for patently political reasons—in 1938. To ascribe a vital

---

[1] *Revoliutsiia i molodezh*, (*Youth and the Revolution*), p. 54; Kline, p. 624.

[2] A. I. Zis, *O kommunisticheskoi morali* (*Concerning Communist Morality*), 1948, p. 30. Cf. Shishkin, *Osnovy kommunisticheskoi morali*, pp. 144f and 257f, where he stresses the priority of the social interest and collectivism over individual interests, but balances this by devoting an entire section (p. 230f) to socialist 'respect and care for man'.

and creative role to Soviet morality would have been to depart even more dangerously from the Marxian slogan that 'social being determines social consciousness' and that morality only reflects the material life of man. Then, with Stalin's *Marxism and Questions of Linguistics* (1950), the supreme authority himself opened the way for treating the superstructure, including morality, as a vital and active force on the path to Communism. Official encouragement was given to the creation and propagation of the theory and norms of Communist morality. In 1951, a conference of Soviet and Czech philosophers agreed that the teaching of Marxist ethics was inadequate and confused, that it was not set out in logical terms and that it neglected moral theory before Hobbes: a specialist course, such as M. I. Lifanov had outlined in *Voprosy Filosofii* (no. 2, 1951), was badly needed. In the same year, Sharia published his *Concerning Some Questions of Morality*, in which the active, creative role of consciousness was stressed even more strongly than Stalin had stressed it:

Marxism-Leninism teaches that not only the building of the new Communist economy, but also the formation of the new Communist consciousness of man is not self-propelled, not a process dictated by fate, but follows from the many-sided, completely devoted educational work of the Bolshevik Party and the Soviet administration.

(Introduction, p. 3.)

Sharia, in his emphasis on conscious decision and limited free will, had perhaps gone somewhat further than Soviet authorities were willing to countenance; he has written nothing on ethics since. But the emphasis on moral theory and propaganda continued. Shishkin, now the doyen of Soviet moral philosophers, published his *Foundations of Communist Morality* in 1955 and the first reasonably serious work on the history of ethical theory for many years, *From the History of Ethical Doctrines*, in 1959. At the same time, a conference of moral philosophers and party, industrial, educational and Komsomol leaders met in Leningrad under the auspices of the Soviet Academy of Sciences and of the Ministry of Higher and Specialised Secondary Education to discuss the role of ethics in Soviet life. It ended by formulating a draft syllabus for ethical teaching in higher educational institutions and publishing the papers presented before it.[1] All of them stressed the profoundly ethical nature of Communism and the need for the most intensive moral education to overcome the vestiges of capitalism and

[1] *Voprosy marksistko-leninskoi etiki* (*Questions of Marxist-Leninist Ethics*), Moscow, 1960.

of anti-moral and amoral conceptions in human consciousness. N. S. Khrushchev, in his report to the XXIst Congress of the Communist Party of the Soviet Union, had underlined the importance of moral education:

We must develop among Soviet people Communist morality, at the foundation of which lie loyalty to Communism and uncompromising enmity to its foes, the consciousness of social duty, active participation in labour, the voluntary observation of the fundamental rules of human communal life, comradely mutual help, honesty and truthfulness, and intolerance of the disturbers of the social order.[1]

To these excellent sentiments the Soviet philosophers and educational leaders assembled found little to add.

Soviet moral philosophers, then, have come down heavily on the conception we saw Marx and Engels develop in the *German Ideology:* the conception that morality is concerned with *social interest.*[2] The morality of the new world is thus full of the abstract moral concepts of the old: duty to society, care for fellow-men, upholding of the social order, etc. To establish a difference, Soviet philosophers rely on the economic interpretation of history. The abolition of private property means that the social interest has truly been established, while in the capitalist society of private property and class distinctions it remains an illusion or a hypocritical cloak for the interests of the ruling class. Even in the period of the proletarian dictatorship, when morality still represents a class interest, morality loses completely its hypocritical character: the proletariat, the overwhelming majority of mankind, needs no hypocrisy to cloak its interests, which are the interests of the vast majority of mankind. But its morality, before the Revolution and after, is a mighty force, organising and fusing the masses, helping to destroy the old order and lay the foundations for the new.[3] Ever-increasingly, Soviet leaders emphasise the power of ideology, of moral exhortation and moral education.

The abandonment of ethical radicalism, of contempt for conventional moral slogans and of the insistence that all moralities passively

[1] *Materialy vneocherednogo XXI s'ezda KPSS* (*Materials of the Extraordinary XXIst Congress of the C.P.S.U.*), p. 46.

[2] 'The relationship of individual and society, the relationship between personal and social interests—this is the *chief* content of morality' (Sharia, op. cit., p. 23, his italics).

[3] *Istoriia VKP(b). Kratkii kurs.* (*History of the C.P.S.U. (Bolsheviks). A Short Course*), p. 125; Shishkin: *Osnovy* . . . pp. 13–14.

reflect the economic conditions that give them birth, has finally led to the extension of the 'Popular Front' ideology to the field of moral philosophy. Soviet philosophers in recent years not only insist—following Engels in Chapter IX of *Anti-Dühring*—that there has been continuous progress in morality, but now emphasise that there are certain basic moral conceptions applicable in all ages and that the 'progressive' thinkers of all times have gone beyond the conditions of their time to the morality of the future. Lenin, in *The State and Revolution* (HM 759), speaks of the 'elementary rules of social life' which have been taught in school books for generations and which Communists will make into a social habit; Krushchev, as we have just seen, echoed the phrase in his address to the XXIst Congress, where he called for the 'voluntary observance of the fundamental rules of human communal life'. To a Soviet philosopher, these are eminent and 'safe' authorities, even if Engels (and Marx) were quite unequivocal in insisting that any moral principles that had appeared 'eternal' did so only because they expressed those forms of dependence common to all past societies. At the same time, a new generation of specialists in the Soviet Union tends naturally to become increasingly aware of the specific problems and characters of a specialist's field and to demand for it a certain intellectual independence. Even so, only one Soviet philosopher—as far as I know—has drawn the full logical implications of the Lenin-Khruschev position. V. P. Tugarinov, of Leningrad University, has been arguing since 1958 that in the various sciences we will find a part determined by the categories of historical materialism, but also a part based on the special categories of the science concerned—categories which are applicable at all stages of historical development. Thus in ethics, he argues in his *O tsennostiakh zhizni i kultury* (*Concerning The Values of Life and Culture*), there are 'moments' expressing what is common to all humanity and 'moments' expressing class interest. Tugarinov, of course, does not simply divide ethics into eternal truths and disguised class interest; he portrays the relationship as an intricate one, insists that abstract judgments expressing universal ethical notions become subservient to class interest in the manner of their application to concrete situations, and generally holds that 'moments' of a universal kind are stronger in aesthetics than ethics. (Op. cit., pp. 23–4.)

Even Tugarinov, however, promising as his position might appear, is prevented from making any genuine contribution to ethical theory by his uncritical acceptance of moral rules as normative rules and of ethical judgments as tied to—unexamined—'interests'. Precisely because no Soviet philosopher has either questioned or even seriously examined this identification of ethics with interests, Soviet philosophy has consistently substituted evasion and conformism for any genuine tackling of the problems of ethical theory. Working with a doctrine of interests, they have been in an impossible position. Like the legal writers, Soviet moral philosophers have faced the basic difficulty that the need for moral or legal obligation can only be explained if individual and social interest do not truly coincide, while the difference between Communist morality and other moralities can only be explained by saying that under Communism individual and social interest do coincide. Sharia, indeed, tries to argue that individual and social interest in Communist society harmonise without being identical: If they were identical, he concedes, there would be no moral 'alternatives' and therefore no field for morality (p. 70). Morality hence has to be based on the combination of two criteria:

True moral evaluation cannot take place on the basis of the purely objective criterion of the usefulness of an action for the development of society, neither can it take place on the basis of the purely subjective criterion of personal pleasure—only the bringing together of both these criteria gives us the underlying morality of action. Priority always belongs to the objective content of behaviour. This Marxist thesis refutes both the *a priorism* of moral norms and creeping empiricism, i.e., the actual denial of moral principles altogether. *In this Marxist thesis the dialectical-materialist principle of the unity of subject and object finds its concretisation in the field of morality.*
(P. 62, Sharia's italics.)

The reference to dialectical materialism, of course, is sheer mystification. Sharia's promulgation of two criteria does nothing to solve the problem—if this is a genuine problem—of harmonising individual and social interest: it merely restates that problem. Neither does any other Soviet ethical writer solve or seriously tackle this problem; the others gloss it over more skilfully—and more dishonestly.

What does appear from Sharia's position, from our earlier quotations from Shishkin, from the papers at the Leningrad conference and from every recent Soviet pronouncement on ethics is the pervasive treatment of morality as a *normative* system, concerned with establishing principles and guiding behaviour. And this, as Marx often saw, cannot be anything more than the attempt to achieve the harmony of discord and harmony, to bind evil with chains that are themselves evil and that create nothing but further evil and further instability. The morality of freedom erects no principles and proclaims no obligations; it finds itself in the struggle with evils and not in their suppression.

Of recent ethical writers in the Soviet Union, Sharia certainly makes the most serious attempts to see the discipline which he places at the foundation of moral conduct as conscious, self-imposed discipline. But in his work, too, the discipline is not the free and coherent working of an activity; it is the set of requirements imposed by an external need:

In socialist society every right of the citizen which is real, and not formal, is linked with a corresponding duty. The right to work is linked with every-one's duty to work . . .

The supporters of 'free love' strove to support their anti-moral 'theory' by saying that since in bourgeois society a woman's freedom in expressing her feelings is paralysed by her lack of economic rights, therefore in socialist society she must be free of every limitation. In saying this, the nihilists in the field of morality failed to see that socialism is not the weakening of the social bonds between people, but on the contrary, the strengthening of these bonds, and in so far as love is not only an emotional-psychological event, but necessarily includes in itself social relationships, it cannot be anarchic, but must subordinate itself to the developing socialist relationships. In other words, Marxism-Leninism, repudiating the compulsive discipline (it matters not whether the compulsion be legal or economic) of the society of exploiters, upheld by the stick in feudal society and by hunger in capitalist society, sets against this compulsive discipline conscious discipline, i.e., the conscious striving toward the upbuilding of Communist society.

(Pp. 99–100.)

The pedestrian character of Soviet ethics, its tedious preaching of ends and duties, emerges even more clearly in Shishkin's *Osnovy*, where he sets out the 'principles and norms of Communist morality'. His section heads give an adequate idea of the contents:

1. The victory of socialism in the U.S.S.R. and the new conditions under which Communist morality is formed.

2. Collectivism as a principle of Communist morality:
   (a) The superiority of collectivism over bourgeois individualism
   (b) The social interest—the main interest of Soviet man
   (c) The concept of duty, honour and conscience in Communist ethics
   (d) Labour—a duty and matter of honour

3. Patriotism and internationalism:
   (a) Attitude to the homeland as a moral problem
   (b) Devotion to the homeland and to the international brotherhood of toilers—the main demand of Communist morality

4. Socialist humanism:
   (a) Socialist humanism—the highest type of humanism
   (b) Respect for the worth of man and care of man
   (c) Hatred for enemies and vigilance—an inescapable feature of socialist humanism

5. The moral foundations of friendship, marriage and family:
   (a) Society and personal life
   (b) Friendship
   (c) Marriage and family

6. The moral qualities and character traits of the fighter for Communism

In all this, of course, there is not even a hint of the fundamental problems and difficulties of normative morality: no discussion of the logical and empirical basis of 'obligation', no consideration fo the problems of moral 'justification', no hint of the necessary vagueness of normative principles. The true basis of moral 'obligation' in Communist society emerges clearly enough when Shiskin heads the seventh and final section of his book: 'The Communist Party—the Mind, Honour and Conscience of Our Time.'

Conclusions

Ethics and the
Foundations of Marxism

MARX'S belief in the rational, free and completely co-operative society of the human spirit, we have seen, was the foundation and driving force of his intellectual and political development. The structure that followed was high and broad. As it grew it disturbed the foundations, but the basic thrust and design remained. The goal was the same. Man would pass from the realm of conflict and dependence into the realm of co-operation and freedom.

The concern with minimising conflict and maximising co-operation *in the abstract* is no stranger to moral and political theory, and never has been. It has not normally stemmed from the concern with freedom, however. Liberty, as Croce has said, lives 'a perilous and fighting life'; the concern with minimising conflict of any kind, with making the world safe for harmony, is more typical of the desires for security and sufficiency, of the motives concerned to establish domination and seek the shelter of submission. It is such movements, such concerns to escape from the conflicts and dangers of history, that moral and political philosophers have all too often been willing to serve. One of Marx's important contributions to ethics is his bringing out of the despotic conceptions, and the resultant incoherence, underlying their work. There is no harmony of discord with harmony, no way of binding man into freedom. There can be no coherent principles of moral or political obligation. The source of moral obligation, the legal and political sovereign, cannot be exalted above the conflicts and divisions of history. As long as movements and interests conflict, any attempt to bind this conflict cannot be anything more than an attempted domination of some of these movements and interests over the rest. If the community of interest proclaimed by the sovereign were real, there would be no point in such proclamation and no basis or need for the exercise of 'sovereignty'.

Marx is often accused of having minimised the interdependence of competing movements and interests in society—an interdependence from which, it is claimed, overriding moral and political principles can be elicited. A pluralist view of society—for which Marx helped to lay the foundations—would not have to treat interests as fixed and separate, though Marx's doctrine of class struggle itself came close to such treatment. The interrelation of movements and interests in a society will reveal affinities as well as conflicts; certain interests may be able to reach adjustments with other interests which will enable both parties to go forward vigorously and amicably. Even where interests seem totally opposed to each other, there will usually be certain boundaries beyond which the conflict cannot be pressed without destroying *both* the participants. This sense of the affinities between different movements, or of the boundaries to fruitful conflict, is called 'statesmanship'. But there is nothing in all this to show that there is a public interest 'higher' than special interests, or an interest common to all movements which they must satisfy first. The adjustment of interests is not something that precedes and determines the characters and aims of specific interests. On the contrary, it can only follow from them The legal and political structure of a society, its sanctioned rights and duties, represent partly the actual adjustment reached between interests and partly the mechanism arrived at for further adjustments. (No sharp line can be drawn between adjustment and mechanism, since the mechanism itself is reached by adjustment and may be changed by future adjustment.) As Marx saw there is no impartial adjustor standing outside all interests and all history. The adjustments and even the most basic mechanism of adjustment in a society will be formulated in the clash—in the conflicts and the alliances—of specific movements. Just as there is no finite number of movements in a society, just as there are no fixed, separate and unchanging interests, so there is no total adjustment, no overall plan, to which all movements and interests can be subordinated or through which they can be expressed. The belief in the possibility of an overall social plan requires the erroneous treatment of interests as atomic, as capable of being counted and moulded into a pattern. The belief in the possibility of 'rational principles' for adjustment requires the commercial notion that all interests can be reduced to a common currency. It requires the political theorist to elevate co-operation without considering *what* it is that co-operates. It requires him to ignore the positive characters of the movements he wants to control and the qualitative distinctions in the interests he wishes to reconcile. This is why his principles can never be concrete. This is why conflict and incoherency break out the moment we seek to 'apply' these principles to any specific social situation.

There may, of course, be certain social situations—such as war, or alien domination—when a wide range of movements within the society faces a common impediment or fears a common danger. It is in such situations that talk of the 'national interest' or 'the common good' gains its maximum degree of plausibility. But even here we find consistently that the concrete policies concealed in these phrases cannot command total support and have to resort to ambiguity, hypocrisy and physical suppression in order to maintain a semblance of social solidarity. In fact, the greater the claims that a common social interest exists, the more urgent the need to manufacture the evidence for social unity, the more vicious the repression of the inescapable protestors and dissidents. That such a common interest is not a true common interest is sufficiently indicated by this need for suppression and the stifling of criticism, by the *fetishism* invoked to protect the State, the army or the movement of national liberation. That what co-operation does take place is extrinsic and temporary is sufficiently indicated by the invariable disunity, by the struggle for power, that follows victory in war or the attainment of national 'independence'.

Neither is there anything in the interdependence of movements or social provinces to show that all the participants must have a common policy or a common end. It is true that one party in conflict could cause its own destruction as well as its opponent's by pressing its demands beyond a certain point. There is nothing in this to produce co-operation while the two competing parties do co-exist, and their co-existence is not a policy to be aimed at but a fact, often pleasing to neither. The point at which mutual destruction will result cannot be laid down by general and immutable principles: it will vary as concrete social situations and alignments vary. In any case, the frequent suggestion that moral and political principles are necessary to save society from chaos and self-destruction is quite false. Movements operate in concrete social situations and formulate policies within these situations; they do not as a general rule press their demands to the point of destroying themselves. The moral and political principles that arise in a society are not the barrier between blindly self-seeking movements and destruction. It is because movements already recognise their mutual dependence that they formulate social codes and political principles: codes and principles that nevertheless vary and conflict as movements vary and conflict, which seek working arrangements and limits to conflict but in no way presuppose that there is an ultimate working arrangement or a final limit.

The main point is that any specific interest in adjustment as such is not higher, but lower than specific interests. There are no 'rational' principles on which it can rest or base its supremacy. It does not precede specific interests, but follows them. It is in general not creative but parasitic. It is not above society, but part of it: it, too, is historical, socially determined and partial. Its notion that it controls society instead of being controlled by it is an illusion.

The illusion that policies, or moral and legal principles, are controlling factors in society is one to which the moral and political theorist is especially prone. The chief merit of Marx's economic or materialist interpretation of history, with all its confusions and difficulties, lies in its exposure of this illusion. Causally, policies will be factors in any given social situation and may affect the changes that take place in that situation. But all the evidence shows that they are not controlling factors in history: they do not precede and determine all historical development. Above all, they are not the policies of 'reason' or 'morality' or 'society'; they are the policies of specific, existing movements, the characters and social situation of which precede and determine their aims. Normative ethical and political theory, as Marx realised, has depended largely on obscuring this point: on treating ends, policies and principles as ends, policies and principles *in themselves*. Once we show that this is not so, that they are ends, policies and principles *of* specific and historical subjects, conflicting among themselves, the normative pretensions of much moral and political theory are fatally undermined. The vagueness and incoherence that break out in theories of moral and political obligation stand revealed as inescapable results of the illusion on which normative theories rest and not as the mere consequences of an individual theorist's incompetence. To this conclusion Marx has shown us the way.

Marx's exposure of normative conceptions was not marred by the crass inconsistencies of Engels. Whatever Marx's followers may have done, Marx did not proclaim historical evolution, or Marxist science, or the coming revolution, as normative criteria establishing new obligations and new principles for conduct. He was too able and coherent a thinker for that. Nevertheless, his exposure of normative ethics was not as thorough-going as it might have been; not as clear-sighted as it needs to be for the establishment of an ethical science.

Marx prided himself, already in his youth, that he did not confront 'the world' with doctrinaire principles of what 'ought to be'; he did no more than show it the end to which it was inevitably developing. The end Marx foresaw, we have argued, was not a mere utopia, based on nothing but metaphysical illusions. It had a genuine empirical content, an empirical content which ethical theory cannot ignore and on the basis of which a positive ethical science becomes possible. Marx's positive contribution to the working out of such an ethical science is not great. It rests on unsystematic flashes of insight, on an emotional character in which the morality of freedom and the ability to see qualitative distinctions and ways of living were strong. It does not rest on any reasoned working out of the distinctions that Marx was able to appreciate intuitively or of the cultural tradition in which he himself was an uncompromising participant. Marx perceived, in himself and in others, the characteristic ways in which goods work. He saw that evils were divisive and goods co-operative, that apparent harmony between evils always involved an element of resistance, always re-quired coercion on one side and submission on the other. He saw the connexion between freedom and the productive morality; he himself used scientific and artistic creation as the paradigm of free labour. He saw the incoherence and dependence enshrined in any morality that elevated ends and subordinated activities: he realised the different roles played by 'rules' in the morality of freedom and the morality of security and protection. The distinctions in the operation of movements, motives and ways of living with which ethical science begins are all displayed in his work. In his comments on religion and punishment, in his analysis of the social effects of capitalism, we find a depth of psycho-logical and historical insight impossible to the man who is not able to grasp the positive distinctions between freedom and slavery, between enterprise and servility, between the untrammelled morality of production and the fetishistic morality of security.

Why could Marx take this no further? Why could he not associate the distinctions he saw so clearly with distinctions in quality? Why could he not see the struggle for freedom as a concrete historical struggle between free movements and unfree movements, co-existing and competing at any one time? To recognise that goods and evils, free and unfree activities, co-exist is to recognise that neither are metaphysically higher, that a struggle which has gone on throughout history points to no ultimate end or resolution. Marx was committed to such an end, to such an ultimate resolution. It required him to treat freedom as the true and self-sufficient state of man, servility and dependence as temporary phenomena that did not stem from any positive human character or any permanent feature of social activity. In his early period he did so frankly by elevating the essential human spirit above the empirical and determined man. In his later period he concentrated on the instability and incoherence of evils, glossing over the concrete foundations and positive character of goods.

What made this evasion possible was Marx's idealist upbringing and his confused doctrine of freedom as self-determination. Self-determination as a philosophical concept enabled him to treat goods purely negatively, as that which occurs when external dependence and domination have been removed. Man's character, the nature of his activities and the social organisation in which he lives thus become entirely irrelevant, provided all external determination has been removed. What it is that now determines itself is left—and has to be left—entirely unclear. For self-determination, as we have seen, requires the ultimate removal of all distinctions, the paring away of all qualities, the assumption of an underlying but unspecific human substance into which everything is absorbed.

The belief that evil and the conflict of evils could be eradicated also required a reductionist doctrine—a single course from which all evils and all conflict sprang. That source, for the mature Marx, was private property.[1] In this, and in his allied definition of classes in terms of their relation to property, he proved himself thoroughly the intellectual child of the capitalism he criticised so unsparingly.

The most obvious failure of Marxism has lain in the incorrectness of Marx's predictions. In each case, this incorrectness has stemmed from his over-estimation of the importance of private property. He failed to see the gains which the working-class might make under capitalism because he saw the worker's divorce from property as a divorce from all enterprise, control or political power. He failed to

[1] Marx did see private property as following inescapably from the division of labour. But he cannot coherently distinguish the division of labour from the organisation of labour which will emerge under Communism except in terms of the ownership of tools which the former allegedly implies. Hence I take private property as fundamental in Marx's analysis.

recognise the emergence of centralised power in the State because he could not seriously conceive a political, non-property-owning institution gaining or keeping any significant power in a society he saw as dominated by property. He grossly underestimated the social importance of nationalism because he saw the conflict of the propertied and the propertyless as the only fundamental and significant conflict. His followers have been totally unable to give a plausible account of fascism, as they were incapable of appreciating its importance when it first emerged, for similar reasons.

The pattern which Marx saw in historical change was a pattern suggested almost entirely by the transition from the *Ancien Régime* to capitalist 'democracy'—above all, by the French Revolution. It simply did not, and would not, fit Asia. Admittedly, Marx did not see Asia as a disturbing factor in capitalist development because he visualised Asia being throughly penetrated by European capitalism, its institutions overthrown, its governments toppled, its social life radically commercialised. He saw this, indeed, as the precondition for freedom after 2,000 years of Oriental stagnation and despotism. But on what did the despotism rest? On private property, on which Marx saw all despotism resting? Climate and territorial conditions, Marx wrote in the *New York [Daily] Tribune* in 1853, made artificial irrigation by canals and waterworks the basis of Oriental agriculture. The construction and control of these vast waterways 'necessitated in the Orient, where civilisation was too low and the territorial extent too vast to call into life voluntary association, the interference of the centralising power of the government.' 'The key to the Oriental heaven,' Marx and Engels agreed in an interchange of correspondence in June 1853 (Marx, M III, 1, 477; Engels, ibid., 480), is 'the fact that there was no private ownership of land.' A penetrating observation, as Wittfogel has shown,[1] but an observation which entirely destroys the basis for Marx's belief that a society without private property must be a society of freedom. If the power of the Oriental State rested on its powers of direction and management, then another despotism can be built on the same power. Many people, Wittfogel among them, have seen Soviet society as precisely such a despotism.

The realities of Soviet life and the character of the Communist Party as a historical institution are not best brought out by examining the moral theory proclaimed by Marxism alone. But there can be little

[1] In his *Oriental Despotism*. See esp. chapters I-III and IX.

doubt that Marx's reductionism, his proclamation of an ultimate goal supported by history and his failure to emphasise positive distinctions in ways of living have done much to facilitate the Philistinism and the servility that characterise contemporary Marxism. The neglect of positive distinctions, the elevation of historical 'tasks' and 'ends', enabled the Communist Party to seize centralised power and exercise unprincipled tyranny in the name of a new metaphysical sovereign: history itself. It removed any barriers to opportunism, it facilitated the elevation of ends above forms of organisation and ways of life: it thus reduced all concrete institutions and activities to a subordinate status and a dependent existence. The concentration on the 'one thing needful' rested on the same utilitarianism and produced the same dependence and stagnation of enterprise as the capitalist emphasis on material reward. Together with the doctrine that all things are reflections of a fundamental conflict—a doctrine that proved almost fatal to science, speculation and art in Soviet society—it was a godsend to those concerned to stifle independence and creativity, to establish uniformity and total control.

There has recently been something of an advance in Soviet scientific and speculative thought. It is, indeed, one of the features of tyrannies that they are parasitic upon scientific, industrial and artistic movements basically incompatible with the fetishisms of political and intellectual domination. The tyranny requires science and production: in fostering these, it constantly runs the danger of fostering the scientific and the productive spirit as well. It is no accident that serious speculation and intellectual competence in the Soviet Union found their greatest theoretical barrier in crude economic reductionism, in the doctrine of 'reflections'. Intellectual pressure from men having a certain competence in specific intellectual fields certainly did much to lead to the collapse of thorough-going reductionism. But it is one of the ironies of contemporary Marxism that it has been outweighed by the crude voluntarism which the abandonment of the doctrine has also made possible. The stabilisation of Soviet tyranny has led to a widening of the area of inessential liberties: it has also led to increasing reliance on fetishism, on moral exhortation and moral sanction. It is fast leading to the normative illusion that policy can control society and solve the conflicts of international relations. In all this, there is no significant trace of the freedom and spontaneous co-operation envisaged by Marx. Capitalism, as Marx saw, split man into two: in liberating him as a political citizen it also liberated the avarice and commercialism that could reduce man to dependence. But it did liberate him as a political citizen: it increased the possibilities for movements and institutions to function independently in the social struggle, it made possible organisation and, above all, publicity. The struggle with evils is one in which goods are strengthened as frequently as they are destroyed; in a society in which there was no such struggle there would be no goods. In fact, the struggle continues in all societies, in the societies of Communism and of past Oriental despotisms as it continues under capitalism. But in so far as Marx is right in distinguishing between the alienation of man under capitalism and the enslavement of the whole man in Oriental despotism and feudalism, the Communist society of to day and of the foreseeable future stands with the latter.

Bibliography of Works Cited

A. TEXTS BY MARX AND ENGELS

Marx-Engels Gesamtausgabe, ed. Marx-Engels Institute, Moscow; Frankfurt a.M., 1927f., Section I, vols. 1–i, 1–ii, and 2–7, Section III, vols. 1–4.

Marx-Engels: *Sochineniia*, Institute of Marxism-Leninism, Moscow, 1939f.

Marx-Engels: *Selected Works*, 2 vols.; Foreign Languages Publishing House, Moscow, 1951.

Marx-Engels: *Basic Writings on Politics and Philosophy*, ed. Lewis S. Feuer; Anchor Books, New York, 1959.

Marx-Engels: *Correspondence 1843–1895*, ed. Dona Torr; International Publishers, New York, 1936.

Marx-Engels: *The Holy Family, Or Critique of Critical Critique*, trans. R. Dixon; Foreign Languages Publishing House, Moscow, 1956.

Marx-Engels: *The German Ideology*, Parts I & III, ed. R. Pascal; Lawrence & Wishart, London, 1939.

Marx-Engels: *On Britain*; Foreign Languages Publishing House, Moscow, 1953.

Marx: *The Poverty of Philosophy*; Foreign Languages Publishing House, Moscow, undated. [A superior translation, in my view, to that in the Kerr edition, Chicago, 1920.]

Marx: *Grundrisse der Kritik der politischen Oekonomie*; Dietz Verlag, Berlin, 1953.

Marx: *A Contribution to the Critique of Political Economy*, trans. I. N. Stone; Charles H. Kerr & Co., Chicago, 1918.

Marx: *Das Kapital, Kritik der politischen Oekonomie*, vols. I–III; Dietz Verlag, Berlin, 1957.

Marx: *Capital: A Critique of Political Economy*, vols. I–III, trans. Samuel Moore and Edward Aveling; Charles H. Kerr & Co., Chicago, 1912.

Marx: *The Civil War in France:* Lawrence & Wishart, London, 1941.

Engels: *Herr Eugen Dühring's Revolution in Science (Anti-Dühring)*, trans. E. Burns; International Publishers, New York, undated.

Engels: *The Origin of the Family, Private Property and the State*; Lawrence & Wishart, London, 1940.

B. WORKS RELATED TO MARX AND MARXISM

Acton, H. B.: *The Illusion of the Epoch*; Cohen & West, London, 1955.

Adams, H. P.: *Karl Marx in His Earlier Writings;* Allen & Unwin, London, 1940.

Barth, Hans: *Wahrheit und Ideologie*; Manesse Verlag, Zurich, 1945.

Berman, Harold J.: *Justice in Russia*; Harvard U.P., 1950.

Black, C. E. (ed.): *The Transformation of Russian Society*; Harvard U.P., 1960.

Burns, Emile: (ed.): *A Handbook of Marxism*; International Publishers, New York, 1935.

Carr, E. H.: *Karl Marx: A Study in Fanaticism*; J. M. Dent & Sons, London, 1934.

Eastman, Max: *Marx, Marxism and the Science of Revolution*; Allen & Unwin, London, 1926.

Hazard, John *et al.*: *Soviet Legal Philosophy*; Harvard U.P., 1951.

Hilferding, Rudolf: *Das Finanzkapital*; I. Brand, Wien, 1910.

Hook, Sidney: *Towards the Understanding of Karl Marx*; Victor Gollancz, London, 1933.

Kautsky, Karl: *Ethics and the Materialist Conception of History*; Charles H. Kerr & Co., Chicago, 1918.

Kelsen, Hans: *The Communist Theory of Law*; Stevens & Sons, London, 1955.

Lenin, V. I.: *Sochineniia* (4th Edition); Gospolitizdat, Moscow, 1948.

Lichtheim, George: *Marxism: An Historical and Critical Study*; Routledge & Kegan Paul, London, 1961.

Lukács, Georg: *Geschichte und Klassenbewusstsein*; Malik-Verlag Berlin, 1923.

Marcuse, Herbert: *Reason and Revolution: Hegel and the Rise of Social Theory*; Routledge & Kegan Paul, London, 1955.

Mehring, Franz: *Karl Marx: The Story of His life,* trans. Edward Fitzgerald; Allen & Unwin, London, 1948.

Nicolaievsky, Boris and Mänchen-Helfen, Otto: *Karl Marx, Man and Fighter,* trans. Gwenda David and Eric Mosbacher, Methuen & Co., London, undated.

Popitz, Heinrich: *Der entfremdete Mensch. Zeitkritik und Geschichtsphilosophie des jungen Marx*; Basle, 1953.

Popper, Karl: *The Open Society and Its Enemies,* vols. I and II; Routledge & Kegan Paul, London, 1957.

Rosenberg, Arthur: *A History of Bolshevism from Marx to the First Five Years Plan,* trans. Ian F. D. Morrow; Oxford U.P., 1934.

Rubel, Maximilien: *Pages Choisies pour une Éthique Socialiste*; Librairie Marcel Riviere et Cie, Paris, 1948.

Schlesinger, R.: *Soviet Legal Theory*; Routledge & Kegan Paul, London, 1951.

Schumpeter, Joseph A.: *Capitalism, Socialism and Democracy*; Allen & Unwin, London, 1959.

Sharia, P. A.: *O Nekotorykh voprosakh kommunisticheskoi morali*; Gospolitizdat, Moscow, 1951.

Shishkin, A. [F.]: *Osnovy kommunisticheskoi morali*; Gospolitizdat, Moscow, 1955.

Shishkin, A. F.: *Iz istorii eticheskikh uchenii*; Gospolitizdat, Moscow, 1959.

Sorel, Georges: *La Décomposition du Marxisme*; Paris, 1908.

Stalin, I: *Marksizm i voprosy iazykoznaniia*; Izdatelstvo 'Pravda', Moscow, 1950.

Trotsky, L. D.: *Terrorizm i kommunism*; Petrograd, 1920.

Trotsky, Leon D.: *The Living Thoughts of Karl Marx*; Cassell & Co., London, 1942.

Tugarinov, V. P.: *O tsennostiakh zhizni i kultury*; Leningrad University Press, 1960.

Vyshinsky, A. Y.: *The Law of the Soviet State*, trans. Hugh W. Babb; Macmillan, New York, 1954.

Wittfogel, Karl A.: *Oriental Despotism*; Yale University Press, 1956.

Zis, A. I. *O kommunisticheskoi morali*; Gospolitizdat, Moscow, 1948.

Istoriia VKP(b). Kratkii kurs; Gospolitizdat, Moscow, 1952.

Materialy vneocherednogo XXI s'ezda KPSS; Gospolitizdat, Moscow, 1959.

Voprosy marksistko-leninskoi etiki. Materialy nauchnogo sovechchaniia; Gospolitizdat, Moscow, 1960.

Anderson, John: 'Marxist Philosophy', *Australasian Journal of Psychology and Philosophy*, vol. XIII (1935).

Anderson, John: 'Marxist Ethics', *A.J.P.P.*, vol. XV (1937).

Anderson, John: 'Critical Notice of H. B. Acton's *The Illusion of the Epoch*,' *A.J.P.*, vol. 37 (1959).

Kamenka, Eugene: 'The Primitive Ethic of Karl Marx', *A.J.P.*, vol. 35 (1957).

Kamenka, Eugene: 'The Baptism of Karl Marx', *Hibbert Journal*, vol. LVI (1958).

Kamenka, Eugene and Tay, Alice Erh-Soon: 'Karl Marx's Analysis of Law', *Indian Journal of Philosophy*, vol. I (1959).

Kamenka, Eugene and Tay, Alice Erh-Soon: 'Karl Marx on The Law of Marriage and Divorce—A Text and a Commentary', *Quadrant*, no. 15 (Winter, 1960).

Kline, George L.: 'Changing Attitudes Toward the Individual', in C. E. Black (ed.): *The Transformation of Russian Society*, cited above.

C. OTHER WORKS

Chernyshevskii, N. G.: *Sochineniia;* Gos. Izdat. Khudozhestvennoi Literatury, Moscow, 1948f.

Feuerbach, Ludwig: *The Essence of Christianity,* trans. Marian Evans; London, 1854.

Hare, R. M.: *The Language of Morals*; Clarendon Press, Oxford, 1952.

Hegel, G. F. W.: *The Phenomenology of Mind,* trans. J. J. B. Baillie; Swan Sonnenschein, London, 1910.

Hegel, G. F. W.: *The Philosophy of Right,* trans. T. M. Knox; Clarendon Press, Oxford, 1953.

Passmore, J. A.: *Ralph Cudworth*; Cambridge U.P., 1951.

Spinoza, B.: *The Ethics,* trans. R. H. M. Elwes; Tudor Publishing Co., New York, 1941.

Stevenson, C. L.: *Ethics and Language*; Yale U.P., 1944.

Anderson, John: 'Determinism and Ethics', *A.J.P.P.,* vol. VI (1927).

Anderson, John: 'Realism versus Relativism in Ethics', *A.J.P.P.,* vol. XI (1933).

Anderson, John: 'The Problem of Causality', *A.J.P.P.,* vol. XVI (1938).

Anderson, John: 'Art and Morality', *A.J.P.P.,* vol. XIX (1941).

Anderson, John: 'The Meaning of Good', *A.J.P.P.,* vol. XX (1942).

Anderson, John: 'Ethics and Advocacy', *A.J.P.P.,* vol. XXII (1944).

Simpson, C. A.: 'Old Testament Historiography', *Hibbert Journal,* vol. LVI (1958).

Urmson, J. O.: 'On Grading', in *Logic and Language* (Second Series), ed. by A. G. N. Flew, Basil Blackwell, Oxford, 1953.

Index

Marx's early writings, preceding the *Economico-Philosophical Manuscripts* of 1844, are indexed under 'Marx' and letters under the name of the recipient. Otherwise, all works by Marx and Engels are indexed under their titles, generally rendered in English. Works by other authors appear only under the author's name. Details of editions are given in the 'Bibliography of Works Cited' on pages 200 ff.; references in the bibliography are not included in this index.